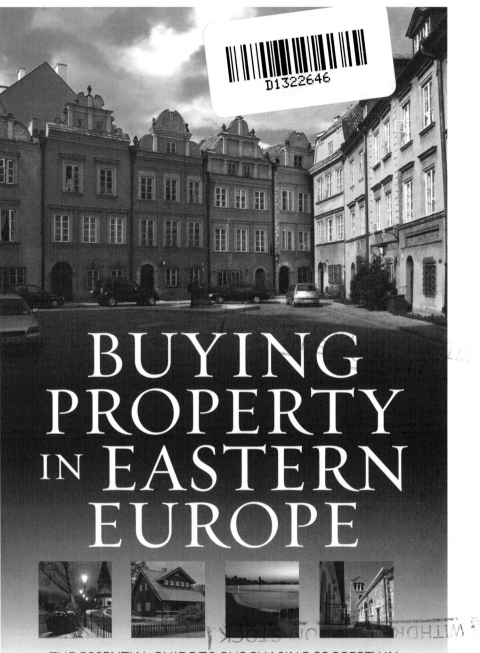

BUYING
PROPERTY
IN EASTERN
EUROPE

THE ESSENTIAL GUIDE TO PURCHASING PROPERTY IN
13 COUNTRIES, FROM THE BALTIC TO THE BALKANS

L E A O N N E   H A L L

howtobooks

Acknowledgments

My thanks go to Mark Wheatley. Without his help and support the production of this book wouldn't have been possible.

I must also thank the large number of estate agents and lawyers who helped me with my research and constant questions. These include the team at SomeplaceElse.co.uk, Ivan Bakaltchev at Bulgarian Gateway, Peter Ellis at Croatia Property Services, Nathan Brown at CzechPoint101.com, Zoltan Szemes and Ernest Nagy at A1 Real Estate, Ann Ilic-Ferrier at Montenegro Properties, Damien Thiery at Romanian Properties Ltd, Frances Sargent at SlovenianProperties.com, Petra Gajdosikova at Slovakia Investment Property, Philippe Robin at Selection Property, the team at The International Property Law Centre and the team at Blevins Franks.

My thanks also go to the team at howtobooks.

Published by How To Books Ltd,
Spring Hill House, Spring Hill Road,
Begbroke, Oxford OX5 1RX, United Kingdom
Tel: (01865) 375794 Fax: (01865) 379162
info@howtobooks.co.uk
www.howtobooks.co.uk

First edition 2007

British Library Cataloguing in Publication Data
A catalogue record for this book is available from the British Library.

ISBN: 978 1 84528 198 4

Produced for How To Books by Deer Park Productions, Tavistock
Typeset by *specialist* publishing services ltd, Montgomery
Cover design by Baseline Arts Ltd, Oxford
Printed and bound by Bell & Bain Ltd, Glasgow

Note: The material contained in this book is set out in good faith for general guidance and no liability can be accepted for loss or expense incurred as a result of relying in particular circumstances on statements made in the book. The laws and regulations are complex and liable to change, and readers should check the current position with the relevant authorities before making personal arrangements.

Contents

Appendices:

Preface

A huge number of people are now looking to buy second homes. With a volatile stock market and worries over pension schemes, property is seen as an appealing way in which to invest. What's more, many of us aren't satisfied with simply owning a home abroad – we want to live there permanently, seeking a more relaxed life, a better climate for retiring, or somewhere safe to raise a family. With house prices in the UK rocketing, property overseas is becoming increasingly attractive, especially for first-time buyers, and Eastern Europe is currently one of the world's hotspots.

So why is that? Well, what I love about Eastern Europe is the infinite variety. Whether you want sea, sun and sand, clean mountain air and skiing opportunities, a beautiful, affordable countryside home or a chic city centre pad, you'll find it in Eastern Europe – and generally at a fraction of the price of Western Europe.

The variety of places, peoples and cultures in Eastern Europe, along with the virtually inexhaustible amount of property, really does mean there's something for everyone. While the concept of living or buying in an area which, up until recently, was under the shadow of communist rule may put some buyers off, it's worth noting that these countries have developed incredibly quickly, with many cities becoming European economic leaders and international business hubs. Turn the corner, though, and you'll still find people living off the land, as their ancestors did before them, giving an irresistible mix of the modern and the traditional.

If you're seeking to buy somewhere with a little more diversity and adventure, Eastern Europe really is the ideal option for you.

Leaonne Hall

Map of Eastern Europe

1
Introduction to Eastern Europe

INTRODUCTION

The Eastern European property market is one that has really come into its own in the last five years, for reasons that include the growth of budget flights, EU membership and increasing levels of foreign investment. With everyone from families and retirees to investors and second home buyers purchasing property in a region that has only recently managed to shed the shackles of communism, it's unsurprising that people are asking questions about property purchase and the logic or otherwise of buying into such an immature market. That's where this book comes in. Here you'll find answers to all the questions you may have about the regions: investment potential, average prices and conveyancing system, as well as handy hints about relocating to, and living in, a largely alien environment.

We have featured the top 13 countries located in Eastern Europe that are experiencing the most demand and which are showing feasible market growth and also have a relatively safe legal system. Although Turkey isn't technically part of Eastern Europe, we have included her as she shows the same market features as countries such as Bulgaria and Poland – last year alone saw between 10,000 and 15,000 Europeans buying in the country.

Despite many marked similarities, each of the 13 countries included here has different characteristics and features, which make them a worthy choice for a second homebuyer. These are all covered in more detail in the individual country chapters found in the second half of this book.

Whatever advice you may find, don't be fooled into thinking you can go it alone. What is presented in this book is a guideline of what you can expect and how to go about making your dream a reality. However, there is no substitute for experienced professional advice, so in order to avoid becoming the next 'horror story', make sure you surround yourself with a team of experienced professionals – and do your research!

All currencies were correct at the time of going to print. However, always check conversion rates, as they are liable to change. A good site is www.xe.com.

Factfile

- Population: 348 million
- Area covered: 19 million square km
- Largest and most populous country: Turkey (71 million people, 783,562 square kilometres)
- Longest river: Danube (2,800 kilometres)
- Major mountain range: Carpathian Mountains: covering an area of 190,000 km^2 they run for 1,500 km along the borders of Romania, the Czech Republic, Slovakia, Poland, Ukraine, Austria, Serbia, and northern Hungary
- Most expensive city: Istanbul, Turkey (5th out of the 144 countries included in *Mercer Cost of Living Survey 2006*, www.mercerhr.com)
- Cheapest city: Vilnius, Lithuania (116th out of the 144 countries included in *Mercer Cost of Living Survey 2006*, www.mercerhr.com)
- Largest house price rises 2005-2006: Poland, 34%

BUYING ABROAD AND WHAT IT CAN OFFER

Once reserved primarily for the rich or rootless, today the culture of owning a property abroad is a dream lived by more than 750,000 Brits. The overseas purchase has now become a straightforward and safe process – so much so that it is anticipated that two million Britons will be living on foreign shores by 2020, with over 11 million expected to buy foreign properties within the next five years. Owning a holiday home abroad is top of the British wish list, with HIFX Foreign Currency exchange (www.hifx.co.uk) reporting that 68% of adults – 29 million people – would like to buy abroad. And the reasons why we seek to live in foreign climes? These are generally two-fold: 37% of us are looking to move abroad in search of better weather, while 32% of us are searching for a better quality of life.

Twenty years ago buying abroad was considered a difficult and risky business – and that was even before you considered looking beyond the Iron Curtain. With the lack of freedom of movement limiting a buyer's sphere of choice it wasn't until the advent of the package holiday and the mass development of the Spanish property market in the 70s and 80s that the idea of owning a home in the sun became a feasible prospect. Things have changed drastically since then and today property has become the cornerstone of our investment portfolio as we have seen our faith in the pensions and stock market undercut by increasing volatility in the equity markets.

The introduction and expansion of the EU means that buyers now enjoy unlimited choice, with the increase in household internet access and budget flights encouraging us to be more adventurous, whilst TV shows and the media cajole us into exploring new markets. Today you can find a plethora of companies which specifically cater for buyers seeking to purchase in 'off-the-beaten-track' countries, helping to make the conveyancing process a much smoother ride than it would have been five years ago. Meanwhile the fly-to-let phenomenon means that a well-researched purchase close to an airport receiving budget flights can more-or-less guarantee to cover your costs. On a more practical note, by buying abroad you'll generally get more for your money – £250,000 in the UK will buy you a one-bedroomed flat in the centre of Bath, while in Eastern Europe you could live like a king in a six-bedroomed coastal villa.

Many have asked the question, why risk buying a second home abroad when you can own a holiday home in the UK and take advantage of a 'safe' market and guaranteed price appreciation – and all in your own back yard? Well, for a start, just because property prices in the UK are high, this doesn't automatically translate into guaranteed market growth. UK capital growth currently sits at around 5%, meaning if you went out tomorrow and bought a property in the UK, hung on to it for one year and then sold it, your profit would be less than 10% of the property value. Compare this with an Eastern European market where annual appreciation rates regularly hit 30% – more in Poland, where an investment of £100,000 today may well have quadrupled within a decade – and it's easy to see which scenario offers the best investment.

Enough of the practicalities: for most, the lure of a home overseas is the attractive lifestyle and low living costs. Brits, disillusioned with the weather, their wages and the spiralling cost of property and living, see the solution to their problems as a move abroad – and in many cases it has proved successful, leaving the buyer with a nest egg for the future and a home away from home for holidays. What's more, living in the sun is proven to have a beneficial impact upon your health.

A new but significant trend is the increasing numbers of people who are relocating abroad in search of a new and exciting lifestyle. Keen to learn about the culture of a country, buyers are becoming more adventurous and this has particularly benefited the markets in Eastern Europe, where buyers aren't just finding themselves living in an expat enclave, but actually among the local people. Still perceived as being 'foreign', Eastern Europe is a long way from becoming a 'Little Britain', Costa del Fish and Chips, or Chiantishire.

EAST VERSUS WEST: WHY BUY IN EASTERN EUROPE?

The Eastern European property market makes a lot of sense: EU accession, improved infrastructure and continued foreign investment are all helping to secure and build upon the growing political and economic stability these countries now enjoy. With stability comes confidence, all of which helps to bolster the property market and encourage a continuation of the already high appreciation rates. While this is very much an over-arching view of the market, it explains why thousands of investors are focusing their attention on Eastern Europe. Throughout Western Europe many people have found themselves priced out of the property market.

Another major advantage of Eastern European countries is the cost of living. In Bulgaria, GDP is one-third that of the UK and while this doesn't mean prices are three times cheaper it's a fairly good assessment of the situation. You can enjoy a meal out with wine for £5, while in Poland a meal out will cost about £11. Prices in Romania are an average of 50% cheaper than the UK. Even the forward-thinking market economies of the Baltic States sit roughly 40 places below London in the *Mercer Cost of Living Survey* for 2006.

While Spain and France remain a safe bet and still experience market growth of between 4% and 8%, when measured against price rises of 17% in Estonia, 12.5% in Bulgaria (in 2005 this figure sat at a staggering 36.5%) and 9% in Hungary – figures which are set to continue to grow for the foreseeable future – there is no competition. Whereas a two-bedroomed property in St-Tropez will set you back by 730,000 euros, in Kaş in Turkey such a budget would buy you three separate three-bedroomed villas, while in Bulgaria you can purchase a two-bedroomed ski property for 45,000 euros!

What really makes Eastern Europe so appealing is not just the growth in property prices, but the economic growth and political stability that go with it. The Baltic States are a shining example of this. All three are rising stars in the tourist market, receive budget flights, are experiencing average economic growth rates of 7–10% per annum over the last few years and are politically stable democracies. All of this is what has helped make their property markets so attractive and will continue to do so for the next ten years.

Despite all these positives, as with everything, there are negatives and these are impossible to ignore. Many question the impact historical stigmas have left on these countries and their political circumstances. Corruption is – quite rightly – a concern to many, as are the questionable land registry systems in operation and the threat of defective titles. These are all things to be aware of and to take into consideration when choosing where to buy. However, with the right advice and careful planning, you can avoid becoming a victim.

While the buying process has become easier in many countries thanks to EU membership wiping away restrictions to foreign buyers, you should be aware that mortgage rates are still high – 6% in Hungary, compared with 3% in Spain – but these will drop over time and as demand increases. Finally comes the question of market uncertainty and whether the investment bubble will burst. While the 20–50% appreciation rates won't last, prices still remain cheap compared with UK levels and, as long as demand continues to outstrip supply, then your investment is likely to be a sound one. However, do be aware that these countries are past the point of appreciating by 20% overnight. The markets have calmed down and in many instances now represent a better medium- to long-term investment than a market where you can buy an off-plan property and double your money by selling it on completion.

Top ten reasons to buy in Eastern Europe

1. With more countries set to join the EU and the euro, investors can expect to see prices increase. These factors have led to considerable house price inflation in markets which have already joined, and investors are optimistic that the pattern will be repeated.

2. The tourism sector is growing rapidly as the infrastructure and marketing of destinations improves. This will lead some areas to develop a valuable short-term lettings market, helping buyers to supplement their income.

3. While budget airlines have yet to serve many Eastern European destinations, many are adding routes which will make the region more accessible and drive up prices.

4. House prices are low, as is the cost of living; many pensioners retiring out East will see their pound stretch further.

5. International and media attention is being increasingly focused on the Eastern European region. For example, being a popular ski destination, Sofia – the highest capital in Europe – is bidding for the next winter Olympics. Consequently, Bulgarian resorts have been getting face lifts, and new facilities are being developed: good news for potential rentals.

6. In the capital cities and major industrial centres, after 50 years of communism, there is a dramatic shortage of high-quality apartments. With many multinationals relocating to Eastern Europe, this makes the potential

6

for long-term rentals excellent and also means demand for property is high, thus sustaining price appreciation.

7. Eastern Europe contains a wealth of attractions, with stunning coastlines, mountains, lakes and historical cities, making it ideal for those seeking a bit of culture to go with their second home.

8. Parts of Eastern Europe remain relatively unexplored, allowing buyers to totally submerge themselves into a new culture and avoid the 'Little Britain' effect, while taking advantage of the low prices.

9. Though the infrastructure is far behind that of Western Europe, inward investment from the EU and government initiatives are improving accessibility. This leads to the opening up of new locations and the creation of activities such as golf, sailing and skiing.

10. Affordability means that extras which would normally sell for a premium – such as a detached property, a swimming pool, coastal location or view – are more within many people's budgets.

A BRIEF HISTORY OF EASTERN EUROPE

The history of Eastern Europe is a complex affair dominated by a series of national quarrels and clashes. Consequently, these countries would never co-exist harmoniously as a unified region. An area of considerable ethnic diversity, Eastern Europe's population of 348 million is comprised of 14 major nationality groups and nine smaller ones, including the Slavs, Romans, Bulgars and Magyars. Since the 1500s the countries of Eastern Europe have been subjected to centuries of foreign rule, which finally culminated in 50 years under communist control and an isolationist policy which severed the region's ties with the outside world. The 19th century saw the development of intense nationalistic feelings, culminating in the failed and bloody 1848 revolts, while the 20th century saw two World Wars.

It was with the end of World War I and the disintegration of the four defeated empires of Austro-Hungary, Germany, the Ottoman Empire, and Russia that Eastern Europe as we know it today began. The peace settlement saw the creation of Czechoslovakia, Yugoslavia, Latvia, Lithuania and Estonia, and in the case of Poland, re-creation, as she became an independent country after more than a century of foreign rule. Turkey replaced the Ottoman Empire, with the creation of other Middle

Eastern countries in the following years.

Undeveloped and under-resourced, as the 30s came along and the world was hit by economic depression, these new states were unable to cope with the aggression of Germany, and during WWII they found themselves caught between the forces of Nazi Germany and Russia. By 1945 they were under Russian rule, and despite repeated promises from Stalin that they would be granted independence, they soon found themselves under the yoke of communism and hidden behind the Iron Curtain.

Stalin's death in 1953 signalled the beginning of a series of revolts – such as in Hungary in 1956 and in Czechoslovakia in 1968 – which signalled the beginning of the end for communism in Eastern Europe. Independence from Russia eventually came in 1989, with the toppling of the Berlin Wall and the final collapse of the Soviet Union on December 25, 1991. Almost immediately the countries of Eastern Europe began declaring their independence and today enjoy parliamentary democracies, following many years of heartache and bloodshed.

CORRUPTION AND THE LEGAL SYSTEM

Whereas buyers in France and Spain are following a well-trodden path, by choosing to buy in Eastern Europe you are still, to some extent, a pioneer, and could be faced with corrupt officials and demands for backhanders. While such dealings may be more prevalent in some countries than others, you should still be prepared for officials who pass you from pillar to post, especially in countries such as Montenegro, which currently has a poor land registration and mortgage system in place, although they are working to rectify this.

Many countries with weak governments have seen their justice system infiltrated by organised crime groups, who bought up land during the property boom and sold it on at inflated prices and with dodgy titles. However, such occurrences should prove of little concern to the average property buyer – just ensure you check the land registry and property title thoroughly.

Thankfully, pressure from the EU is making many countries clean up their act and Croatia is one example of a government taking steps to deal with corruption and mafia activity. Unfortunately, in Bulgaria foreigners are still being charged over the odds for property – despite legislation outlawing the previously acceptable practice of charging locals less than foreigners – while Montenegro is hugely reliant on Russian money, with many mafia figures having bought up swathes of coastal land.

Bribery and black money are more commonly encountered, a common method of greasing the wheels of industry and avoiding getting your planning application buried under mounds of 'paperwork'. While this problem is better than it was five years ago, don't be surprised if you encounter such demands – the best thing to do is employ someone who knows how the system works. The justice system in Eastern Europe can be creaky to say the least, and while countries such as the Czech Republic are adamant the system is free of corruption, to take a dispute to court is usually a three-year process.

THE EU AND EASTERN EUROPEAN ECONOMY

In May 2004, the countries of Cyprus, the Czech Republic, Estonia, Hungary, Latvia, Lithuania, Malta, Poland, Slovakia and Slovenia all joined the EU. The result was the opening of borders, a relaxation in visa laws and restrictions on foreign property buyers, the embracing of a market economy and the introduction and acceptance of civil rights. More importantly, it has also led to massive EU funding for the new members, which in turn has translated into improved infrastructures and facilities. Since this newfound freedom of movement was introduced, more than 15 million EU citizens have relocated for work or retirement reasons to another member state.

In the three years since 2004, Estonia has averaged one of the best economic growth rates in Europe, reaching nearly 10% GDP growth per annum, with increases of 89.9% since 2000, an average GDP of 6.23% and low inflation. Such economic prosperity has fuelled huge levels of foreign direct investment and price rises of 30% per annum in the last few years, making the property market one of the most popular investments in Europe. PriceWaterhouseCoopers carried out a recent survey which highlighted that 42% of 201 companies surveyed forecast a growth in Eastern European operations, with 46% of companies considering investing in the newly-joined Eastern European countries.

However, while positive growth can be witnessed, with new member states experiencing an average economic growth rate of 6% – seven times that of the original EU members – it's important to remember that we are only three years into EU membership and there is still a long road ahead. GDP rates among new members currently sit at between 35–75% of Western European levels. *The Economist* predicted that even if the new member states continue to grow at a rate double the original EU15, it would still take an average of 50 years for them to reach economic parity.

Slovenia adopted the euro on 1st January 2007 and the euro is soon to be embraced by many eastern countries – the Baltic States are looking at 2008–2010. Consequently, travelling between countries is destined to become increasingly easy. It's also good news for investors who will no longer be required to ride the rollercoaster of exchange rates, while those looking to secure a mortgage can expect a drop in inflation and interest rates as Eastern European countries seek to fulfil the requirements of the Eurozone. Finally, this is all good news for the property markets, which should expect to see a significant rise in prices and demand.

Recent admissions

Bulgaria and Romania joined the EU on the 1st January 2007, but what will it mean for investors? Accession and its relationship to residential property prices is one of the most pervading questions surrounding membership. Bulgaria saw property price rises in anticipation of EU membership with real estate one of the country's fastest-growing sectors, up 5.3% in 2005.

While EU membership doesn't guarantee inflation within the property market, it does allow for economic stability and prosperity, which in turn allows the market to flourish. Lessons on this score can be learnt from Spain. In 1986 it joined the EU and faced challenges over its economic stability. However, tourist numbers increased dramatically – a similar picture to that of Bulgaria, up 22% annually – and foreign property purchase began in earnest and continued over the last 20 years. Over the last few years, Romania has seen capital growth of 30%, with rental yields as high as 15%, along with the development of a mortgage market. Thanks to EU membership, this growth is likely to have been safeguarded and PriceWaterhouseCoopers have earmarked Romania as the one place in Europe where investors can make money fast.

THE TOURISM BOOM AND BUDGET FLIGHTS

It was the advent of package holidays that gave holidaymakers the idea that the lifestyle of sun, sea and sand could be enjoyed year-round – all they had to do was buy a property on foreign shores. It's a well-known fact that as the number and regularity of budget flights have grown, so the overseas property market has expanded. The introduction of new flight routes has been responsible for the creation of new property markets and as more and more Eastern European countries join the EU, so the routes will continue to grow.

Between 2000 and 2004, there has been a 45% increase in the number of UK households owning a second home abroad. This correlates with the rise in passenger numbers. Since the 1980s, the number of international passengers per year has risen from 43 million to 167 million, and today 80% of Brits hold a passport compared with 24% in 1984. Ryanair has seen passenger numbers grow from 5.5 million in 2000 to nearly 31 million in 2006.

2006 saw aviation activity in Eastern Europe in double figures for the first time, with an overall 12% rise from 2005. Flights to Poland were up by 21%, Turkey by 19% and operations in and out of the Baltic States increased by a staggering 87% in summer 2006.

In the future, demand is unlikely to lessen. Between 2004 and 2005, tourism figures rose by 22% annually in Bulgaria and 22% in Turkey, with Poland seeing tourist figures hit 15.2 million in 2006, making it the 12th most visited country in the world. For investors looking to buy to let, this is good news – it's also good news for the property market. Tourism means increased awareness of each country's market, which in turn stimulates demand for property, and so those buyers looking to secure a good investment should keep an eye on the new and planned budget routes, as they are certain to stimulate the property market.

Travel and Tourism Demand, 2007–2016
(% predicted annualised real growth)
1. Montenegro 10.2%
2. China 8.7%
3. India 8.0%
4. Romania 7.9%
5. Croatia 7.6%
6. Vietnam 7.5%
7. Latvia 7.3%
8. Maldives 7.2%
9. Albania 7.0%
10. Cambodia 7.0%
Source: World Travel and Tourism Council

2
Where to buy in Eastern Europe

INTRODUCTION

The first hurdle you'll be faced with is deciding where to buy, and you should note that the old adage 'location, location, location' still rings true. The most important thing potential buyers should bear in mind is that these markets are still developing and may appear extremely alien to the western eye. Consequently, you should choose carefully and decide just how deeply you're willing to immerse yourself in an unfamiliar culture – for example, if you move to Bulgaria you will have to learn that shaking your head means 'yes', and nodding means 'no'!

To many, the thought of buying a home in the former communist bloc seems daunting, but in reality, the purchasing process in Eastern Europe is very similar to that in the UK. Yes, there are different problems to be faced, issues to be aware of and safeguards to take, but as long as you go into the process armed with the facts, things should run smoothly.

Nevertheless, there will be an element of pioneering involved. While the EU has embraced some Eastern European countries, others can still be comparatively naïve in terms of property legislation, with many lawyers and agents having never dealt with a foreign buyer. As a result, the purchasing process in rural Romania may well be fraught with frustration when compared to Turkey's western coast, and you should consider this when choosing your final location.

GETTING TO KNOW EASTERN EUROPE

As disparate as they are similar, Eastern European countries are unknown to many. While you may be aware that the property market is blossoming, you may not know much about the countries themselves. However, it's essential to get to know a country prior to purchasing there. With the borders between the various countries open, you can happily tour Eastern Europe by car and visit potential relocation sites armed with a pen and paper. Take notes and photos, and ensure you visit during both winter and summer. Most importantly, spend time with the locals, as opposed to the relative comfort of a clutch of expats. You must be aware of the realities of life in a country only in the early stages of westernisation, and you have to learn to mingle with the people who may well become your neighbours – and eventually your friends.

i) Geography

Ask most people to identify Poland or Romania on a map and they struggle. While the countries of Eastern Europe are increasingly easy to reach, geographically we remain ill informed. Eastern Europe can be loosely defined as the region lying between Central Europe and Russia. Generally encompassing countries that once made up the former Eastern Bloc, they also include many Balkan states and Central European countries, such as Poland, the Czech Republic, Slovakia, Hungary and Slovenia. Covering an area of approximately 19 million square km, with a population of roughly 348 million people, this vast region runs from the sun-drenched tip of Kaş on Turkey's southwestern coast to the Estonian marshlands in the north. The majority of these countries are coastal, although Hungary, the Czech Republic and Slovakia are landlocked. You should be aware of this if you intend to let your new home, because the lack of a coastline may make it much harder to rent out your property. Some areas are mountainous, which can result in harsh and isolated winters. Alternatively, this can mean ski resorts and a healthy rental income. Essentially, you can choose your terrain and be lakeside in Slovakia, coastal in Bulgaria or among the mountains in Romania. Whatever you decide, you must consider your future intentions, with regard to letting or selling, as well as your own personal preferences.

ii) Climate

In a nutshell, what you need to ask yourself is whether you're moving abroad in order to find better weather than in the UK – in many Eastern European countries the winters can be worse. If you are an out-and-out sun-seeker then you need to look to the south, where Turkey, Bulgaria's southeastern coast and Croatia offer a hot Mediterranean climate. If you dislike the heat, look to the crisper, milder weather of the Baltic States or mountainous Slovakia. By deciding what kind of climate you seek, you are deciding whether to look to Eastern Europe's north or south.

Generally speaking, the climate in the southernmost countries of Eastern Europe is Mediterranean, with hot, dry summers and mild winters, while the northern countries have cool and cloudy summers with wet, snowy winters. Whatever your choice, the temperate nature of many areas of Eastern Europe can be surprising.

The following chart compares the annual average temperature, rainfall and hours of sunlight you can expect.

	Country Av. monthly temperature (°C)	Av. monthly precipitation (mm)	Av. hours of sunlight per day
UK	14	49	4
Bulgaria	11	53	6
Croatia	17	71	7
Czech Republic	12	67	5
Estonia	8	49	5
Hungary	11	35	6
Latvia	10	47	5
Lithuania	10	55	5
Montenegro	18	138	7
Poland	11	46	4
Romania	11	51	6
Slovenia	15	115	4
Slovakia	10	63	6
Turkey	16	52	7

iii) Politics, the EU and the economy

The cloud of communism that once hung over Eastern Europe is now gone, thanks to the accession of the Czech Republic, Estonia, Hungary, Latvia, Lithuania, Poland, Slovakia and Slovenia to the EU on May 1st 2004 and Romania and Bulgaria on January 1st 2007. Currently, Turkey and Croatia are undertaking negotiations and introducing a number of reforms to smooth the way. Only Montenegro remains isolated from the EU although, following a national poll, Montenegro has split from Serbia, meaning her economic and political future is more certain. Nevertheless, some commentators believe she would have had a better chance of joining the EU had she remained unified with Serbia.

With most Eastern European countries governed by stable parliamentary democracies, the political outlook is relatively calm. As a result of this and EU accession, member states have seen a strengthening of their economy and an upturn in the demand for property, making these markets ideal for the investor. For example, in Slovakia, foreign investment into Bratislava attracted investors from overseas, who in turn drove up property prices and encouraged appreciation. Similarly, increased stability across Eastern Europe has seen many countries taking steps to open their markets to westerners. For instance, Turkey is currently introducing new property legislation.

However, while stability is apparent, economic prosperity is not. The gulf between east and west is still vast in many areas, although foreign investment is on the rise. It is expected that countries which enjoy a healthy, tourist-based economy will gain more from EU membership in terms of property appreciation, so if you are buying to invest, choose countries with a heavy economic reliance on tourism.

It is also important to look at the currency. Currently, the euro is in use by Montenegro (which previously used the Deutschmark) and Slovenia. Few Eastern European countries offer foreigners a local currency mortgage, so currency fluctuations should be closely monitored. In many cases, the most secure option is to pay for the property upfront. For more details on securing a mortgage, see page 42–3, and for currency information, see page 44.

iv) Language

Without question, you will be buying in a location where English is not spoken as widely – or as well – as it would be on the Costa del Sol or the Côte d'Azur. In an Eastern European country, be prepared for a communication barrier, especially if attempting to learn the language. Slavonic languages are notoriously difficult to grasp as they are based on the Cyrillic alphabet and employ unique nasal vowels. However, making the effort to grasp a few key phrases is worth it as it will allow you to become involved in local life, to avoid feelings of isolation and to communicate during the buying process or in an emergency.

MARKET PERFORMANCE AND INVESTMENT POTENTIAL

With traditional favourites such as Spain and France becoming saturated with investors, and their markets currently experiencing sluggish levels of growth, buyers are looking for alternatives, and in the majority of cases, want to experience something of the country and culture in which they choose to purchase. Eastern Europe offers these opportunities, whether it is a villa in Turkey, an apartment in Bratislava, or a traditional stone-built house in Croatia.

While the concept of buying in Eastern Europe may seem like a new phenomenon to many, most people are aware of the staggering price hikes that have occurred due to the media spotlight the area has been under. Investors and budget flights have already made huge progress in attracting the attention of a wider audience, spurred on by the accession of eight countries into the EU. Prices are still leaping up – sometimes at a rate of 30% to 40% per annum – and in some areas, such as Prague, property prices are already on a par with the UK.

While Eastern European countries are seeing some of the largest price rises in Europe, don't assume high rates of appreciation are guaranteed. In some countries, such as Bulgaria, market growth has slowed from 37% to 4% in some areas. Nevertheless, it is not unheard of for investors to experience appreciation rates of 20% in six months. In Romania it's possible to buy a parcel of land, leave it untouched for two years and then sell it on for twice the price. Parts of Turkey have seen price hikes of 30% to 40%, while in Dubrovnik they have risen by 50% over the last two years. However, some countries have yet to experience a boom period like those of Prague and Croatia in early 2003, so investors should keep their eyes open.

The question to ask is whether or not the market will continue to expand at such a high rate, and if this has any relevance to your purchase. Experts believe that the market will continue to grow – albeit at a slower rate – simply because property prices remain low when compared to the UK. However, when looking at a country, you should realise that in rural areas where demand for property is low, you will not experience the same rate of appreciation as you would in a major city or resort. Also, if you are looking to make money from renting your property, the market will not perform uniformly. A stone-built house in inland Konya in Turkey will not generate the same income as a coastal villa in Bodrum. Do your research and ensure you buy in an area which experiences high demand for holiday rentals if you intend to let, and experiences healthy appreciation and a high turnover rate if buying to sell in the future.

At the end of the day, if you are looking to make money from your property, your own feelings must be superseded by what will appreciate well and sell easily, and you should go on to choose your location based on these findings. You must assess how vulnerable the market may be and whether the risk is worth it – most investors say yes, as the financial rewards can be substantial. The best advice on offer is to invest in several markets and not, as the saying goes, put all your eggs into one basket.

PERSONAL PREFERENCES

It is essential that wherever and whatever you choose, you buy a property that fits your requirements and intended usage. If you're looking to invest, you need to assess whether the current market climate will suit buying off plan or a plot of land. If you are purchasing a holiday home then you need to decide what you will be spending your time doing and what your motivation for purchasing is. If your intention is to relax on the beach, then ensure you know which country offers the best stretches of coast – for example, Bulgaria's Black Sea Coast and Croatia's Istrian Peninsula. Do you want to be near mountains or in the countryside? Do you intend to let your property? If so, you will need to ensure the furnishings are appropriate and the property is close to attractions and the airport. How far do you want to be from the UK and how easy is it to get there? This applies both to flight times and time spent travelling to the property from the airport. Whatever your specifications, it is important to choose a country and a property that suit your personal tastes and requirements. For example, those seeking an easy-to-reach holiday home should consider Croatia, the adventurous DIY enthusiast should look to Montenegro, while Turkey is a popular destination with retirees due to the large expat community. With Estonia currently topping the charts for price growth, the Baltic States are a good location for investors, while Bulgaria has been dubbed the new Spain due to the new-build phenomenon on its Black Sea coastline.

Ask yourself the following questions to help you narrow down the choices:

1. What will I be using my new home for?
2. Is there a specific country or culture I like above others?
3. Is a sunny climate important to me?
4. What can I realistically afford?
5. Am I aiming to make money from my property?
6. Will I be looking to retire to my second home one day?
7. Do I want to be within two hours of the UK?
8. Do I want to be able to speak the language?

BUDGET

One of the most important factors to establish is your budget. Whether you have £10,000 or £1 million you must have a detailed idea of how much you can spend and also what extra costs you will be faced with. Some areas of Eastern Europe are obviously more expensive than others, due to the existence of regular budget flights, an established local market and high demand with low availability. However, if your budget is tight, it is important to remember that cheap doesn't always make for the best buy. It may mean accessibility is poor, or that the property requires renovation – which can mean large construction bills – and generally you should factor an extra 15% on top of your renovation budget as a safety net. If you do buy cheap, you should ensure you have done your homework and are aware of the potential for growth in the market, enabling you to make your money back in the long run.

Many people fall into the trap of thinking that letting their property can cover all the costs of their mortgage and upkeep. While this will bring in a nice lump sum, you should not rely solely on it to cover all your costs – ensure you can pay the bills yourself. In terms of added costs, you should always secure quotes from a variety of estate agents to ensure that you aren't paying extortionate fees – they can range from 2 to 6% – so shop around to get the best deal. It is also worth seeing if you qualify for any fiscal or tax benefits from purchasing in one country over another, or for a certain kind of ownership – for instance, if you buy through a company.

Finally, there is no point in buying a second home if you are only going to land yourself in debt back in the UK. Think carefully, budget wisely and always ensure that you take expert advice.

TRAVEL AND TRANSPORT

Always think about travel costs and the ease of access when doing your research. You should ensure the country has international airports, which are easily accessible from your new home. This will help determine where you buy and is an essential factor when looking to secure rentals – experts in the travel industry state that a journey of more than one-and-a-half hours following a flight will stop many people from travelling. It is also worth being aware that the easier the access to Western Europe, the more expensive property is likely to be. While this is a very broad statement, it is an accurate one – in areas such as the Czech Republic and parts of Bulgaria, prices are almost twice as high as in less accessible areas such as Montenegro. Think of others and of the future. Are you so inaccessible that friends and relatives will be put off from visiting? Is your property located in an area that may be difficult to reach once you are in your dotage?

It's also worth noting that while flying is the most common way of travelling abroad, driving and taking the ferry are becoming increasingly popular, especially as motorways through Western Europe are excellent, and Eastern European roads are dramatically improving. Consequently, taking the scenic route to your new property can be a pleasant and eye-opening experience, and is recommended when you're trying to establish exactly where you want to buy.

Budget flights

In recent years, budget flights have been extremely influential in opening up new markets throughout Eastern Europe and encouraging the second-home boom. In the next couple of years, it's estimated that there will be a 20% increase in the number of budget flights available and these are set to focus on countries that have recently joined the EU. As they make rentals more viable and strengthen new property markets, these planned routes can have a major impact on the amount of appreciation a country or resort experiences. For example, Romania and Montenegro currently have no budget flights so they experience a slower rate of property price growth and demand for holiday lettings, yet the Czech Republic has received them for a number of years, causing the Prague market to become well established – and expensive.

Obviously, a destination appears more attractive to potential renters if it's served by budget flights and so, when looking to buy a second home, you should be aware of newly planned routes and obtain a list of locations served by current budget airlines. As far as possible, you should also examine the vulnerability of flights and whether or not routes are likely to be withdrawn, resulting in a drop in rental demand and also damaging investments.

While budget flights have helped develop and sustain demand in many overseas markets, investors should be aware that in the long term air travel may become unsustainable. Increased awareness of global warming and concerns over the impact of air travel on the environment may either result in a constriction of the market, or drive prices up to a point where they no longer appear 'budget' to the average flier. Wherever possible, avoid investing in a destination solely because it is served by budget flights. If nothing else, the airline may one day simply decide to cancel the route, leaving you with a worthless investment and a property which will rapidly lose its value.

A final consideration is how much it costs to reach the country of your choice. Some routes are less popular and consequently more expensive than others – it also depends on the day, month and time of year you choose to fly. If expensive plane tickets are going to hamper your enjoyment of your new home then ensure you buy somewhere where flights will be affordable.

Getting around

In terms of travelling, once you reach your destination, you should be aware that the infrastructure might still be relatively poor. If you get annoyed when UK public transport runs late then you should think twice about buying or living in an area where, in certain rural locations, the bus may only turn up twice a week!

Generally speaking, areas popular with western tourists are fairly well equipped with roads and public transport, but you should try out public transport before you buy – especially if you don't intend to own a car.

EXPAT COMMUNITIES AND FACILITIES

Moving abroad can potentially be an isolating and alienating experience, whether you choose the Dordogne or Dubrovnik. Wherever you buy, there will be an acclimatising period, where life may seem difficult and living in a foreign country trying. Be prepared for this as, while it may seem romantic to buy a tumble-down traditional home on the Istrian coast, there will inevitably be downsides.

In some Eastern European markets, communities will be devoid of expats, so people aiming to live close to an expat community should do some serious research and check the facilities on offer. Alternatively, if you are looking to be immersed in the local culture and want to put a safe distance between yourself and any other Brit, then there will be an Eastern European community that will suit your purpose. While major centres such as Sofia, Budapest and Prague will have experienced a certain amount of westernisation and may well have English bookshops, papers and cinemas, it is important to also think about the shopping facilities and what kind of produce you will have access to. Will it be difficult to get hold of a jar of Marmite or a tin of beans and are you prepared for this? Will you need to cook using local produce? If so, you may need to practise and hone your skills, learning how to make a mean goulash or gut a fish.

A buyer also needs to think of the amenities they may want on hand. If you have children then you will need to locate yourself close to an international school. Will you need internet access? Do you have to be close to a major town or city? Will you have a car or will you need to rely on local transport? Many people buy and retire abroad in order to spend their time golfing or boating. Will these amenities be available if you want them?

If you want to be near an expat community then be prepared to pay extra, just as you would for a coastal property or a nice view. However, while property in a local area will be lower in price, you must decide whether a cheaper home is more important than the security offered by an established expat community.

Whatever your final decision, if you believe you have the spirit of adventure and are confidant enough to make an effort to mix with the local community, then you are certain – with a little patience and perseverance – to find your dream home in the location you've always desired.

3
Finding and buying a home

PART 1: CHOOSING A PROPERTY

Once you've established where you are going to buy your new property, the next decision is to choose what you're going to buy.

FIXING A BUDGET

This is always the most important part of planning your property purchase and whatever type of property you intend to buy, before you begin house hunting, it is essential to have established the parameters for your budget, and ideally have even factored in a contingency plan should things become more costly than you originally intended.

So, how do you establish how much to spend? It all depends on your usage and where you choose to buy. If you intend to relocate to Eastern Europe, you may already own a property in the UK that you can sell, investing the equity in your new home overseas. Have you got any savings or a source of rental income that can go towards a purchase? Do you need to save a certain amount of money before you begin your property search and, if so, how much? Knowing where you are planning to purchase allows you to pre-empt any additional costs – such as property tax and notaries' fees – allowing you to sit down and do the sums, detailing all the costs you may incur along the way. Additional costs are generally as follows:

- Agents' fees – between 2% and 6%

- Stamp duty – varies

- Property tax – varies

- Deposit – generally 10%

- Legal fees – generally 1%

- Mortgage repayments

- Land registry fees

- Survey costs

- VAT (on new buildings)

- Fittings and furnishings.

Before committing to a purchase, if you aren't going to be buying the property outright, then always check you will be able to raise any required cash through a mortgage or loan, and work out how much you'll be entitled to borrow. Many mortgage sites offer an online budget planner service which will give you a rough guide as to how much you will be allowed to borrow. You also need to factor in the cost of the deposit; this varies depending on where you decide to buy and is usually between 10% and 20%, so ensure you find out exactly how much you'll be required to pay when you sign the provisional contract to avoid any nasty shocks. Certain countries may also require you to be able to invest a certain amount of your own money into the purchase.

If you are buying a newly-built property, figuring out how much you will be required to shell out is a straightforward process – most of the costs are covered in the list above. Don't forget details such as paying a community upkeep fee, though this will vary depending on where you choose to buy, but is generally between £5–£10 per square metre per year.

If you are looking to renovate a property then budgeting for the process does get slightly more complicated. Renovation requires a strict budget and regardless of where you buy, the rules are the same as if renovating in the UK. You shouldn't always assume that just because you are renovating in Eastern Europe this means lower costs. In Bulgaria, the demand for workmen and the rise in the number of restorations means that renovating a house might cost almost as much as it would in the UK. Always do your research and price-up potential renovation costs, making sure you get a thorough survey done prior to agreeing to buy. Generally, a renovation budget should allow for an additional 15% contingency to allow for the process costing more than you accounted for – and it generally does.

Whatever your final decision may be, never throw caution to the wind, don't listen to persuasive, slick-talking agents and don't be rushed into anything. There are very few people who don't have to worry about sticking to a budget, so take care. You certainly wouldn't buy a property in the UK if you didn't have the money, so why should Eastern Europe be any different?

Managing your budget

As we have already established, careful handling of your budget is a top priority when it comes to buying a second home. International financial experts Blevins Franks (www.blevinsfranks.com) offer some top tips to help you manage your budget wisely:

1. Before buying, always consider the maximum you can afford to pay for your property, whether you are buying in cash or raising a mortgage. If purchasing by the latter, make sure you allow for a significant rise in interest rates. If you don't and interest rates rise, you are jeopardising your ownership.

2. Don't let sweet-talking estate agents tempt you into buying more than you can afford. Buying off plan in order to make money on completion of the build is a high-risk strategy and can lead to significant losses.

3. Always secure your mortgage in your local currency (i.e. the pound sterling in the UK). If you don't, you run the risk of suffering from a sudden fluctuation in the exchange rate. For example, if you borrow in Estonia Kroon and the pound suddenly (or progressively) weakens against the Kroon, you would be faced with paying a lot more than you originally borrowed.

4. Always appoint an independent lawyer and, if possible, don't use the vendor's lawyer – if a problem arises, who is the lawyer advising objectively? If the developer or vendor is passing a number of clients onto a lawyer or is a 'local', then you may become the victim of poor – or less than objective – legal advice.

5. Never pass money for a deposit to any intermediary other than the lawyer acting for you. Even then, ask for proof that they have a separate client account in which the funds are held, so you have some protection in the event of the lawyer running off.

6. If buying a new property, always ask the developers if they have insurance against insolvency so that if they go bust, you can claim for the lost deposit(s) and/or the right to funds to complete the project.

7. Always check the land registry to ensure that there are no legal charges against the land or property you are considering buying, as many builders allow a bank to have a charge against the asset pending the completion. If the builder goes bust during the build, the bank can call in the security and you may get nothing.

RESEARCHING THE PURCHASE

There are a variety of methods and sources available to you when you're researching the purchase of your dream home, but the recommended – and most common – starting point is the internet. There is a wealth of material out there and by surfing the net you can get a better idea of the type of agent you need, the kind of property and prices you'd be looking at, as well as a cache of contacts you can arrange to meet. Never commit to an agent or property online and don't put any money forward, even if you're assured that it doesn't tie you to anything.

Search engines such as Google are the best starting point for your web-based research. Terms such as 'Turkey property' or 'Bulgaria estate agent' will throw up hundreds of listings, so try to be more specific if you've already tracked down the location of your choice. Keep a list or bookmark all your favourite sites so they can be easily found again.

There are numerous books, property magazines and newspapers out there that are filled with useful advice and contact details for lawyers, estate agents and property finders, and they are a mine of information – for example the weekend broadsheets and the wealth of magazines in your local newsagents are all good starting points, as are online resources such as *World of Property*.

For more personal advice you can attend exhibitions. These give you the chance to meet some of the agents face-to-face and also allow you to pick up literature on developments, countries and the purchasing process, and provide you with the opportunity to discuss the market and get advice about the right investment for you. Many also offer useful seminars which can help you get to grips with the state of affairs in a specific country. A list of these and all the exhibitors are available online. Go armed with a list of questions and a large bag to carry all the brochures home in, but beware the seductive spiel of some agents who will try to commit you to a sale then and there.

Exhibition contacts

- A Place in the Sun – www.aplaceinthesunlive.com
- Homes Overseas – www.homesoverseas.co.uk/Exhibitions
- International Holiday and Overseas Property Show – www.premierexhibitions.com
- www.internationalpropertyshow.com
- Overseas Property Expo, www.overseaspropertyexpo.com
- Property Investor – www.propertyinvestor.co.uk
- The First Time Buyer's Property Show – www.firstrungnow.com
- The Homebuyer Show – www.homebuyer.co.uk
- The Sunday Business Post Property Expo 2007 – http://www.propertyexpo.ie
- Worldwide Property Show, Resale & Rental Property Show – www.dslexhibitions.ae

Read up on the countries you are thinking of buying in, learn about the geography and culture and get hold of some guide books such as Lonely Planet, Rough Guides and Bradt Guides. Look at the political and economic state of the country and find out what the future prognosis for the property market is. Take a look at budget flight options (see www.flycheapo.com) and any new routes that might open up or further develop the market, and where possible, take a trip out to the country and arrange to view as many properties as you can. Make sure you visit during both summer and winter as a property can take on a wholly different character during the cold winter months and during peak/off peak season.

FINDING AN ESTATE AGENT

So, you've established a budget, done your preliminary and background research and now you want to move to the next stage – finding an estate agent to help you in your quest to secure a pad overseas.

The essential thing to remember is to always do your homework on prospective agents before getting underway with any property searches or purchasing. It is vital to do your background research when it comes to agents as different companies may offer the same property at different prices and also charge different fees. Some agents may even try to charge to show you around properties, which is an undesirable practice and one that is best avoided.

Always try to go with a company who has come recommended from friends or family. Visit the AIPP (www.aipp.org.uk) and Fopdac (www.fopdac.com) websites and check out their list of vetted agents and lawyers. There's also the International Real Estate Federation (www.fiabci.com) and the Confederation of European Real estate Agents (www.webcei.com).

Recommendations for choosing an estate agent:

- Always ask an agent if they are regulated and ask if you can see their certification, as the governing body will safeguard you against getting ripped off or losing your money.

- Employ someone who knows the area well and knows how the purchasing process works in the country – this could save a lot of hassle in the long run when it comes to paperwork and red tape.

- Many agencies are paid by the seller or developer of the property, meaning their services to you will be free. However, some agents will then charge the buyer a finders' fee which can be up to 3–5%. Before you start to work together, check what their policy is.

- Make sure the agent has a good selection of property on their books – this will not only provide you with ample choice but also reveals that they are a proactive company.

- Whoever you choose to work with, always make sure you keep a record of your conversations and dealings with them and keep pestering – the last thing you want is to be forgotten under a pile of other clients.

- The key to avoid being ripped-off is to do your research. If you go to an agent armed with background knowledge, this will make them realise that not only are you serious as an investor, but that they can't pull the wool over your eyes. They will also be able to do a better job for you if they know your budget, limitations and exactly what you are looking for.

TRY BEFORE YOU BUY

You wouldn't buy a car without taking it for a test drive, having already visited numerous garages, and nor should you commit to buying a property without having first visited the area and looked at a number of different properties. The biggest mistake you can make is to commit to buying a property without travelling out to the country and checking the area – and the property – first. Even if you have employed the services of a house search agency, get them to narrow the options down and then you should take a week out to go and view them all.

Getting to know Eastern Europe before you buy is essential – and also the most fun bit of the purchasing process. Try to travel extensively around your country of choice before making any firm decisions. Buy a map and guidebook and make notes, take photos and check out exactly what facilities would be available to you if you bought there.

The best way to see everything is to take as much time as possible, to rent a property in the area, hire a car and spend time living as you would if you bought a home there. This is the closest you can get to experiencing what life would be like in Eastern Europe, and also gives you a chance to meet and talk with the locals, and try to discover what life in the area is really like. Pick up the local papers to look for advertised property and also employ word of mouth – talk to local residents about your property search as they may know of any houses for sale.

Inspection trips are another way to spend time experiencing a country, and doing this can help you to make an informed purchase. However, there are disadvantages and inspection trips have had a bad press in the past, thanks to the use of aggressive sales techniques and the bullying of clients. If you do choose to go on a viewing trip then don't let yourself be pressurised into anything.

On the positive side, there are many advantages to viewing trips. For one thing you will be provided with a portfolio of properties to visit that meet your specifications, you'll get to know your estate agents, you'll be provided with subsidised flights and accommodation and you will get the opportunity to get to know the country and the purchasing process. Be aware that these can be genuinely helpful trips, but do not treat them as free holidays, and ensure you know exactly what costs you are likely to incur.

PROPERTY TYPES

Before you think about the type of property you want, you must ensure that you know what you will need from your future home. How much space will you require? If you have children and want friends and family to visit regularly then you shouldn't choose an apartment, while if you crave privacy, search for a rural home or spacious villa; a young couple keen to be in a central hub should obviously look for a city centre apartment.

Other considerations that will affect the type of property you buy include the heating and air conditioning situation. Eastern Europe can get bitterly cold during the winter, but be aware that you are unlikely to get connected to gas outside of major conurbations, so electric and oil central heating will be the best you can expect. Air conditioning is worth installing, as in summer temperatures can be high. Look at the parking and access situation too. Few city properties come with guaranteed parking and spaces can be expensive to purchase, which may be a problem if you intend to take your car. If you want to buy in a rural area, are the roads accessible enough for you and will they be passable in winter? These are all considerations that it's worth spending a few moments looking at before you settle on a certain type of property.

Apartments

Apartments are one of the most in-demand property types in Eastern Europe, with the vast majority of the urban population living in them. Although the term 'apartment' may conjure up the image of communist concrete monstrosities – and some of these are up for sale – these aren't what a western buyer is looking for, or what you'll be offered. Generally speaking, for investors, city apartments are the best option as they are eminently more rentable than other property types. Ideal for business people looking for a long-term let, and also good for short-term rentals and those looking to spend a long weekend in Prague or Budapest, they can generate a healthy rental income. On the Bulgarian coast and Turkish Riviera there are also a number of newly-built apartment developments that can be picked up for under £40,000.

Apartments tend to be cheaper than villas or houses, offer a high quality finish, have lower running costs and, as with Florida and Spain, if part of a development, will come with facilities such as a gym or pool. Exterior maintenance will be carried out for you, there will also be neighbours to keep an eye on things and many developers now offer buyers guaranteed rental opportunities for many months of the year. What's more, apartments come with the benefit that you can 'lock and leave' them. However, be prepared for less space and less privacy.

There is also the option of choosing a period apartment. Budapest is a good example of this, with a number of turn-of-the-century buildings transformed into modern apartments. With distinctive architecture, running from Rococo to Art Deco or Baroque, all are centrally located and many contain unique frescoes and balconies.

Villas

Not every Eastern European country will have the right climate, demand or advanced property market to be able to offer a newly-built villa development. However, this doesn't mean there's a shortage on the market, with Turkey and Croatia both full of fantastically-located, modern or traditionally styled villas. Generally found on the coast, this is the perfect option for those seeking a holiday home that can generate a healthy rental income from holiday makers.

Villas have the advantage of offering plenty of space and privacy, with the option of having a pool installed, as well as providing you with private gardens. A number are located in purpose-built developments with onsite amenities and they're popular with Brits, offering space from neighbours and features such as private garages. Be prepared to pay a premium for a coastal spot.

Rural properties

There are numerous rural properties for sale in Eastern Europe, and this can mean anything from a tumble-down cowshed to a custom-built period house on the shores of Lake Balaton. There is a strong custom of Eastern Europeans owning a second home in the country, so there are many on the market, although unlike the western idea of a weekend in the country, this can mean anything from living in luxury to staying in a wood cabin with no electricity. Consequently, if you are willing to put some DIY time in, it is possible to pick up a rurally-located home for next to nothing. Montenegro is a good example of a healthy rural property market. Most properties sold are period, stone-built buildings ripe for renovation. Similarly in Croatia the in-demand property is a traditionally styled, stone-built cottage, although availability is very low.

Historic properties

Eastern Europe has a rich cultural history and part of this historical heritage is manifested in the number of ducal seats and magnificent manors scattered around the country. Fancy buying a Czech castle? If you have a couple of million to spare then you shouldn't be short of options.

Most have fallen into disrepair as the family fortune has dissipated, although given the price tag, the majority are bought as businesses and end up transformed into hotels or spas. Transylvania offers a number of gothic castes and chateaux that are ideal for renovation and they may well prove to be popular in the future, as they are located in the mountainous ski areas. For those on a smaller budget, many of Eastern Europe's larger cities offer traditional apartments with period features in their old town areas.

Newly-built properties

As the property market in Eastern Europe has got hotter, a number of newly-built developments have sprung up to cater for the demand. These are particularly prominent on Bulgaria's Black Sea Coast. The market in Montenegro has seen a similar phenomenon occur, although these developments are all restricted to three storeys. For more details see the section below on new builds vs resales.

Land

Thanks to the explosion of interest in Eastern European property, you will generally find land more readily available inland than on the coast. Investors have been increasingly attracted to plots of land thanks to the low prices that allow them to build their dream property. Land is also a great investment. In Romania, some investors have bought plots and, rather than developing them, have kept them untouched, selling them on after land prices have quadrupled. Most countries can offer inland plots, although be aware that the greatest restrictions foreigners now face are on the purchase and ownership of land – in some countries it is forbidden altogether.

Commercial

For the budding entrepreneur there are many opportunities to purchase commercial property. Most commercial opportunities are in popular coastal resorts or major cities and property can range from shops and hotels to offices and workshops. Be aware that the building will need to be licensed for commercial usage and if purchasing a business, do your background research and ensure the company is still functioning and that you're not buying a dud.

NEW BUILDS VS. RESALES

Historically, as rural depopulation and increased affluence has resulted in Eastern Europeans opting for newly-built, better quality homes to replace those dating back to the communist era, foreign DIY enthusiasts have been left with a plethora of dream homes. However, pressure has been put on the market as many locals have also begun to show an interest in restoration. Nevertheless, now is a good time to look east for your renovation project, as many Western European countries – such as France and Italy – are experiencing a shortage of rural homes due to high demand; what's left carries an extortionate price tag. Eventually, the same scenario will hit Eastern Europe as increasing numbers of overseas buyers plunder the stock of dilapidated buildings, causing price hikes. This is likely to affect areas such as those around ski resorts or in proximity to major towns and cities; the real wilderness is unlikely to dry up for many decades.

With local demand vying with foreign demand in many countries for the purchase of newly-built apartments, brand new property is regarded as a safe investment – except where supply exceeds demand, a scenario currently being witnessed in the tiny country of Slovenia. There are plenty of developments situated in the Eastern region, most located in cities or along the coast, and while prices are still affordable, if space restrictions and demand continues to be an issue, you will see prices rocket.

Pros and cons

Renovating

- There is plenty of choice and prices are low.

- You can build a home to suit your purposes and needs.

- You will have a unique, characterful property that will be popular for rentals (depending on location).

- You'll generally be looking at more space – both inside and out.

- Cost of labour is generally 33% cheaper and materials 66% cheaper than in the UK. However, in some countries, such as Bulgaria, costs are nearly on a par with the UK.

- It is essential you consider the work and cost of bringing a property up to western standards of living: the connection of utilities and the creation of a passable road may be required.

- You'll need to secure planning permission – something that was virtually guaranteed in the days before EU legislation came into play, but rules have been tightened.

- Factor in a cost of between €400–€700 per square metre for renovation.

- Remember that this will be a long-term process and may mean months of living on a building site, and it can be a stressful process.

New build

- It will be fully habitable and ready to live in and you will have the sale completed quicker.

- Less stress and hassle.

- The build quality for a newly-built property will be higher, and you will most likely be provided with extras such as a fitted kitchen and all utilities connected.

- Energy efficiency and insulation will be better.

- Less maintenance will be required.

- Many come with onsite amenities, such as a gym or swimming pool.

- Unlike an older property, it will probably lack character and is unlikely to have a spacious, mature garden.

- You may not feel you have sufficient privacy, as it's more than likely that you will be in a development.

CHOOSING THE RIGHT HOME FOR YOU

When looking to buy a home, in order to help you narrow down your search, you need to decide on your usage – what will you be using your property for? There is a such a broad range of landscapes, locations and property types to choose from and so being clear on what you want will make the search a lot quicker and easier, saving you time and money in the long run.

Ask yourself some serious questions such as: Do you want to be near a beach? Do you want to have neighbours or would you rather live in an isolated area? Are you looking to let your home and if so, do you want to buy within half an hour's drive of the airport, which will ultimately be more expensive. Are you buying a holiday home or purchasing as an investment? Are you going to be relocating or retiring to your property? If so, you need to consider proximity to schools and hospitals.

Finally, how much are you prepared to risk when purchasing? Are you happy to look at immature markets which may carry some risk, but potentially more gain in the long run, or are you after a more established market?

Issues to consider

Where?

- Do you want to live in the city or countryside?

- Do you want to be inland, near the coast, or close to the mountains?

- Is your wish to live in an isolated community or do you want to have neighbours?

- Is good weather important to you or are you happy to endure cold, snowy winters?

- How far are you prepared to be from the UK/home/family/friends?

Why?

- Why do you want a second home? Are you going to be using it for weekend breaks/months away/holidays, or are you looking to relocate?
- Do you want to make money from your home?
- Do you eventually intend to retire there?
- If you intend to sell the property on later, are other properties in the area selling well?

Travel

- Are the cost of flights expensive? If you intend to rent the property, make sure you buy close to an airport that offers budget flights.
- Are you happy to go to the same place every year?
- Is accessibility an issue? If you intend to retire there, will it remain just as easy to access when you are older?

Amenities

- Do you want public transport, shops, restaurants, etc. on your doorstep, or are you happy to travel to reach them?
- Do you have hobbies/sports you want to pursue?
- What entertainment could you enjoy in the area?

Health

- Does anyone in the family have long-term health concerns – e.g. diabetes – or heart problems that will need to be regularly monitored?
- How good is the health service?
- How near will you be to the doctor/dentist/hospital?

Practicalities

- Is it important to be able to speak the language? If so, are you prepared to learn?

- Do you want to take your pet? If the Eastern European country of your choice is now part of the EU, you only need a pet passport. If not, then you need to consider that they will have to spend time in quarantine.

- Do you know your neighbours and what they are like?

- Are there expats in the area? If not, are you prepared to integrate yourself into local life?

Type

- Who will be staying/living in the property? Will it just be yourself and your partner or are you likely to have family and friends round? If so, you will need to ensure there is space/spare rooms.

- Will you need to modernise the property? If so, have you budgeted for renovation costs?

- Do you want a property with character or something new and pristine with all mod cons?

4
The buying process

HOW THE EASTERN EUROPEAN BUYING PROCESS DIFFERS FROM THAT OF THE UK

At first glance, the legal system in the UK and Eastern Europe may seem very similar. Although they both follow the same principles, generally speaking, the system employed by Eastern European countries is very different, being based on a different civil and legal code. Consequently it is vital that you secure independent legal advice and look into the taxation, inheritance and other implications of your being a foreign buyer. The most obvious differences are that in the UK there is no need to sign a preliminary contract – you merely see a draft contract and agree to it – and until the exchange of contracts takes place, you are not legally bound to purchase the property.

When buying a property, you should also expect financing for UK nationals to be much more limited than in Western Europe, and in some cases non-existent, meaning that raising finance in the UK will be necessary. Although progress is being made to improve the system in countries such as Romania, the mortgage market is still very immature and there is a long way to go before foreigners will have the choice offered in the UK market. With a limited availability of finance comes the problem of less competitive lending terms. This can be manifested in the form of lower loan to values (LTVs), higher interest rates, lower mortgage terms and higher pre-payment penalties.

One of the first differences you'll be faced with will be the language problem, and this in turn will translate into cost – the cost of getting documents translated or getting your lawyer/estate agent to deal with issues that you would otherwise have been able to handle had you spoken the language. Secondly, you have the currency differences. Only Slovenia and Montenegro currently use the euro, and so there are issues of currency conversion and oscillating exchange rates to be aware of. However, with EU membership has come increased stability as many Eastern European currencies are now pegged to the euro. Also, while purchase costs for property might be lower, acquisition costs are generally higher than in the UK: these include costs such as taxes, notary and estate agents' fees, and other costs required to close the sale.

Other factors to consider include ownership. In many instances there are restrictions upon foreign buyers which may require them to purchase as a company. For more details, see p46.

Main stages of UK conveyancing

Stage 1: Prior to the Exchange of Contracts
The draft contract is received and negotiated, enquiries are made about the property and the formal mortgage offer is received.

Stage 2: Exchange of Contracts
The contract is signed and you hand over a 10% deposit. Final accounts are prepared and the mortgage deed requested for you to sign.

Stage 3: Completion
You obtain the keys to your new home and receive the title deeds. Stamp duty is paid and the transfer is arranged at the land registry so the house is now registered in your name.

Main stages of Eastern European conveyancing

Stage 1
The signing of the reservation contract and payment of an initial reservation fee – generally 0.5% of the property's value.

Stage 2
The preliminary or future contract. This binds both parties to the sale and the buyer can use this in the mortgage application process. Signing this document is equivalent to an exchange of contracts in the UK. Once this has been signed, a deposit of between 10% and 20% needs to be paid.

> **Stage 3**
> The signing of the final purchase contract in the presence of a notary. This is
> the equivalent of completion of a sale in the UK. Once the final contract has
> been signed, the remaining funds need to be paid in order to finalise the sale.
> However, you are not technically the legal owner of the property – not until all
> the necessary paperwork is submitted to the land registry and they have
> acknowledged the sale and lodged you as the new owner on the registry
> records.

HOW TO FINANCE YOUR PURCHASE

There are a number of ways in which a purchase can be financed in
Eastern Europe. The first is (if you are fortunate enough) to pay up-front,
thus owning your home outright. The alternative is through raising the
cash in the UK, either by re-mortgaging your home or applying for a
mortgage with a UK bank. Finally, you could apply for a mortgage in the
Eastern European country where you are buying.

The mortgage market is currently emerging in Eastern Europe and as
such, interest rates are slightly higher than the established markets such
as Spain and Portugal and, in most cases, UK buyers prefer to re-
mortgage in order to raise the funding. It should also be pointed out that
in some Eastern European countries, local banks do not advance
mortgages for off-plan properties due to the lack of security.

Alternative methods for raising finance include securing a short-term
loan. This is particularly popular if you know you have a lump sum of
cash coming to you – such as a pension – and need a stop-gap to help pay
a deposit or other fees. There are also facilities such as an overdraft
extension or the use of a credit card, but again, while the use of these is
personal preference, make sure you do not lumber yourself with more
debt than you can repay.

Eastern European vs. UK mortgages

* You generally only get a mortgage of a maximum of 70% of
  property value in Eastern Europe.

- Generally, Eastern European mortgages are only for 15 years, although 25-year mortgages are becoming increasingly available.

- Not all property types and locations will be eligible for a mortgage, e.g. off-plan purchases.

- The lending process and repayment schedules differ, as do the restrictions. Typical repayments, based on 25 years, with an interest rate of 6.5%, are as follows:
€ 100,000, repayment = € 675 per month
€ 200,000, repayment = € 1,300
€ 300,000, repayment = € 1,975.

Sample mortgage rates, provided by Fidentia: www.fidentiagroup.com

Bulgaria
Max LTV: 80%
Rates from: 6.25%
Max term: 25 years
Max age: 65

Hungary
Max LTV: 70%
Rates from: 5.99%
Max term: 25 years
Max age: 68

Poland
Max LTV: 80%
Rates from: 3.21%
Max term: 20 years
Max age: 65
Commercial mortgages: Yes

Latvia
Max LTV: 80%
Rates from: 4.49%
Max term: 20 years
Max age: 65
All mortgage loans are subject to status.

CURRENCY CONVERSION

The best way to negotiate and successfully navigate currency exchange is to search for the best exchange rate deal. There are numerous specialist currency exchange companies out there who will often beat rates offered by the main banks. You can choose from a risk-free option – to buy all of your currency in one go and fix the cost of exchange, or a high-risk strategy – to buy euros each time you need to send them to the developer/seller. There are also a number of forward-buying contracts, where you fix your foreign exchange rate for a specified amount today and elect a date in the future to pick up and pay for your currency. A deposit payment of between 3% and 10% is generally required on agreement of the contract.

There are also a number of sophisticated currency swap arrangements that individuals can enter into, but these are probably not going to be suitable for most and do not always provide complete protection.

Useful contacts:

www.fidentiagroup.com
www.currencies.co.uk
www.globexfx.com
www.travelex.co.uk
www.currenciesdirect.com
www.hifx.co.uk

TAXATION

As with any tax situation, it's always tricky to establish exactly how much you will be liable to pay, when, and – if you have assets in more than one country – to which tax office. Thankfully, member states within the EU have double-taxation treaties with the UK and so you shouldn't end up paying two lots of tax. The following Eastern European countries have such an agreement with the UK:

• Bulgaria

- Croatia (Croatia does not have a unique agreement with the UK, but does have an agreement in place which dates back to the days of the Yugoslav Republic. This covers income tax, capital gains tax and corporation tax.)

- Czech Republic

- Estonia

- Hungary

- Latvia

- Lithuania

- Montenegro

- Poland

- Romania

- Slovakia

- Slovenia

- Turkey.

Currently no Eastern European country has a double taxation treaty which covers inheritance tax. See www.hmrc.gov.uk/si/double.htm for more details.

Buyers should always consult experts to get the best, up-to-the-minute tax advice, while UK nationals should consider their tax position with both HM Revenue & Customs (www.hmrc.gov.uk), as well as the foreign tax authorities, as you will be obliged to report any worldwide income to UK authorities, regardless of whether they tax you on it or not.

The main taxes you will be liable to pay in Eastern Europe are:

- Stamp Duty

- Capital Gains Tax

- Tax on rental income

- Council Tax.

Rates vary. See Section 2 of this book for country-specific details.

Tax residency

Your position as a tax resident is what determines where you will be taxed and on what income, although the rules governing tax residency vary from country to country. The rule generally states that if you are resident in a country for 183 days out of the tax year (this doesn't have to be continuous) you will be taxed on income in that country. Residency doesn't require you to be a legally recognised resident of the country, nor does it require you to own a home there, (although in both cases this will generally mean you are classed as a tax resident) – it merely depends on the number of days spent residing in a country. To take Bulgaria as an example, you are considered to be a tax resident in Bulgaria if you have a permanent residence in the country or if you are a permanent resident, i.e. if you spend more than 183 days in Bulgaria in any year. If you aren't a permanent resident and are only working in Bulgaria temporarily, then tax is payable only on your income earned while you're there.

Gains may or may not be taxable in the overseas country, depending on the circumstances, but are likely to be taxable back in the UK. In the UK, you will also be considered a resident if you spend more than 183 days here (excluding days of arrival and departure) in any given tax year, or more than 91 days on average per year, over four UK tax years.

Property ownership through a company

Many countries only allow foreign individuals to acquire property through a local company due to restrictions on property ownership by foreign buyers. If you remain UK resident and use the property you've purchased as a holiday home, the UK Revenue and Customs department may charge you tax on an annual 'benefit in kind', even though you will have financed the property and the running costs. Also, depending on the circumstances, a foreign company effectively managed and controlled in the UK by you could, itself, be viewed as a UK tax resident and become subject to UK company taxation and compliance requirements.

Country examples

Details provided by Blevin Franks Mortgage and Tax advisors, www.blevinsfranks.com.

Croatia

- For individuals, rental income is taxed at an effective rate of either 7.5% or 10.5%. There are also surcharges for residents of up to 18%.

- Companies pay tax at 20% on rental profits, and rental losses can be carried forward for up to five years.

- Capital gains are taxed at 35% for individuals and at 20% for companies. Assets held for more than three years on your first home are exempt.

- VAT is levied at a rate of 22% on leasing of real estate, except on real estate used for residential purposes.

- 5% transfer tax is levied on transfer of real estate ownership.

- Annual property taxes are levied based on the size and the location of the property.

Czech Republic

- Foreign investors can only invest through a Czech company, although this restriction has to be removed for EU residents by May 2009.

- Rental income and capital gains are taxed at progressive rates of up to 32% for individuals, and for companies as part of corporate income at 24%.

- Rental losses can be carried forward for up to five years.

- Real estate transfer tax is payable at 3% and is payable by the vendor (or purchaser as the guarantor).

- Real estate taxes are payable at variable rates.

Estonia

- For individuals, rental income is taxed at 21%. Companies pay tax at a flat rate of 28.2%.

- Capital gains are taxed as part of other income at 21%.

- Land tax is payable at 0.1%, up to 2.5%, and is payable by the owner of the land.

- There are no transfer taxes or stamp duties, but state fees and notary fees are due.

Hungary

- Usually it is easier to acquire property through a property holding company.

- For individuals, rental income is taxed at either 25% of gross rental income or at progressive rates of 18% to 38% (in this case actual business accounts have to be prepared).

- The corporate tax rate of 16% (plus 2% local tax) is payable by companies.

- Capital gains are taxed at either 25% with a 10% reduction after five years or for companies, capital gains are taxed as part of income.

- Share sales are exempt from capital gains tax.

- Building tax is payable by the legal owner at 3%, or a maximum of HUF 1,006 per square metre.

- Land tax is payable at a maximum of 3% or HUF 224 per square metre.

- Transfer tax is payable by the person acquiring the property at 2% up to HUF 4 million and 6% above that.

Latvia

- Net rental income is taxed at a corporate income tax rate of 15% or personal income tax rate of 25%.

- Capital gains on real estate are exempt from capital gains tax provided that the property has been owned for more than 12 months.

- Capital gains tax for companies is 2% of the proceeds of the sale.
- Real estate tax is payable on land at 1.5% and on buildings at 1.5%, but houses and apartments which are used for residential purposes are exempt from real estate tax.
- Registration duty is payable between 0.5% to 3%.

Lithuania

- For individuals, rental income is taxed at progressive rates from 15% to 33%. Companies pay corporation tax on rental income at 15% plus 3% social tax.
- Tax losses can be carried forward for up to three years.
- Capital gains are treated as part of income and non-residents are taxed at 10% on gains on real estate. However, residents are exempt provided they only purchase one piece of real estate per year.
- Real estate is subject to 1% real estate tax.
- Land owned by a legal entity is subject to land tax at 1.5%.
- Notary dues of between 0.5% and 1% upon transfer of real estate.
- State use imposed upon transfer of real estate is charged from LTL100 to LTL10,000, depending on the value of real estate.

Poland

- For individuals, rental income is taxed at progressive rates up to 40%. Net income received by corporate taxpayers is taxable in Poland at 19%.
- Capital gains on real estate is taxed at 10% of the sale price, but the payment of tax on gains is exempt provided you have owned the real estate for over five years.
- Sale of land and buildings is generally subject to VAT at 22%.

Romania

- Rental income is subject to individual income tax at a flat rate of 16%. Net income is determined by deducting 25% of the gross rental income.

- Companies pay corporation tax at 16%.

- Capital gains are taxed at 16% but share sales are subject to a special 1% rate under specific conditions.

- Rental losses can be carried forward for five years.

- Stamp duty and notary fees are payable on purchase of real estate.

Slovakia

- Rental income is taxed as ordinary income and is subject to a tax rate of 19%. For companies, the standard corporate tax rate is also 19%.

- Capital gains tax is also payable at 19%, but gains are exempt after five years under certain conditions.

- Real estate tax is levied on individuals and companies owning real property at approximately SKK280 per square metre.

- Real estate transfer tax has been fully abolished.

Slovenia

- Rental income is taxed at progressive rates from 16% to 50% and companies pay corporation tax on rental income at 25%.

- Rental losses can be carried forward for up to seven years.

- Capital gains are taxed as part of other income and are exempt if the property has been held for three years or more.

- Immovable property transfer tax is levied if VAT has not been charged on the transfer (at 2% of the market value of the transaction).

- New real estate tax is likely to be introduced soon.

Turkey

- Rental income is taxed at progressive rates from 15% to 40%.

- Companies pay corporation tax at 20%.

- Capital gains are taxed as part of other income and gains on property are exempt after four years. There is also an annual exemption of approximately £4,000.

- Title deed charges are imposed on the acquisition of legal title at 1.5%, and the same charge applies when the property is sold.

- Stamp tax is calculated on the sale price of real estate at 0.75%, with a ceiling of YTL800,000.

- Property tax is levied on the owner of real estate at 0.2% on buildings. If in residential use the rate is reduced to 0.1%.

Montenegro

- Rental income is taxed at progressive rates from 0% to 23%.

- Companies pay corporation tax at 9%.

- Capital gains are taxed as part of other income, but only 50% of the actual gain is taxable.

- Rental income received by non-residents is subject to withholding tax at 15%.

- Annual property tax of between 0.08% and 0.8% is levied (in most cases, 0.2% on buildings).

- Property transfer tax of 2% is payable by the purchaser on the acquisition of real estate.

- Transfer of newly-built property located in Montenegro is subject to VAT at 17% but the lease of residential real estate is not subject to VAT. Any other transfer of real estate is subject to property transfer tax.

Bulgaria

- Foreign individuals can only acquire land through a Bulgarian company.

- Transfer tax at 2% is payable on transfer of property.

- Registration fees at 0.1% of the price of the property are payable.

- The notary fee is calculated as a percentage of the agreed price (between 1.5% for property up to BGN1,000 and 0.1% for values above BGN 100,000).

- VAT is charged at 20% if the seller is registered for Bulgarian VAT purposes.

- Real estate tax is payable at 0.15%.

- There are also garbage collection fees imposed by the local authorities.

- Rental income is subject to 15% withholding tax on gross income and no expenses can be deducted.

- Capital gains are subject to 15% Bulgarian withholding tax. Two properties are exempt after five years.

- Property inherited by a spouse or heirs of a direct line is tax exempt, but inheritance tax is levied on a property exceeding BGN250,000 at 0.7% if the property is inherited by brothers, sisters and their descendants. An additional 5% is charged for other heirs.

- Significant changes are expected to Bulgarian tax laws following EU accession.

FINDING A LAWYER

The best way to go about finding a lawyer is to contact the London-based embassy of the country you're buying in, asking them for a list of recommended lawyers. Another simple method of hunting down a reliable professional is to gain a personal recommendation, either from family or friends, or by posting a notice on an expat website forum.

The services provided by your lawyer will include drawing up the necessary documentation relevant to the sale in the language of the country of purchase. Even though not all Eastern European countries require you to employ the services of a lawyer, it is recommended you do so as your lawyer will be able to carry out a proper background search of the property and its title to ensure it's clean. They will also prepare the contract of purchase for you.

Most agents will offer to find you a lawyer, but this is not a recommended course of action, as they will probably be acting for the vendor, too. It's essential that you employ the services of an independent lawyer and always make sure they're registered. You will generally have the choice of choosing between a UK-based or local lawyer, but the advantages of having someone operating on the ground in the country of purchase – especially as they can act on your behalf, if given power of attorney – far outweigh the benefits of being based in the UK. Local lawyers generally have a superior working knowledge of the country's legal system, requirements and loopholes.

THE GENERAL BUYING PROCESS

Eastern Europe is a staggeringly beautiful and diverse region that has a wealth of attractive properties on offer, and it can be easy to let your heart rule your head and succumb to agent pressure or your own feelings without doing the proper research and thorough checks on a property. Never allow yourself to do this. Always ensure you give the property a going-over before parting with any money, and don't worry if you lose the property as a result of your diligence – there's sure to be another.

Almost all of the Eastern European countries employ a continental law system, which is completely different from the UK common law system. The standard residential conveyancing transaction generally follows a threefold process: the reservation, the preliminary contract and completion.

The first stage is the reservation of the property. Depending on the price of the building, reservation fees vary, but are usually in the region of €1,000 to €2,000 for properties costing up to €100,000. Once the reservation contract is signed and the reservation deposit is paid, the buyer is provided with the preliminary sale contracts, either by the agent or the seller's solicitor, management contracts and all the other relevant documents in relation to the purchase, such as title deeds, construction licences and habitation licences.

The second stage of the transaction is the signing of the preliminary sale contract. In cases where you are purchasing an old or resale property this is the stage at which a survey should be arranged. Buyers should be aware that before they sign the preliminary sale contract, they should always seek independent legal advice, as once the contract is signed they will be committed to the purchase, and in the majority of cases, there are heavy penalty clauses in case the buyer pulls out once the contract is signed. Also, buyers should bear in mind that the preliminary sale contract is a private contract and as such, the title of the property does not transfer at this stage. You will generally now be required to pay a deposit of between 10% to 20%, and with an off-plan property, this will make up the first instalment. The preliminary contract should contain details of the payment timeline if you are purchasing a newly-built, off-plan property, and buyers should know that in Eastern Europe, the stage payments in off-plan cases are not protected by bank guarantees, as in Spain or Portugal. Because of this, it is crucial that the content of the contract is specific about the details of payment and in what situation payment should not be offered.

The final stage is the signing of the title deeds, which is executed in the presence of a public notary. A state official, it is his/her role to witness the signatures of the parties on the deeds and also to check that both parties have the legal capacity to enter into the final contract or deed. Buyers should be aware that the notary is independent and does not act for either of the parties. At this stage, if buying a resale or old property, the payment of the remainder of the property price is required, along with the payment of estate agents' fees in some cases. If you are buying in a country such as the Czech Republic, where it can take a significant amount of time for the land registry to recognise the sale (and thus legally declare you as the owner of the property), the final payment can remain with the notary or in a separate bank account, only being transferred to the seller on receipt of the title deeds.

Restrictions on foreign buyers

As many Eastern European countries are part of the EU, other EU citizens are generally allowed to purchase property with limited restrictions or no restrictions at all. Where there are restrictions, these tend to surround the ownership of land and most can be circumnavigated by setting up a limited company. In some cases, such as Turkey, you will need to check with the government or military that they are happy for you to buy.

Additional costs

Several fees and taxes will be payable on top of the cost of the initial property purchase price. It's recommended that you budget for an additional 4–5% of the cost of the property – this should cover the additional fees required.

Costs may include:

- Transfer fees: 2–2.5%
- Notary fees: 0.5–1%
- Legal fees: 1–1.5%
- Surveyor's fee (optional)
- Mortgage fees (if applicable)
- Foreign exchange costs (if applicable)
- Estate agents' fees (if applicable).

Surveys

It is advisable that you get a survey carried out on your property, especially if it is an older or resale property. Although newly-built properties come with a guarantee for a certain period of time, it's still recommended that you get it checked out. Your lawyer or agent should also complete a background check on the property, including checking court records and mortgage records to ensure there are no debts transferable with the property. Normally, a visual survey will be arranged and the cost of this is often included in the overall fee paid to your lawyer or estate agent. A structural engineer will also view the property to inspect the construction in detail. The type of report you decide to get will vary from a UK survey and is generally not as thorough. The survey can be carried out by either a surveyor or an architect, but you may have to get it translated. However, there are increasing numbers of local companies, especially in the larger towns and cities, which are offering English-style surveys and are gearing themselves towards the foreign market. A full structural survey can be arranged if the house is particularly old or there is some doubt about the land the building has been built on. This will cost you between £200 and £300.

The following is a list of things to ensure the surveyor looks out for:

- That the title corresponds with the property's size and number of rooms.

- Whether the plot boundaries are correct.

- Check the walls and roof for obvious signs of disrepair or cracks.

- Check the property for damp or dry rot.

- Check which fittings and furnishings come with the house and garden and which don't.

- Do the doors and windows fit and lock properly?

- Are you connected to all utilities?

- Where are all the plug sockets and telephone points, and are there enough?

- Do you have fully-functioning heating and air conditioning, or is this something you will have to rectify?

- Is the bathroom in good condition? Are the tiles damaged? Is the bathroom ventilated?

- Does the drainage system function properly?

- Are there any strange smells in the house?

- Are there any signs of insect infestation in the woodwork?

Background checks

With certain types of property there are different considerations to take into account before you purchase. For example, with an apartment always check out the management costs you may be levied with for upkeep of communal areas, security and general caretaking. For a business, make sure the proper background checks are done and you are permitted to trade and use the property or land you have purchased for the intended business venture. If buying a newly-built or off-plan property, dig around and ensure the developer has obtained building permission. In all cases, you should ensure that all the planning permission and permits you require have been granted. Finally, it is worth checking to see whether there are any plans for the development of the land surrounding your property; is a road or airport planned over the next few years? Will your view be blocked by a new development?

FINAL CHECKLIST

- Always establish a budget and stick to it.

- Always view the area and as many properties as possible before committing to buy and consider renting in the area to get to know it better. Try to view a property you are considering buying at different times of day and year.

- Think twice before you buy: is the area right for you? Make sure the answer is yes before you sign the legally-binding preliminary contract.

- Make sure that the property corresponds to its description with both the estate agent's details and the title in the land registry, and get your lawyer to carry out a thorough background check before purchase.

- Make sure you're paying market value for the property and aren't the victim of overcharging, as foreigners in Eastern Europe can be.

- Always check the additional costs of the purchase, such as taxes and fees for the notary, estate agent and lawyer.

- Make sure that planning permission has been granted for the property and that any future work you want to do will also be given the OK.

- Always clarify what is, and what is not, included in the sale, such as fittings and furnishings.

- Have any documentation translated into English before you sign it.

- Appoint a power of attorney to the preliminary and final contract on your behalf if you can't attend.

- Make sure that there are get-out clauses in the preliminary contract for any issues such as the seller backing out, or failure by the developer to complete an off-plan property.

- Never sign a document unless you know exactly what you're signing.

- Be sure of any key dates or deadlines and adhere to them – missing a stage payment could lose you your property.

- Always use a professional to check that the paperwork relating to the property is in order.

- Have a survey done on the property and check the exact boundaries, clarifying all rights of way and access routes.

5
Buying to let

Thanks to the regularity and affordability of budget flights throughout Eastern Europe and the relaxation of visa rules, jetting off for a holiday in the region has become increasingly easy – and popular. Eastern European countries are experiencing the largest tourist growth in Europe, with countries such as Montenegro, Romania and Croatia leading the way.

Consequently, the concept of buying a property in order to make money from letting it out has become a massive phenomenon. The vast majority of people who purchase overseas buy with the intention of holidaying there for four to six weeks of the year and renting it out for the remaining 46-odd weeks. As a UK resident you will have the benefit of being able to tap into the foreign market, as you will have an understanding of the needs and standards a foreign renter will expect and can market and furnish your home accordingly.

However; a word of warning. Many markets in Eastern Europe simply can't generate the kind of yields investors have come to expect from France and Spain. For one thing, most Eastern Europe countries have very short peak/summer seasons due to the weather. Secondly, many of the tourist markets in the region are too undeveloped to fill beds, and those that can often have deals in place with travel agents, as tourism is predominantly organised by package holiday deals – this is especially the case in Bulgaria. While this will no doubt change, be aware that your purchase will be a long-term, rather than short-term investment, and it will take time to build up a rental portfolio.

Many people also fall into the trap of thinking that they can buy slightly above their price range as income generated from rentals will cover their repayments, but this is simply too risky a strategy. Only buy what you can afford to sustain and be aware that the majority of income from lets will go on maintenance costs, furnishing, cleaning, property management and general wear and tear, as well as any advertising you choose to do.

SHORT- OR LONG-TERM?

Whatever you decide to do, if you are going to be reliant on rental income in order to make your investment a stable one, then it is imperative you look at the future of the market. Talk to lettings agencies and travel agents and ask them where they think the best investments are to be made. Any planned increase in budget flights is a good sign that the market will be opening up to tourists, providing you with future demand for short-term lettings.

There are many locations in Eastern Europe – generally the capital cities or larger towns – where a healthy foreign student and business population will mean long-term rentals are feasible. While this will severely limit the time you can spend in your home, in the long run, it means the property is being looked after and you have a healthy and regular income generated from it. The Baltic States are an excellent example of a market where massive foreign direct investment and the growth of multinationals in the region is resulting in a growing foreign workforce, all of whom are looking for accommodation.

THE IMPORTANCE OF LOCATION

You may think it is a cliché, but that old adage again 'location, location, location' will never wear thin in terms of choosing a property with the intention of letting. If you buy somewhere too far from the airport, you're unlikely to secure many lets; if you buy in 'no-man's land' too far from the coast, ski resorts or major cities, then the likelihood is that very few people will show an interest. Buying a home to let has to be a business decision and, as such, you need to think very carefully about the location and put your own tastes to one side.

The first thing to do is to ensure that the area you are looking to buy in is not saturated with rentals, as this minimises your chances of securing a healthy number of bookings. This doesn't mean you should pick an area which is virtually unknown – the best bet is to look at the newly-developing areas where budget flights are fairly regular.

The next thing to do is get to know the area and see what kind of amenities and infrastructure are in place. The kind of amenities you are looking for obviously depends on whether you are trying to attract short- or long-term rents. Most holiday-makers will either want the property to have a pool and large garden for barbeques, or to be near the beach, so are prepared to pay a little extra for a premium location. Proximity to the airport is a must, as most people are not prepared to travel for more than 90 minutes to reach their rental accommodation.

Long-term renters will want to be close to supermarkets, their office and possibly schools, if renting with their family. City centre apartments, close to the transport network, clubs, bars and restaurants are the prime locations.

Today it is even possible to buy newly-built property with guaranteed rental income for a fixed number of years. While this is good if it's true, be wary of taking a developer at their word and make sure you get proof and written confirmation before entering into a purchase.

SETTING A PRICE

Firstly, you must think about whether you intend to make a living out of renting property, or if you are just trying to cover your costs. For instance, you will be able to generate more income from the ski resorts of Bulgaria than you would for a coastal house in Montenegro. Similarly, if you are letting long term, you will be making less per week, but you'll have a guaranteed income over a longer period.

The best thing to do is find out how much other properties of a similar size and in the same area are charging, allowing you to estimate the kind of income you can expect to generate. This is important so that you don't price yourself out of the market, and by possibly undercutting the competition, you could end up securing more rentals and thus making more in the long run.

FURNISHING THE PROPERTY

Regardless of where you buy and what the area can offer, if you don't furnish your property properly then you are unlikely to secure large numbers of bookings, and the prospect of re-bookings will be very low. This is just as important with long-term rentals, especially as you are probably going to be looking at renting to single business people or young couples, who will want a modern look and feel from their home.

The first rule for short-term rentals is to make sure everything is clean and tidy and in working order. Ensure that all facilities, such as a television, fridge, freezer and cooker are in place and that there is fresh linen and towels – no one wants to have to bring these in their luggage. The standard of your furnishings generally dictates how much you can charge, but be prepared for breakages and wear and tear – furniture should be hard-wearing and easy to clean. Bedrooms should have comfortable beds and space for clothes to be hung, and providing a sofa bed in the living room will also allow you to up the rent charged, as you can provide accommodation for more people.

Added extras such as a washing machine or tumble dryer are always handy and it's recommended that air conditioning is available for the hot summer months – and heating for the winter! If you can, put together an information pack on the area with details of things to do, attractions to see and the best places for food and drink. Providing dry supplies such as tea and coffee will also help make your guests feel more at home.

MARKETING

If you intend to let your property then you need to be prepared to spend some time and money on marketing it correctly. The first few years are always likely to be tough, but if you ensure you put the work in early on and spend time making your property feel welcoming and homely, then you are sure to build up a regular client base which will probably sustain you for the foreseeable future.

To start with, you need to get your property advertised – there are numerous ways of doing this. One of the best ways are holiday websites. For a small fee – and, in some cases, no fee at all – you can upload details about your property to the website, and allow people to view and book online. There are also numerous magazines and newspapers where you can place advertisements, and a wealth of property management companies that will handle all the marketing, booking details and cleaning of the property for you.

If you intend to let your property then it's probably sensible to set up your own email address and phone number – especially if you don't want to publicise your home phone number. There are also a number of cheap and easy website packages out there so you can set up your own website.

If you decide to market your own home, be prepared to do the following:

- Follow up on queries straight away.

- Check your email and phone messages daily.

- Be prepared to advertise, but make sure you do your research and advertise in the right medium, depending on the type of tenant you are trying to attract.

- Think about having your own brochure printed and do an annual mail-out to previous tenants.

- Make business contacts in the local area and arrange an advertising deal with them – in return, you could recommend them to your clients.

- Advertise your property by word of mouth back in the UK. There are always rentals to be secured by sending emails around at work or getting friends to recommend your property.

- Keep an inventory of the contents of the property so you know if anything has been broken, damaged or stolen.

MANAGEMENT COMPANIES

If you don't feel you have the time or expertise to manage the letting of your property, then you can employ a property management company to do it for you. This is especially handy if you are not residing in the same country as your rental property is located. Generally speaking, if you manage the letting of your property yourself, you'll be able to generate more income and be more successful in letting your property. This is because you will be giving the project your undivided attention, unlike most management companies who have a large number of clients on their books and generally charge a fairly hefty rate of commission.

Nevertheless, a decent company will be able to take care of the marketing, maintenance, client liaison and booking of the property, and deal with all the bureaucracy and red tape that might come with the territory, making them value for money if they are good at their job. While most will be able to generate a large number of rentals during peak season, you need to be aware that they will have a number of clients on their books, so you won't get priority treatment. Also, don't take promises of year-round bookings and hefty yearly yields too seriously, as in reality, this is unlikely to happen.

Costs vary, although you are normally looking at up to 20% of your earnings. Make sure you tie them down on their promises and get guarantees about the number of weeks and level of income to expect. Finding a decent company isn't always easy, although your estate agent should be able to recommend someone to you, and word of mouth recommendations are always a good starting point. Note that if you are going to be living in the UK, it may well pay to have someone based in the same country as you, to avoid being ripped-off and to make communication easier.

LEGAL ISSUES

If you intend to let your property then the best starting point is to ensure you notify the authorities in the relevant country that you will be doing so. You should also brush up on local tenancy laws; these vary from country to country, but you will still be required to meet certain safety standards, so take legal advice.

Generally speaking, you will be taxed on your rental income in the country where the income was earned, i.e. the country where your rental property is located. This will generally be charged at the going income tax rate (see Chapter 3 for more details on tax), which will be lower than the UK rate. You will not be liable for taxation in the UK on rental income if there is a double taxation treaty in place with the UK and you pay tax in the country where your rental property is situated.

THE PROS AND CONS OF RENTING

Pros

- You can make money to cover repayments.
- Your home will be occupied and cared for during your absence.
- You can employ a holiday letting company to do the hard work and marketing for you.
- You have secured a nest egg for the future.
- The Eastern European markets are constantly growing, fuelled by media interest and EU membership. Tourist boards are reporting massive growth, with Bulgaria alone reporting a 42% increase in the number of British holiday-makers in 2005.

Cons

- You may find that you cannot spend time in your home during peak or summer seasons as that's when you experience the most demand and make most money.
- You will need to employ the services of a maintenance and cleaning firm which can sap your income.
- You will need to look into tenancy legislation and the health and safety standards demanded by law.

- Furnishings and facilities will need to be provided.

- The garden will need to be tended.

- If something breaks or there are problems, then you may not be in the country to deal with them.

> **Top tip**
>
> In order to assess whether renting your property will be a viable option, figure out how much income you will be likely to generate a week, and how many weeks' worth of rentals you can generally expect per year. Divide the net annual rent by the value of the property and if you end up with a figure less than 6% to 7%, then your property is not going to be a profitable or good buy to let investment.

6
The Baltic States

Factfile

Lithuania
Area: 65,200 sq km
Population: 3.4 million
Currency: Litas
GDP growth rate: 7.5%
Capital City: Vilnius (population: 542,287)
Inflation: 3.4%
Unemployment: 5.6%

Latvia
Area: 64,100 sq km
Population: 2.31 million
Currency: Lat
GDP growth rate: 10.2%
Capital City: Rīga (pop: 747,200)
Inflation: 6.7% (2005)
Unemployment: 7.8%

Estonia
Area: 45,227 sq km
Population: 1.35 million
Currency: Kroon
GDP growth rate: 9.8%
Capital City: Tallinn (Pop: 411,600)
Inflation: 4.1%
Unemployment: 7.9%

COUNTRY PROFILE

Despite the fact that the three Baltic States have short summers, long winters and an almost impenetrable language barrier, the three countries of Latvia, Lithuania and Estonia are topping the charts when it comes to economic and property market growth. Dynamic and well organised, these small countries have generated huge levels of interest, and experts predict that the market will continue to develop over the next ten to 20 years until prices are on a par with Western Europe.

Did you know?

- Only 16% of Estonians believe in God, giving Estonia the smallest percentage of believers in Europe. However, a staggering 54% claim to believe in some sort of spirit or life force – this is the highest percentage in Europe (Europe's average is 2%).
- The world's first Christmas tree was decorated and displayed in Rīga, in 1510.
- The world record for the greatest weight lifted with a human beard is held by Lithuanian Antanas Kontrimas. He lifted a girl weighing 62.05 kg ten centimetres off the ground.

Why the Baltic states?

Undoubtedly one of the biggest success stories of EU membership, the Baltic Tigers – so called because of the aggressive periods of economic expansion they've experienced since 2000 – have seen astronomical growth over the last few years, and topped all the polls in price appreciation and popularity when it comes to buying overseas.

All are stable parliamentary democracies, while NATO membership and the pegging of their respective currencies to the euro has helped to perpetuate the prosperous economy upon which the stability of their property markets is based. In terms of economic growth rates, all three have been close to 10% for the last few years, making them the fastest-growing economies in Europe. In comparison, the average increase of the original EU members was a mere 1.6%.

This is no mean feat when you look back to the early 90s and see how the collapse of the Soviet rouble, and the consequent inflation and financial crisis of Russia in 1998 damaged the Baltics. What's more, it was only in the early 1990s that Baltic nationals were entitled to buy their own property.

Today, inflation and interest rates are exceedingly low, which has encouraged the locals to get a foot on the property ladder, helping to stimulate price rises, which are destined to approach Western European levels within ten years. Estonia, Lithuania and Latvia are aiming to enter the euro zone at some point between 2008 and 2010, and this will further boost the popularity of the region with foreign investors and tourists.

Their collective property markets have topped the polls for price appreciation, with Estonia leading the charge at 54% for price increases in 2006. For the third quarter of 2006, estate agents Knight Frank reported that Latvia experienced growth of 39.2% and Lithuania 15.5%, putting all three countries in the top ten for worldwide house price growth in 2006.

Looking at all three countries in terms of tourism, up until 2004 very few UK tourists holidayed in the Baltic States. The three capitals of Rīga, Tallin and Vilnius remain the focal point for tourists and investors alike, with stag parties becoming increasingly popular. Consequently, all three capitals have been touted as the next Prague. Culturally, the Baltic States offer fine architecture, and all three capitals have been declared UNESCO World Heritage sites.

Economy and politics

Members of the EU and NATO since 2004, the Baltic States are Europe's leading growth economies, with foreign direct investment hitting €806.9 million in Lithuania in 2005, €507.9 million in Latvia and €837.9 million in Estonia. Enjoying a period of sustained economic growth, which began in 2000, all three countries have undergone economic transformation, thanks to their implementation of economic reforms and liberalisation. This, coupled with their skilled labour force and fairly low wages, saw the beginning of mass foreign investment, which helped to propel the Baltic Tigers to the position of Europe's economic leaders. It is predicted that this growth will continue at rates of between 5–10% until at least 2010, when they are expected to adopt the euro. The countries are also expected to experience a rise in GDP similar to that seen by Ireland during the 1990s. Despite the fact their GDP per capita is currently between 50–60% of the EU average, and unlikely to rival or match it in the near future, the fact that it has doubled since 1999, rising from 25% to 50% in eight years, is remarkable.

Lithuania

The keys to Lithuania's continued strong economic growth have proved to be foreign direct investment, a strong exports market and EU structural funds. While Lithuania no longer enjoys the highest rate of economic growth in Europe, economically, the country has continued to perform well for the past few years and currently enjoys an annual growth of over 7%, and an inflation rate of 2.3%. GDP is expected to continue to grow at above 7% past 2007, with the country earmarked to receive €9 billion in EU structural funds between 2007–2013.

Politically, the country has seen very little change since its independence from the Soviet Union in 1991. Stability is the over-arching theme, which is great in terms of investment.

Lithuania is a parliamentary democracy and the Prime Minister is Gediminas Kirkilas.

Latvia

Suffering from inflation rates that hit 951% in 1992 and a 50% crash in GDP following the collapse of the Soviet Union, Latvia has clawed her way back and today is regarded as the rising star of European economies. In 2005 growth rates hit 8.5%, the highest of any EU country, with interest rates as low as 4.5%. It was accession to the EU that helped bolster the country's flagging economy. Coupled with EU funding and foreign investment, in the third quarter of 2006, the economy of Latvia recorded the highest growth rate of the Baltic States. GDP hit 11.8% year on year, while Latvia currently tops the pay increase ladder with 11.1% projected rises in 2007. All this makes it a lucrative investment market, as current rates of inflation – 6.5% – are predicted to decrease further, while economic growth continues to rise, currently standing at 10.2%. The key question being posed is whether the Baltic States can sustain such growth. In Latvia, things have been seen as getting slightly out of hand and accordingly, in order to slow growth, interest rates have been increased. Nevertheless, as the economic and property market growth are going hand in hand, Latvia remains a sustainable country in which to invest.

Latvia is a parliamentary democracy and the President is Vaira Vike-Freiberga.

Estonia

Enjoying the strongest economy per capita of all three Baltic States, despite enduring severe financial crises, Estonia managed to turn things around much quicker than her Baltic neighbours thanks to her close relationship with Finland, which was responsible for a large amount of foreign investment, and this helped get Estonia back on her feet.

The most affluent of the Baltic States, Estonia has the highest rate of mobile phone and computer ownership of the three. With GDP growth rates of 9.5% in 2006 and low rates of inflation – currently 4.1% – the economy has grown strongly and analysts predict that this growth will continue, making it a sound investment prospect for property buyers. Estonia is a parliamentary democracy and the Prime Minister is Andrus Ansip.

Annual GDP growth rate									
	2000	2001	2002	2003	2004	2005	2006	2007 (e)	Annual GDP growth rate 2000 2001
Estonia	7.9%	7.7%	8.0%	7.1%	8.1%	10.5%	9.5%	8.0%	89.9%
Latvia	6.9%	8.0%	6.4%	7.5%	8.5%	10.2%	11.9%	9.0%	92.6%
Lithuania	4.1%	6.6%	6.9%	10.3%	7.3%	7.6%	7.4%	6.5%	72.8%
Data from International Monetary Fund. e= expected values									

Geography and climate

While the Baltics are three of Eastern Europe's smallest states, it is actually their small stature which has helped them undergo such rapid economic revival. It has been suggested that the Baltics share more in common with Northern Europe and while they are commonly grouped together, the Baltic people see the three countries as being very disparate – they regard the title of Baltic States as referring more to their geographical proximity than their cultural and historical similarities.

Bordering Russia and Belarus, and surrounded by the Baltic Sea to the west and Gulf of Finland to the north, Estonia is the smallest of the Baltic Tigers, covering 45,226km and with a 3,794km-long coastline, which is studded with over 1,500 islands. The most northerly of the three states, her close relationship with Finland is one bolstered by geographical convenience, as the two countries are only separated by the Gulf of Finland.

Latvia is sandwiched between Estonia and Lithuania, and has a smaller coastline of 531km. Covering an area of 64,589 square kilometres, it has a population of 2.3 million. Lithuania is the largest and most populous of the Baltic States, with a land area of 65,303 square kilometres, coastline of 90km and a population of 3.6 million people.

There's more to these countries than their three striking capitals, and outside of these you'll find vast forests, expansive wetlands which provide a habitat for many birds and animals, and extensive tracts of beaches. The countryside is peppered with rustic villages and isolated farmsteads, and the people of the Baltics have a close relationship with nature and the countryside – a countryside which explodes with greenery and colour during the spring.

Generally wet, with mild summers and dark, snowy winters, the climate in the Baltics can be incredibly unpredictable. The climate in Estonia is colder and wetter than her other Baltic counterparts due to her exposure to the Baltic Sea. Winters are dark – some days only see six hours of daylight – with the first snow coming in November and unlikely to let up until spring when the thaw sets in. December marks the start of winter in earnest, and during this period temperatures rarely top 0°C and regularly drop to –20°C; this continues right through until March.

The summer months of June until August are when the Baltics are at their best, enjoying many days of sunshine – although showers are equally common. Temperatures average around 20°C throughout this period. During spring, the climate is moist and the landscape lush and green, with many colourful flowers. Autumn is similarly beautiful, when the leaves begin to turn a golden brown.

History and culture

Despite following very different paths to reach their current independence, the history of the Baltic States is very similar. A story of foreign rule and subjugation of its peoples, having been controlled by the Soviet Union from 1940–1941 and then again from 1944/45 until 1991, all three finally gained independence with the collapse of the Soviet Union on August 21st 1991.

Having ruled their own country for only 30 years out of 800, Estonia's history has been shaped by its neighbours, with the Danes, Germans, Swedish and Russians ruling in turn. The mid-nineteenth century saw Estonia undergo a cultural and linguistic revival, which was soon followed by the collapse of Germany and Tsarist Russia, and a fleeting moment of Estonian independence in 1918, which ended again in 1940. The people weren't to savour self-rule again until the collapse of Soviet Russia in 1991 when independence was declared.

Latvia underwent a similar history of occupation and foreign rule. Germany, Sweden and Russia all took it in turn to rule the country. However, during the 1900s, the Latvians asserted their independence, fighting off the Russians and Germans and achieving self-rule following WWI. But, they too fell victim to Soviet annexation in 1940 and despite increased calls for self-government during the 1980s, it wasn't until the Soviet collapse in 1991 that Latvia once again became an independent state.

Lithuania has seen more days of independence than her neighbours, existing as a unified state in the 14th century and a combined Polish-Lithuanian state in 1569. However, by the end of the 18th century, Lithuania had fallen under Russian control, which was never really shaken off – the end of WWII saw a brief flurry of independence – until Lithuania declared independence in 1990, almost a year earlier than its Baltic neighbours.

Far from being countries scarred by their communist past, the three Baltic capitals are in fact UNESCO World Heritage sites and boast some of Europe's finest architecture. Lithuania is characterised by the pine forests and lakes of its national parks and the charm of its capital Vilnius, with its Baroque churches and cobbled streets, while Latvia, with its scenic countryside and southern farmlands, is famous for the art nouveau architecture of Rīga, whose old-town buildings also reflect the eight centuries of its varied occupation and history. Lithuania and Latvia share more in common with each other than Estonia, where the Finnish influence is evident in both the language and heritage. Its capital is a blend of medieval and modern and boasts a fine array of bars and restaurants. To the east, the coastline is rugged and rocky, while to the west, the coastal towns are popular resorts. Inland is rolling countryside, and everywhere are quaint villages, which attest to the cultural and religious diversity of the country. In both Latvia and Estonia, the once oppressive Russian influence remains evident, with Russian widely spoken and many immigrants from the former USSR living here.

Religion

79% of the Lithuanian population are Roman Catholic and only 1.9% Protestant. The Catholic Church has played an important part in the country's development and many Catholic leaders were central to the anti-communist movement. 4.9% of the population belong to the Orthodox Church, mainly the minority Russian population.

The Latvian population is fairly equally divided between Lutheranism, Catholicism and Orthodoxy, the former representing the largest segment of the population with 24%, Catholicism 19% and Eastern Orthodoxy 15%.

Another 6–7% indicate affiliation to other religions, while 35% profess to follow no faith.

Estonia's dominant religion is Evangelical Lutheranism, although at present less than a quarter of ethnic Estonians, 31%, define themselves as active believers. In a survey carried out in 2005, only 16% of Estonia's stated they believed there was a god, making Estonians the least religious people in the EU.

Tourism and getting there

The property market in the Baltic States has certainly been bolstered by the introduction of budget flights following accession to the EU in 2004. 2006 saw a breakthrough in the Baltic market, with OAG (The Official Airline Guide, www.oag.com) reporting that the number of low-cost operations into and out of Estonia, Latvia and Lithuania has rocketed by 87% compared with July 2005, while Tallinn airport saw visitor figures rise by 40%. 2005 saw visitor numbers to Vilnius and Tallinn rise by 30%.

The World Tourism Organisation (WTO) reported recent growth in the tourism market of 20% for Latvia, 15% for Lithuania and 7% for Estonia. Such rapid growth is good news for those buying to let, although the main focal points are centred around Tallinn, Rīga and Vilnius.

By putting themselves on the tourist map and increasing awareness and interest in their tourist industry, all three countries will only help to secure their positions as burgeoning economic and property-market centres. The World Travel and Tourism Council has announced that Latvia has joined the top ten list for countries expected to see the biggest growth in tourism between 2007 and 2016.

The inevitable growth in budget flights has helped create and sustain the property market in all three countries – easyJet (www.easyjet.com) fly to Tallin and Rīga, and Ryanair (www.ryanair.com) to Rīga, as well as to Kaunas in Lithuania. Lithuanian Airlines (www.lal.lt) fly to Vilnius from throughout the UK.

Cost of living

According to the 2006 *Mercer Cost of Living Survey* (www. mercerhr.com), Vilnius is ranked 116th in a list of 144 cities (with 1st being the most expensive, and 144th being the cheapest), confirming that it's highly affordable, with a cost of living index of 69.2, 100 being the most expensive ranking. Tallinn came 96th with 73.7 and Rīga 81st with 77.2; all three had dropped in their ranking within the survey, making them some of the cheapest European capitals to live in.

In Latvia, a meal for two costs £8 and a pint of beer £1.50. In Estonia a pint of beer costs £1.30, while in Lithuania a three-course meal for two will set you back £20.

Food and drink

Given the cold nature of the climate in these three countries, dishes tend to be fairly heavy and laden with calories and carbohydrates, with pork and potatoes the most popular fare. Be aware that coffee and tea will generally be served black and that outside of the capitals your choice of beverages will be mainly limited to beer and vodka.

Estonia

The average Estonian would like nothing better than to sit down to a meal of pork, salted herring and rye bread, all washed down by a glass of beer. Sauerkraut and potatoes are also popular choices, with beer and vodka the most popular alcoholic beverages. While vegetarians may not fare well among the meat-laden menus, western influences are having an increasing effect and lighter dishes and international cuisines are creeping into the capital.

Latvia

Dairy products feature highly on the menu in Latvia and while pork, beef, cheese, sour cream and baked potatoes play a key role in meals, salad dishes and lighter meats such as chicken are beginning to feature regularly on menus.

When eating out, Rīga provides the best array of restaurants, bars and cafés, and thanks to the tourist demand there has been a move away from the hearty Latvian fare to a more international feel.

In terms of beverages, Latvia is renowned for its sparkling wines, known as *Rīgas sampanietis*, although the most common drink remains beer – *alus* – while vodka is also popular. Rīga Black Balm is a must-try when in Latvia and this bitter tipple is based on a recipe two-and-a-half centuries old. It's extremely fragrant, brewed with local grasses and herbs.

Lithuania

As with both Latvian and Estonian cooking, pork and potatoes are also staple ingredients in Lithuania dishes, with most food based on peasant recipes. Typical dishes include chops or roasted cutlets, and sausages or stews. Pizzerias and international restaurants are springing up throughout Vilnius and although vegetarians aren't faced with a wide range of options, cheese and mushroom pancakes are an example of the type of food you can now expect to find.

The country is not known for its wines, but imported vintages are regularly available. Again, beer is the most popular tipple, with vodka also widely consumed.

THE PROPERTY MARKET

People have been buying in the Baltics since the 1990s, but it wasn't until EU membership removed any obstructions to foreign purchases that the market really began to take off. Since the 90s, prices have risen by an estimated 1,000%, making Latvia, Lithuania and Estonia three of the most popular investment markets in Europe. The focal points for investors are the capital cities of Rīga, Vilnius and Tallinn as these offer the best returns, both in terms of rentals and price appreciation.

Examining the prospects for future returns, *A Place in the Sun* Magazine concluded that over the next ten years, the Baltic States would offer investors a 356% rise in prices. While this might be an exaggerated claim, there is no doubt that prices will continue to appreciate as the countries head for adoption of the euro, and tourist numbers and the economy remain among the fastest growing in Europe.

Currently, the average property price sits at £46,000 and while prices in the capitals may seem high already, most analysts are confident that within ten years they will have reached Scandinavian levels, meaning a doubling or even tripling of current values. Consequently, a property worth £100,000 today could be worth around £456,000 in ten years.

However, some of these astronomical price hikes are beginning to slow. Growth in 2005 was 66% in Latvia, 21% in Estonia and 14% in Lithuania, while in 2006 appreciation was 39% in Latvia (Rīga), 15.5% in Lithuania and 10.5% in Estonia, meaning people are asking the question, have we missed the boat? When you consider that the Baltic States are only three years into EU membership, analysts are certain that there is still another 10 to 20 years' growth in the market.

The facts that mortgages are available for up to 85% of a property's value, taxes are low and affluence is on the increase are all factors that help to explain the explosion in investor interest. Couple this with the fact that the quality of newly-built property is high and the cultural and lifestyle appeal strong, and it is clear why investors are keen to sink their money into Baltic property.

The property market is sustained by both high foreign and local demand. As earnings and the amount of disposable income among the local buyers has increased, the desire for better living standards has added pressure to the market. Consequently it is unsurprising that it has expanded so quickly.

The future for the Baltic property markets looks very good. They continue to offer excellent medium- to long-term growth potential, despite the fact that the most canny investors bought into the market long ago. However, thanks to the press coverage, low-cost airlines and EU accession, overseas buyers are still queuing up to take advantage of the excellent returns, so much so that some developers raise their prices by as much as 30% between one phase of a development and another.

In terms of who's investing, the Baltic States are a different market from countries such as Bulgaria or Croatia. As tourism is still a new entity, this is not the place you'd choose to buy your second home. Estonia, Latvia and Lithuania are much more of a pure investment and generally speaking you expect to see the more sophisticated buyer with a property portfolio purchasing here.

Lithuania

Vilnius has experienced the highest growth in the Lithuanian market, with apartment prices in the capital's suburbs rising by 15% to 25% per annum since EU accession, and newly-built properties in the city centre jumping in value by as much as 50%.

With one of the lowest ratios of houses to people, the demand has added to the high rates of price growth, and despite almost 3,000 new homes being built in 2004, 5,500 in 2005 and 6,000 in 2006, the lack of supply doesn't seem to be abating. With the market driven by buyers rather than sellers, the lack of demand and high turnover of property, evidenced by the fact that Lithuania has the highest level of home ownership in Europe, is good news for investors who intend to buy off-plan and sell on completion.

Over the last year, prices for land plots jumped by between 20% and 50%. 25% of the market comprises pre-1960s properties, 90% of which require renovation, making newly-built properties highly sought after. Interest rates on mortgages are relatively low – attractively so – at 4.2–5.3%. Finally, price changes for 2006 have exceeded appreciation rates of 2005 by roughly 2%, meaning there is a continued growth in property prices in the country.

Latvia

Knight Frank has reported that Latvia is heading the European property market in terms of price rises, with the third quarter of 2006 seeing increases of 39.2%. While the mortgage market here is still a long way off that of the EU – in Latvia it accounts for 4.6% of GDP, compared to 48% across the EU – this has not slowed the development of the market.

Since 1998 prices have risen by 300%, averaging between 15 and 20% per annum. The most significant increases have been seen in Rīga, followed closely by the coastal resort of Jūrmala. It is to safe to say that Rīga remains undervalued in terms of an EU capital, but if prices continue to rise at the current rate – many areas have witnessed increases of over 30% within the last 12 months – then it won't be long before they are on a par with their European counterparts.

Mortgages are available up to 85% and are offered to both locals and foreigners in lats, euros and US dollars. Interest rates start at 4.5% and there is no capital gains tax levied on properties that have been privately owned for more than a year.

The same problems of supply and demand evident in Lithuania are also apparent in Latvia and as the country's property prices are reported as being low, the potential for long-term investors is massive given the projected economic and price growth quoted over the next ten years.

Estonia

Estonia has so far been the favourite market with investors, being the first of the Baltics to attract the attention of foreign buyers, with prices averaging growth of 15% year-on-year. Prices in the Old Town of Tallinn are the highest of all the Baltic capitals, but not prohibitively so.

Apartment prices in the capital's suburbs have recently risen by 25% to 45%, while newly-built apartments in the city centre have appreciated by a staggering 70%. Currently, you can expect to buy a decent, newly-built apartment for around £100,000 in Tallinn's centre. While prices have more than doubled since 2003, the rate of increases has dropped from 21% in 2005 to 10.5% in 2006. However, there is no sign that appreciation rates won't carry on growing, albeit at a slightly more sedate pace.

Where to buy

While the capitals remain the most popular property hotspots, other towns and cities are proving increasingly popular as developers begin to move in. Areas such as Jūrmala in Latvia are attracting more investment, but it's likely – with the exception of Lithuania – that property outside the capitals will remain a niche part of the market.

Rīga

As well as being the geographic capital of Latvia, Rīga is the transport hub and economic and commercial centre. It's undervalued when compared to other European capitals, and despite price rises of 30% in the last two years, property is still affordable. Surprisingly well developed, Rīga is currently the subject of much regeneration and modernisation. The Rīga government's development plan is set to run from 2006-2018, with the aim of providing 12 million square metres of living space in order to bring the city in line with western standards. The redevelopment will feature new commercial and residential centres, a bridge to link the north and south sides of the city, and reconstruction of the port area. The development plan will offer considerable opportunities for would-be investors and further encourage the continuation in price growth. The old port area is being opened up as a new residential centre, while just outside of Rīga is Saliena, a satellite town which looks well designed for letting to commuters.

Apartments are the most sought after and widely available property type, although it is possible to find townhouses and old city centre houses. Average prices sit between £60,000 and £130,000, depending on location.

Jūrmala

With sandy beaches and traditional wooden architecture, Jūrmala has been described by some agents as the 'Beverly Hills' of Latvia. Situated to the west of the capital, this coastal resort consists of the three seaside towns of Majori, Dzintari and Bulduri and is situated on Latvia's Baltic coastline, only 45 minutes from Rīga.

Traditionally the reserve of the wealthier of Latvia's inhabitants, its proximity to Rīga has resulted in growing interest from the ranks of foreign buyers. There are a number of new developments being built in the area to cater for the growing demand, and while buyers tend to be predominantly locals, there are also a number of Russians both buying and holidaying in Jūrmala.

Jūrmala sees a massive polarisation in prices, yet property is much more expensive here than in Rīga, with prices averaging €200,000 for a three-bedroomed family home. Despite being coastal, the climate is not akin to that of the Bulgarian Black Sea Coast and so investors should not expect to generate masses of interest from bucket-and-spade tourists. Consequently, rather than looking for a holiday home or rental property, this should be looked at as a longer term investment.

Tallin

Receiving a staggering 81% of Estonia's foreign direct investment, the economic hub of the country is also the major property hotspot. This medieval city offers prices which are marginally lower than those of neighbouring Latvia and Lithuania, but this is unlikely to continue as Estonia has the most promise for foreign investors, with long-term appreciation looking the strongest, as the current lack of high quality real estate is replaced by new developments experiencing high levels of demand.

With 15% price rises in Tallinn last year, values in some districts of the capital are somewhat inflated, with one-bedroomed apartments in the old town selling for over €100,000. While prices in the last three years have more than doubled in Tallinn – a property worth £40,000 in 2000/01 would now retail at over £100,000 – it is still possible to find a bargain. Even so, by buying in the capital's centre, you are likely to experience appreciation rates of around 10% per annum.

In terms of appeal, Estonia attracts more foreign direct investment and is seen as a more attractive place to do business than her neighbours. As for tourism, Estonia also comes out on top, generating €600 per tourist. All of these activities – economic, tourist and consumer – are focused on Tallinn. With a strong infrastructure and largely English-speaking business community, investors will find it easy to operate here.

Pärnu

One of Europe's lesser-known beach resorts, the seaside town of Pärnu is the summer capital of Estonia, thanks to its miles of white sandy beaches. Offering property at prices 30% lower than in Tallinn, yet lying just one hour south of the capital, Pärnu is an up-and-coming hotspot. With two golf courses and several spas, this coastal resort offers property for as little as £20,000.

There are also new developments being constructed, with 18 off-plan riverside apartments being built next to Pärnu River, starting at just £38,000. It's expected that in the near future, budget airlines will consider running flights directly from the UK to Pärnu.

Vilnius

With property prices appreciating by between 15% and 50% since 2004, and with annual average increases of 30%, Vilnius is experiencing high demand for one and two-bedroomed apartments in the city centre. In the future, as long as demand continues to outstrip supply, you can expect to see a similar trend in price growth.

With a massive demand for Western-style residences in Vilnius, many new developments are under construction and the old housing stock is being renovated. While Vilnius' old town is incredibly beautiful and the focus for much demand, the suburbs aren't so attractive and consequently prices fall as you head out of the centre.

Property is selling rapidly, with a number of new developments being built every year. Most property is priced between €150,000 and €200,000, although on the city's outskirts you are looking at around €50,000.

Kaunas and Klaipeda

These two towns have also begun to attract investors and are currently appreciating exceptionally well, although it's still early days.

Kaunas is Lithuania's second city and offers an affordable alternative to Vilnius. Situated 90km to the capital's northwest and connected directly by motorway, today Ryanair flies into Kaunas from Dublin, Liverpool and London. Flights into Kaunas have increased greatly over the last couple of years, leading to increases in tourists and foreign businesses arriving in the Baltic States' second largest city. You can pick up a two-bedroomed apartment in central Kaunas for £112,000.

The coastal resort of Klaipeda is Lithuania's third-largest city and also a transport hub for the entire coastline of the country. Located in the middle of the west coast, it has an attractive old town and a lively social scene. Focus tends to be on one- to two-bedroomed apartments, which retail at around €30,000 on a newly-built development.

What to buy

Generally there are two types of property on the market. Newly-built off-plan properties and historic buildings that can be bought refurbished in the old centres of the Baltic capitals. The problem with the latter is that two to three years ago you would have made a killing had you bought one of these art nouveau properties, but today the prices are much higher. That said, for £100,000 you can pick up a newly-built apartment in the centre, while for £50,000 to £60,000, you can buy in the suburbs.

There is a slight risk that the level of development in the capitals may lead to an oversupply of new-build apartments, although at the moment demand is so high that this seems unlikely for the near future. Good-quality townhouses and apartments are the most popular for rentals, making them likely to appreciate well. There is also the option of renovating Soviet-era property, but this is not likely to resell well or rent well as the market is geared towards newly-built or refurbished property in the old town area of the Baltic capitals.

The recommendation for investment is to always buy in the centre, close to offices, shops and restaurants/bars/clubs. The quality of both refurbished properties and new builds is generally very high and the properties are stylish and sophisticated – on a par with anything you can get in the UK and many bathrooms even come with jacuzzis!

Be aware that if buying a newly-built property, you are likely to be looking at purchasing a grey-finish property; this means you are quoted the property price without the interior fitting included. You would be looking at an extra 15% to get the property completed with all fittings.

THE BUYING PROCESS

Despite being fiercely proud and individual nations, the purchasing process is very similar in all three countries. Thanks to accession into the EU, UK buyers will find no restrictions on purchasing here and no residency permit is required in order to buy.

Stage 1: Restrictions on foreigner buyers

In all three countries, foreign investors are treated equally with citizens of the Baltic States and there are no limits on the purchase of apartments and houses. Land is also freely open to foreign purchase. The main restrictions relate to the purchase of agricultural and forestry land. In all three Baltic States, foreigners must have lived in the country permanently for the last three years and have been actively involved in agricultural activities during that time in order to buy agricultural or forestry land. One exception is Estonia, where no restrictions apply to foreigners purchasing agricultural and forest land so long as the amount doesn't exceed 10 hectares. In Latvia, only a Latvian citizen – or a company with 51% of its shares owned by a Latvian citizen – can purchase such land.

There are also severe restrictions in place when it comes to purchasing a coastal property, so ensure you do all the necessary background research before you buy.

Stage 2: Funding your purchase

Foreigners are able to secure a local mortgage to purchase property in the Baltic States, although the percentage available and interest rates do vary.

In Latvia in order to secure a mortgage, the repayment can't exceed 40% of your monthly income. Latvian banks will offer a loan of up to 90% of the property price, with interest rates as low as 3.5%. The loan term tends to be up to 40 years.

In Lithuania, loans of up to 85% are available to foreigners purchasing property, with interest rates currently under 5%.

In Estonia, mortgages are incredibly affordable with low rates of interest. Euro mortgages are on offer and generally they have a repayment term of between 15 and 30 years, with Estonian banks providing finance of up to 75-80% at interest rates of under 4%. However you have to prove that you have an annual income in excess of £20,000 in order to qualify for a mortgage.

Stage 3: The contract

The process of buying a property is straightforward, with the general timeline being that of the payment of a deposit (between 10% and 20%) on the signing of the preliminary contract, and the payment of the remainder on the formal notarisation or final signing of the contract. Notaries, rather than solicitors, typically oversee the transfer of ownership, although a lawyer is best employed in order to ensure the contract is correct and to assist the buyer in their negotiations.

In Estonia, the ownership of land can be secured through the setting-up of a company, but you will need to secure permission from the County Governor. If you are buying an off-plan property then a deposit of 10–20% will need to be paid during the signing of the preliminary contract, with the final balance to be paid on completion of the build, which generally takes 12 to 18 months. Generally, the payment for property is done through the notary, with the buyer transferring a lump sum into the notary's deposit account prior to the conclusion of the property sale, thus safeguarding the buyer's money until the sale is official. On conclusion of the agreement, or upon registration of the title, the notary than passes the payment over to the seller.

In Latvian legislation, deposits held by a notary are technically safeguarded, although this is rarely the case in practice, with the buyer and seller preferring to use an escrow or bank account for the holding of funds. Until the registration procedure is complete, neither the seller nor the buyer has access to the funds transferred to the escrow account, thus safeguarding the buyer's interests. As with the Estonian process, the payment of a 10–15% deposit is required on the signing of the preliminary contract, with the remaining balance either paid on completion of the property in the case of a new build, or on the final signing of the contract in the presence of a notary. In both Latvia and Estonia, for new-build properties, there are no stage payments, unlike many other countries.

In Lithuania, the purchase price payment is usually divided into two parts: a partial pre-payment and payment of the remaining purchase price. The latter amount is paid after certain steps have been taken – for example, after the transfer acceptance deed has been signed. The deposit must be paid once the preliminary contract has been signed, with the remainder on completion of the development or the final signing of the contract.

In all three countries, you are entitled to sign a power of attorney, which means you have no need to be present in the country for the final signing – your lawyer can do it for you.

Stage 4: Land registration and completion

Despite having signed the final purchase contract and transferred all the relevant funds, it's not until you are listed as the owner of the property with the land registry that you are the full-blown owner of your new property. In Estonia, the registering body is known as the Land Register, in Latvia it's called the Land Book and in Lithuania, the Register of Real Estate. The time taken for registration varies dramatically. In Estonia, it takes between one to four months, but in Latvia and Lithuania it's much quicker – 15 to 30 days in Latvia and 10 working days in Lithuania. Recent legislation introduced in Lithuania in 2007 allows for the signing at the land registry to be done along with the final purchase contract in the notary's office. Not only does this save time but it also cuts costs significantly.

Baltic States legislation requires all property transactions to be finalised in writing, and so – as with many European countries – the final signing of the contract must be done in the presence of a notary. Latvia is the only country where the process differs, as here all that is required is for the relevant parties to sign their application on the Land Book. The signatures can be notarised following the signing. Be aware that it's not uncommon to have to wait a month for an appointment with a notary.

Stage 5: Additional payments

As with any property transaction, both the buyer and seller will be required to make certain payments in addition to the purchase price of the property. This is even more so the case in the Baltics as many property prices are quoted in a grey state (see page 85). Expect to put an additional 15% of the property cost on top of the preliminary quote in order to finish the property ready for habitation.

Typical payments include stamp duty and notary fees, as well as VAT for newly-constructed or reconstructed buildings (although this is usually included in the purchase price). The size of these fees varies among the States. In Latvia, the role of notaries in the conveyancing procedure is limited and their fees low – 23 lats (£22) for testifying signatures for the application to the Land Book and 15 lats (£14) for signing an agreement in their presence. In contrast, stamp duty is high at 2% of either the real estate purchase price or the cadastral value (the value according to the tax office), whichever is the higher of the two figures.

In Estonia and Lithuania, the notary's role is more involved and so their fees are higher, at between 0.5% and 1% of the purchase price. In both Lithuania and Estonia there is no stamp duty, although you may have to pay real estate brokerage fees of 3% and bank fees if an escrow account is opened. Other than that, you'll have the annual payments of property and land tax, plus legal fees which will vary from €150 to €650 depending on the country you buy in.

Typical fees: Latvia

- Transaction costs should come to a total of 4–5%.
- Land registration fees: Maximum € 100.
- Stamp duty: 2%.
- Notary fees: € 300–€ 450.
- Property valuation: € 100.
- Insurance: Average of € 250 (varies depending on property size and type).
- Legal costs: € 250–€ 400.
- Estate agents' fees: typically 5% (normally paid by both the buyer and seller).
- Property tax: 1.5% of the cadastral value, i.e. the administrative value of the land and buildings on it, as assessed by the council. This is paid annually.

Typical fees: Lithuania

- Transaction costs should come to a total of 3–5%.
- Land Register tax: Measured on a sliding scale but shouldn't exceed € 100.
- Notary fees: 0.5–1% of property price.
- Estate agents fees: 3–7%.
- Legal fees: € 500–€ 650.
- Property tax: 1% value of property.
- Land tax: 1.5%.

Typical fees: Estonia

- Transaction costs are low as there is no transfer tax or stamp duty.
- Land registration fee for new property: 0.5%.
- Notary fees: 0.5–1% of purchase price.

- Estate agents fees: 3–7%.

- Legal fees: €222–€444.

- Translation of contract: €103.

- Land tax: 0.1–2.5%. This is decided by the local authority.

THE LETTINGS MARKET

Thanks to the incredibly low interest rates, mortgages are very affordable in the Baltic States and consequently the majority of the population would rather buy a property than look to rent. As demand is limited, rental yields are not high in the Baltic States, and this is not a short-term market as tourism is still in its infancy.

If you look to let, you have three prospective tenants: firstly, the local market and young couples; secondly, a very small tourist market; and thirdly, the largest and growing market of businessmen and expats.

In Lithuania, while rental returns are healthy, generated income has dropped by about 10% in the last year, although current predictions are for a future 15% growth in the market. Rental returns for studios are predicted to grow by 5–10% – surprisingly more than the two- to three-bedroomed apartments – while suburban housing blocks are recording a 17% increase and prestigious property 8%.

In Latvia, returns for a typical city centre apartment range from £350 to £600, representing a yield of 6–8%. Since Estonia joined the EU in 2004, rental yields have been low for Old Town Tallinn, while suburban areas offer much better returns.

In Estonia, the rental market in Tallinn is growing, while on the coast at Parnu you would be paying rental prices almost on a par with the capital.

RENOVATING A PROPERTY

Due to the fact that the typical properties purchased in the Baltic States are newly-built, off-plan homes, there is very little demand for renovations. Generally speaking, most renovated homes tend to be located in the old town of the country capitals. Be careful though – the renovation costs can come out higher than anticipated unless you look into the process carefully before buying. Renovation or resale properties are generally more expensive, situated as they are in premium locations in the historic areas of cities. You can find homes with a white finish as opposed to grey (see page 85), which generally means that they have been plastered but you'll need to install all fittings – allow about € 10,000 for this.

LIVING IN THE BALTIC STATES

Daily life and people

Although geographically close, the peoples of the three Baltic countries cherish their individuality. The Lithuanians and Latvians have the most in common, descended from Indo-European tribes who settled in the Baltics in roughly 2000BC. The Estonians have more in common with their Finnish neighbours, most notably their language. Despite the fact that 69% of Estonia's population lives in urban areas, the Estonians still maintain close ties with the countryside and rural life, as do the Latvians and Lithuanians – until fairly recently the people of all three countries lived in rural villages and farmsteads.

Folk music and festivals are important in all three countries, the most siginificant being the Song Festival which is held every four years or so in each State – attracting singers from all over the country. During Soviet times the revolutionary movement became synonymous with the song and the 'singing revolution' was witnessed as protestors turned to music.

As with many post communist states, the younger generation is marked with an impatience to modernise and move forward. The Estonians are known for being difficult people to get to know, being fairly introvert and shy, especially around foreigners. However the Lithuanians are characterised as friendly and welcoming, as are the Latvians.

In terms of cultures and customs, Lithuania's culture has been heavily influenced by Poland, having once been a combined Poland-Lithuania state. Latvia is the most ethnically diverse and most influenced by Russia, while Estonia sees herself as a European country thanks to the Scandinavian influence.

Visas and residency

As a British citizen travelling to the Baltic States, no visa is required. If you are planning a visit to Estonia, you will be able to travel there freely without a visa or ID card for a visit of up to 90 days. If you intend to live and work in Estonia permanently then you may well need to obtain a Business Visa. To gain temporary residency, an EU citizen must contact the local government authority nearest their residence and register within three months of entering Estonia. Temporary residency is then granted for five years. An EU citizen who has resided in Estonia permanently for five successive years with temporary residence will obtain the right of permanent residence. All details and application forms can be found at www.mig.ee/eng.

In Latvia an EU citizen will not require a visa to enter the country, but will be required to apply for temporary residency if staying in the country for more than 90 days. This can be issued for a period of five years and permanent residency can be sought if a foreigner has lived in Latvia with a temporary residence permit for at least five years. See www.ocma.gov.lv or www.mfa.gov.lv for more details.

In Lithuania the situation is slightly different. As an EU member and British citizen, there is no requirement for a visa when visiting and once you have stayed in the country for three months (90 days), should you decide to stay, you may do so without a permit or visa for another three months. After this period, an EC Residence Permit will be issued for five years if you continue to reside in Lithuania. If you intend to stay permanently you can apply for a Permanent EC Residence Permit. This will be issued to an EU citizen and their family if they have resided in Lithuania for four years. The permit lasts for 10 years before requiring renewal. See www.urm.lt for more details.

Utilities

Estonia

Electricity is supplied in 220v and two-pin plugs are employed, requiring you to bring an adapter for products that require a British-style plug. Once you have purchased a property, in order to connect your electricity, you will need to register with the regional distributor. A technician will then come out to either connect a meter or read the meter in order to determine the property's electricity usage.

Gas is widely available in Estonia and Eesti Gaas (www.gaas.ee) is the provider. To conclude a gas sale and purchase agreement, you will need the following documents:

*   identification document or valid registry card;
*   a document certifying the ownership of the flat/house, or a lease contract;
*   a notarised authorisation document if the owner of the building authorises a representative to enter into the agreement.

If you are renting, you'll be pleased to know that water consumption is generally included in lease agreements. If you have just bought a property then you will need to register with the water and sewerage company that serves the district.

Latvia

Electricity is supplied by www.latvenergo.lv and their website provides all the necessary contacts and details you need to connect them.

Lithuania

The energy company Lietuvos Energija (www.le.lt/en) are the main suppliers of electricity in Lithuania and offer all the relevant contacts for suppliers.

Your estate agent or developer will be able to provide you with details of utility connections and help arrange for connection.

Getting a mobile phone is easy, and there are a number of service providers. If you have a GSM mobile phone then you can simply buy a new SIM card and pop it in your current phone. Alternatively, mobile phones can be rented and bought in all three countries.

As for landlines, phone boxes operate using phone cards, which can be bought from post offices, newsagents and tourist information centres.

In Estonia and Latvia there are no dialling codes and numbers are seven digits long. To dial into Estonia you need the country code, which is 00 372, and 00 371 for Latvia. Lithuania does have area/city codes – seven for Vilnius – while to dial any number from a mobile, you need to first dial 8 and then wait for the dial tone. The country code is 00 370.

Estonia

Mobile phones: Visit www.emt.ee, www.elisa.ee, www.tele2.ee

Telephone: Elion is the largest telecommunications and IT provider in Estonia: www.elion.ee.

Latvia

Mobile phones: Latvijas Mobilais Telefons SIA, www.lmt.lv

Telephone: Lattelecom, www.lattelecom.lv/eng/

Lithuania

Mobile phones: Bite, www.bite.lt, Ominitel, www.omnitel.lt

Telephone: TEO, www.teo.lt/

TELE2 is a mobile phone company that operates in all three countires: see www.tele2.ee in Estonia, www.tele2.lv in Latvia and www.tele2.lt in Lithuania.

Banking and currency

All three countries are currently working towards the adoption of the euro with the estimated adoption dates between 2008 and 2010.

Lithuania hopes to become a member of the European Monetary Union in 2009–2010, but until then, the current currency is the litas (Lt), which is divided into 100 centai. Coins come in denominations of 1, 2, 5, 10, 20 and 50 centų and 1, 2 and 5 litai, while banknotes are available in 10, 20, 50, 100, 200, 500 litai. At the time of going to print, the exchange rate to the pound was 5.12Lt.

The Latvian currency is the lat (Ls or LVL), although Latvia's aim is to become a fully-fledged member of the European Economic and Monetary Union (EMU) as soon as possible.

Each lat is divided into 100 santīms and coins come in denominations of 1, 2, 5, 10, 20 and 50 santīmu, and also 1 or 2 lati, while you can get banknotes of 5, 10, 20, 50, 100 and 500 latu. In January 2005, the lat was pegged to the euro and at the time of printing, £1 was equal to 1.05LVL.

The Estonian currency is the kroon (EEK). Originally, Estonia planned to adopt the euro on 1st January 2007. It has since changed its target date to 1st January 2010.

One kroon is made up of 100 sents and the coins in circulation are 10, 20 and 50 senti, as well as the 1 kroon coin. You can get banknotes of 2, 5, 10, 25, 100, 500 krooni. At the time of printing, the exchange rate was 23.20 kroons to the pound.

Estonia

Setting up a bank account in Estonia is essential and fortunately also very easy. Most Estonian banks offer internet banking with English websites, and an account can be opened at any Estonia bank, so long as you take your passport and make a deposit payment to activate it. However, be aware that there may be a limit on outgoing payments and so, in order to settle a payment or deposit on a property, you may have to go to the bank and do it in person.

Banks are generally open Monday to Friday, between 9am and 4pm. The main banks are Eesti Uhispank (www.seb.ee) and Hansapank (http://w.hansa.ee/eng/). Both have branches throughout the country. Credit cards can be freely used and ATMs are widely available. Visit the

Central Bank of Estonia website at www.bankofestonia.info.

Latvia

Opening a bank account is easy for foreigners – all that is required is a passport and a deposit. You can also open an account via the internet by downloading an application form. However, your passport and signature will either have to be viewed at the bank or authorised by a notary.

Rietumu Bank (www.rietumu.com) is one of Latvia's largest banks, and there is also Unibanka (www.seb.lv), Latvijas (www.bank.lv), Hansabanka (www.hansabanka.lv) and Norvik Banka, which has a department for international customers (www.norvik.lv). The central bank of Latvia can be found at www.bank.lv.

Lithuania

Banks are open between the hours of 9am to 5pm, Monday to Friday, although the larger cities will also see banks open on Saturday mornings. ATMs are easily found throughout the larger towns and cities and credit cards are widely accepted.

In terms of opening a bank account, the website www.bank.lt offers a thorough breakdown of all the banks in Lithuania, with a link to their websites.

In order to open an account, the following will be required:

- passport;
- permit for interim or permanent residency;
- personal identity card;
- driving licence with the driver's signature;
- personal identity document of an EU citizen.

SEB (www.seb.lt) and Hansabanka (www.hansa.lt) also have banks in Lithuania and are among the largest of the country's banks. The Central Bank of Lithuania can be found at www.lb.lt.

Taxes

Latvia

In Latvia, income tax is charged at a flat rate of 25% and corporation tax at 15%. Capital gains tax is generally charged as income and so taxed at 25%, although if you have owned a property for more than 12 months, you are exempt from capital gains tax.

Lithuania

While income tax is generally levied at a flat rate of 22%, some income – such as rental earnings – is charged at a reduced rate of 15%. From 1st January 2008, the government will be reducing the top income tax band to 24%.

Corporation tax is levied at a flat rate of 15% – in some cases this drops to 13% if the company is very small. Residents will be taxed at a rate of 15% for capital gains tax, while non-residents, whether they are companies or individuals, are charged at a rate of 10%. Capital gains tax is not levied on properties owned for more than three years.

Estonia

Income tax is charged at a flat rate of 23%, while corporation tax has been reduced from 23% in 2006 to 22% in 2007, and will fall again to 21% in 2008 and 20% in 2009.

Capital gains is normally taxed as income for both companies and individual investors, although individuals are not liable to pay capital gains on a property if it's their main residence and not a second home/investment.

Insurance

There are a number of insurance companies in the Baltic States which offer comprehensive websites in English, with a plethora of insurance cover, whether it's for your health, your pets or your house.

Estonia

- AS Inges Kindlustus, www.inges.ee, offer various types of insurance.
- Eesti Liikluskindlustuse Fond, www.lkf.ee, specialise in car and traffic insurance.
- Ergo, www1.ergo-kindlustus.ee, offer life, car, pet, home and travel insurance, as well as a number of other services.
- Estonian Insurance Association, www.eksl.ee, has a list of life and non-life insurance companies in Estonia.

Latvia

- AAS Baltijas Apdrošināšanas Nams, www.ban.lv, offer property, travel and specialised insurance policies for individuals and also a portfolio for companies.
- RSK, http://portals.rsk.lv/main.php, offer health, accident, travel insurance and general insurance for foreigners and non-citizens of Latvia.
- Rīga RE, http://www.Riga-re.com/eng/, offer life, health, travel, car and property insurance, as well as other services.
- Latvian Insurers Association, www.laa.lv.

Lithuania

- Lithuanian Insurance Association, www.draudikai.lt, offer useful advice and contacts.
- Baltikums draudimas, www.baltikums.lt, offers motor insurance for individuals.
- Ergo, www.ergo.lt/en, offer house, car, accident, travel and pension insurance.
- Reso Europa, www.resoeuropa.lt, offer home, personal, travel, car, pet and foreign medical insurance.

Healthcare

In all three countries you will be entitled to emergency treatment as an EU citizen, but private insurance is recommended. Bottled water is recommended over tap water and although no vaccinations are specified, it is recommended that you get immunised against tick-borne encephalitis.

In Estonia, dial 112 for an ambulance, and 03 in Latvia, or 112 in Lithuania. Most general medication is available from the chemist, known as an *apteek*. See the section on insurance for useful contacts to secure health insurance.

Retirement

There is nothing to stop you retiring to the Baltic States, but you will be required to apply for residency and may have to prove you receive a certain level of income.

As members of the EU, you will be able to draw your pension in the three Baltic States and it will still be increased to match inflation. As many UK benefits, including income-related benefits such as Pension Credit, Income Support, Housing Benefit and Council Tax benefit, cannot continue to be paid if you move to an EU or EEA country, you will need to rely on the benefits available in the Baltics. As all three countries are members of the European Economic Area, you may well be entitled to certain social security benefits, but these will depend on your circumstances and should be looked into thoroughly with a specialist before you leave. If you are drawing a government pension from the UK, you will be taxed in the UK, while your company and personal pension will still be available to you – although be aware of currency fluctuations and costs for transferring funds to the Baltics that you may incur.

See the websites of the Department for Work and Pensions, www.dwp.gov.uk, The Pension Service, www.thepensionservice.gov.uk, and www.ace.org.uk for details.

Education

Standards of education in all three Baltic States are high, although while English is widely spoken in business and by the population at large, it is rarely employed in schools and the education system. All three Baltic languages are tricky and so it isn't recommended to put your child into a local school, unless they are very young and adapt well to new environments.

There are very few international schools in the Baltic States, but these include:

* International School of Estonia in Tallinn, www.ise.edu.ee
* International School of Latvia, Rīga/Jūrmala, www.isl.edu.lv
* American International School of Vilnius, www.aisv.lt
* Vilnius International School, www.vischool.lt
* French International School, www.efv.lt

Driving

All three Baltic States require you to have an international driving permit in order to drive in the country. Cars drive on the right, headlights must be kept on at all times and seatbelts are compulsory. In general, you must be over 21 to rent a car. Currently, there are no road tolls in force in the Baltics.

The quality of the roads isn't the best in the Baltic States, and a combination of uneven surfaces and potholes when you get into rural areas, and icy conditions with the occasional wild animal thrown in, can make driving treacherous. Latvia has one of the highest rates of automobile accidents and fatalities in Europe, and this is partly attributed to road conditions. Unleaded petrol, diesel and gas are available throughout the Baltic States.

Speed limits, Estonia and Latvia:

* motorways: 100km/h/120km/h (62/74mph);
* open roads: 90km/h (55mph);

- towns: 50km/h (31mph).

Speed limits, Lithuania:

- motorways: 110 km/h (from 1 October to 1 May)/
  130 km/h (from 1 May to 1 October);
- open roads: 90km/h (55mph);
- towns: 60km/h (37mph).

Getting around

Getting to the Baltic States is now quick and easy thanks to regular budget flights which serve the Baltic region. Tallinn Airport had a major overhaul in 2007 which has allowed it to nearly double passenger numbers and host many more airlines.

Getting around the Baltic States is fairly straightforward and buses offer the best options if you want to travel between countries – Ecolines www.ecolines.net offer services throughout the region, as do Eurolines Baltic International (www.eurolines.lt). Trains are quite restrictive and can also be very slow. Car rental is another option, although this is obviously more costly. All major car rental firms, such as Avis, Europcar and Hertz, have agents in the Baltic States. For general travel information, www.balticsworldwide.com/timetables.htm is a really useful site.

Estonia

Given the manageable size of the country, driving is the best way to get around Estonia. However, domestic air travel is available, with Avies (www.avies.ee) offering flights between Tallinn and the islands of Kuressaare and Kärdla, while occasionally they also operate flights between Tartu and Tallinn, Pärnu and the islands of Kihnu and Ruhnu.

Bus services are quick and reliable and Go Bus (www.gobus.ee) operate services throughout Estonia, while at www.bussireisid.ee, you can view timetables for most national routes. www.tallinn.ee details public transport timetables in Tallinn, while www.tak.ee has timetables for Tallinn's bus network.

Three companies provide Estonia's train service, and they are GoRail (www.gorail.ee) who handle international services, Edelaraudtee (www.edel.ee) who provide the inter-city services, and Elektrikraraudtee (www.elektriraudtee.ee) who maintain the local electric trains. Train travel is not popular in Estonia and consequently there have been many cut backs and the system is unreliable. It's almost impossible to travel to Latvia or Lithuania by train and most international services head east. However, trains do travel from Tallinn to Tartu and other Estonian cities.

Lithuania

There are various bus operators in Lithuania, the biggest being Toks (www.toks.lt), who are based in Vilnius, and Kautra (www.kautra.lt) in Kaunas. Bus tickets are cheap and the service is generally well organised.

Trains are operated by Lithuanian Railways (www.litrail.lt), although as with Estonia these have been significantly cut back since the 1990s. There are regular services between Vilnius and Kaunas, but for longer journeys, the bus is quicker and more frequent. If you choose to drive yourself, most of the roads are in fairly bad repair and there are regular hazards, including tractors, animals and decrepit cars.

There are domestic airports at Kaunas, Palanga and Siauliai, though domestic flights are few and far between. Those that are available are operated by Lithuanian Airlines (www.lal.lt).

Latvia

Trains are far more frequent and reliable in Latvia, especially around Rīga. Routes and timetables can be viewed at www.ldz.lv. However, for long journeys, buses are the best bet.

The country offers a comprehensive bus network, with frequent services operating between Latvia's major cities. www.118.lv offers details on routes and timetables.

Some domestic flights are offered by Air Baltic (www.airbaltic.com), but these are limited.

Learning the language

Despite sharing many similarities, the languages of the three Baltic States come from two different backgrounds. Latvian and Lithuanian belong to the Indo-European language family, while Estonian descends from Finno-Ugric, sharing close ethnic and historical ties with the Finnish language. In fact, Estonian is one of the few official languages of the European Union that is not of Indo-European origin.

All three languages are difficult to learn, but it's worth trying to pick up a few basic phrases. Luckily, along with Russian and German, English is another language widely spoken in the Baltic States.

Shopping

Shops tend to be open from 8am/9am to 6pm/7pm, from Monday to Friday, keeping shorter hours at the weekends, with some Sunday opening at larger stores. Supermarkets are widespread and the larger cities offer some international names and products, such as Body Shop and Marks & Spencer. All prices will be displayed in the native currency, although euros are sometimes also included on the price tag. Debit and credit cards are widely accepted, although in smaller, rural areas it may be cash only.

Post

The postal service in the Baltics is improving, with letters taking only a couple of days to reach Western Europe. Post offices are normally open during shopping hours and they generally offer services such as bill payments and express or special delivery. For a better idea of the services and prices, visit the Latvian Post Office at www.pasts.lv, www.post.lt for Lithuania, and for www.post.ee for Estonia.

Crime, corruption and the police

There is little crime in the Baltic States, and although there were problems with organised crime following the collapse of communism, today corruption is limited. Foreigners are unlikely to experience any problems with corruption during the purchasing process.

The police are polite and helpful, although you are unlikely to have any contact with them during everyday life. To contact the police in Estonia, dial 110, in Latvia dial 02 and in Lithuania 112.

7
Bulgaria

Factfile
Population: 8 million
Population growth rate: −0.86%
Area: 110,993 sq km
Capital city: Sofia
Inflation: 6.5%
GDP growth rate: 5.5%
Unemployment rate: 9.9%
Net migration: −4.01 per 1,000
Currency: leva (lv)
Exchange rate: £1 = lv2
EU status: member as of January 2007
Number of foreign residents: 100,000
Time zone: GMT +2 hours

COUNTRY PROFILE

Centrally located in Europe, Bulgaria is a land of tremendous beauty and diversity. The cost of living is low, the food is great and the economy is booming, with the country offering a much slower, more relaxed pace of life – and rock bottom property prices.

Did you know?
- The most popular sport in Bulgaria is football. The country's greatest success – fourth place – was achieved in the 1994 Football World Cup in

the USA. The most popular Bulgarian football player is Hristo Stoichkov.
- The inventor of the computer – John Atanasoff – is of Bulgarian origin.

Why Bulgaria?

With more than 300 days of sunshine a year and skiing to rival the best Europe can offer, it's no wonder the tourist and property-buying market is booming. The scenery in Bulgaria is stunning, the climate superb and there are numerous historic towns and ancient traditions to savour. One of Europe's least populated countries, it boasts 11 blue-flag beaches, 354km of coastline and 37,000km of hiking paths – not to mention nine UNESCO World Heritage sites and a wealth of ancient monuments.

Although property prices are low – where else can you purchase a rural retreat for just £8,000? – it's anticipated that they will continue to rise, fuelled by the growth in tourism and the increasing awareness that Bulgaria can rival Spain, Portugal and Greece as a holiday destination.

Named in a recent report by currency exchange company FC Exchange, as one of the best countries in which to invest in 2007, Bulgaria is one of Eastern Europe's most rapidly advancing and expanding nations. With an average property appreciation rate of 47.5% in 2004, Bulgaria is attempting to shake off its reputation for corruption, dodgy dealing and over-development by only giving the go-ahead to the highest-quality developments, and by protecting its natural parks and resources from the over-development that has so blighted southern Spain. Its investment potential has been attributed to the strength of the economy and currency, balanced levels of supply and demand, low prices and high levels of World Bank and EU funding, which has in turn led to improvements in the infrastructure and tourism industry.

There has been a 90% rise in the numbers of visitors from the EU in recent years thanks to increased ease of access, and now that the country has EU membership and restrictions on budget airlines have been removed, tourist numbers are set to expand.

Politics and economy

As with the majority of Eastern European countries, Bulgaria gained independence in 1989, becoming a parliamentary democracy. Until 1996 it was ruled by the Socialist party, but major economic depression resulted in their collapse. Since then, Bulgaria has been committed to fiscal reform, and has experienced steady economic growth. The current President is Georgi Parvanov and the Prime Minister is Sergey Stanishev.

Thanks to the acceptance of Bulgaria into the EU on 1st January 2007 it is anticipated that the foreign investment that has poured into the country since 2003 will continue, as will the economic growth rate, which is currently one of the highest in Europe, sitting at 5.6%. Annual inflation is at 3.8% and rates of taxation are extremely low when compared with the rest of Europe – 0.15% on property and between 15 and 29% for income tax. Bulgaria's corporate tax rate has been cut to 10%, and the hope is that this will further boost the already healthy business economy and encourage more inward investment.

Geography and climate

Roughly the same size as England, Bulgaria is located on the Balkan Peninsula, surrounded by the Black Sea to the east, Romania to the north, Serbia and Macedonia to the west, and Greece and Turkey to the south. A hilly, mountainous country – more than half of it sits at an average elevation of 480 metres – Bulgaria enjoys a temperate climate, and while chilly in winter, the summers are hot. With glorious, sun-bleached beaches on the eastern Black Sea coast and an excellent skiing season lasting from December to mid-March, in the giant alpine mountains of the Balkan range in the north, this is a country with much to offer.

The Bulgarian capital is the rejuvenated city of Sofia, whose skyline is dominated by the peaks of Mount Vitosha. The country's southwest is home to Bulgaria's highest mountains, which are cloaked in forests and surrounded by lakes. To the north, the Danube flows around the alpine mountain ranges, and nestled among these peaks are many traditional villages. The northwest is famous for Lake Srebarna, a haven for birds and waterfowl.

History and culture

Many people are surprised to find that Bulgaria boasts a huge array of cultural highlights. The country was first formed in AD681 and by 1014 was under the sway of the mighty Byzantine empire, which introduced the Orthodox Church and the Cyrillic alphabet. Soon it was the turn of the Ottomans, who ruled Bulgaria from 1396; the following 500 years saw much persecution of the country's Orthodox monks and the conversion of many Christians to Islam.

During the 18th and 19th centuries there were many revolts and uprisings, and eventually Bulgaria briefly regained independence following the Russian ousting of the Ottomans in 1878. Surprisingly, Bulgaria allied herself with Germany during the Second World War, although the tsar famously refused to send 50,000 Bulgarian Jews to the Nazi concentration camps. Wholeheartedly embracing communism following WWII, Bulgaria remained a communist country until 1991, when democracy was introduced following the collapse of the Soviet Union.

Bulgaria has nine UNESCO World Heritage sites and a number of Greek, Roman and Thracian artefacts and sites. One of the top cultural highlights is the Monastery at Rila, along with the Boyana church and the rock-hewn churches of Ivanovo. The ancient city of Nesebar is one of the Black Sea's most important trading centres and has been labelled a UNESCO Heritage site thanks to its varied architectural heritage, monument to the numerous invaders who occupied it at one time or another.

Religion

Under communism, the country was officially atheist, but today nearly 90% of the country's inhabitants follow the Bulgarian Orthodox religion. A sizeable percentage of the population are Muslim, while there are also small Catholic and Christian groups.

Bulgaria has many monasteries, and during Ottoman rule, these Orthodox centres were responsible for awakening much nationalistic pride, and served as centres for planning and staging revolts. Of the 400 monasteries in Bulgaria today, 160 remain active places of worship.

Tourism and getting there

Tourism in Bulgaria has been growing at a rate of 22% per annum in recent years, although the country has been popular with Germans, Scandinavians and other Eastern Europeans for many years. 2004 saw a 75% increase in the number of British holidaying in the country, and as tourist levels have risen, so has interest in the real estate market.

Between 2005 and 2006, there was a more than 100% increase in visitors to Bulgaria, with 3.7 million tourist arrivals. The World Trade Organisation forecasts that by 2010 there will be 20 million tourists visiting Bulgaria every year, while high street travel agents have reported growth of more than 100% in bookings to Bulgaria. The country has topped travel operator Opodo's top ten emerging travel destinations for 2007 and they reported that bookings to Bulgaria have risen by 40% in the six months prior to EU membership.

Thanks to the continued growth of the holiday market, the number of regular budget flights continues to expand. There are already regular flights to Bulgaria with airlines such as British Airways, Balkan Bulgarian Airlines and Wizz Air. Bourgas Airport's director recently announced that now Bulgaria has joined the EU, additional flights are scheduled by airlines such as Ryanair, easyJet, Germanwings and Myair.

Cost of living

Bulgaria remains one of the most affordable European destinations, with the cost of living sitting at just 30% of Spanish living costs. A meal out can cost as little as £5, while mineral water is as little as 17p a litre and a pint of beer only 35p! Now Bulgaria is a member of the EU, it is widely expected that prices will go up. However, what is very important for potential buyers to be aware of is that the cost of building materials and labour have risen disproportionately in comparison to other costs due to the high demand. Foreigners should also be aware that until recently the law stated that foreigners were to be charged more for things such as property, museums and hotel rooms, compared with locals. This was the official policy of the Bulgarian government until the last year or so, but now this practice is illegal. If you find you are being charged more than the locals, feel free to challenge this.

Food and drink

If you like grilled meat, eggy bread, yoghurt and tomatoes then this is the place for you. Fruit and vegetables are fresh and home-grown and the meals are delicious and varied. The Bulgarians love their salads and popular dishes include *kebahche* (spicy meat sausages) and *kyufte* (flattened, curly sausage).

A typically daily menu starts with pancakes with berries and syrup, or a cheese pastry for breakfast. Lunch can be a *shopska* salad, comprising tomatoes, cucumbers, onions, feta cheese and olives, while a traditional evening meal is *kavarnais* – roasted meat and vegetables seasoned with garlic, onions, tomatoes, oil and spices.

THE PROPERTY MARKET

There has been a media frenzy surrounding the Bulgarian market since 2000, and despite seeing price hikes as high as 40% during the last five years, it's still one of the most popular destinations among British investors, with over 13% of all EU investors saying they would either purchase in Bulgaria or Romania. In 2006 residential property prices appreciated by an average of 4.6% across the country – lower than you might expect – although the number of properties sold surpassed the 260,000 mark for the first time.

There have been reports of the Black Sea coastline suffering from over-supply, due to the high levels of development the area has experienced in recent years. As most buyers there are investors, there are fears that the market will be flooded should everyone decide to sell but, in an attempt to counter this, the government has begun capping development levels.

While it is true that Bulgaria has developed somewhat back-to-front as a market – supply and newly-built developments came before demand, unlike most markets, which grow out of a massive tourism industry –

agents argue that tourism and property demand are rapidly growing, and that with increasing awareness will come growing popularity. However, Bulgaria is still a young market in terms of its property industry and great value and excellent appreciation rates are in evidence. This is demonstrated by the fact that Spain issued 800,000 building permits in 2006 – more than the UK, Germany and France put together – whereas Bulgaria issued no more than 15,000 in 2005.

Now an EU member, Bulgaria has become a byword for property investment, offering many new developments and a Costa del Sol environment for a fraction of the price. Surprisingly, when compared to its Eastern European neighbours, property here retails at prices 50% lower than some areas of Romania and Poland. Mortgages have increased by 166% from 2005 to 2006, with a fall in inflation resulting in a drop in mortgage rates from 16% to 5.5%.

Many have over-rated the Bulgarian market, and it is important to be aware that the massive price hikes that have occurred in the property market cannot be sustained for a lengthy period – appreciation rates have fallen from 47.5% during 2004 to an average of 10.6% in 2005. Of course, it all depends on where you buy and while the Black Sea Coast has slowed, in the mountainous ski resorts prices have risen by 25%. Bulgaria is essentially a long-term investment, and while a few years ago you could have bought and then sold within six months, today you need to wait for three to five years before reaping the benefits, especially if you're looking to build up a reliable rental income.

The EU effect

On 1st January 2007, the entire population of Europe didn't wake up and decide to invest in Bulgaria. Appreciation rates didn't treble overnight, and the likelihood is that they won't for the first few months following EU accession. However, long term, the impact will be positive for property buyers.

EU funds are already pouring into Bulgaria, with a 2007/08 budget of €6.6 billion to be invested. The early 90s saw massive economic instability and a fall in living standards of 40%. EU accession has resulted in economic stability and introduced a stable currency, while increased affluence will be apparent in workers' salaries. This will encourage investment and see secure appreciation rates, making Bulgaria a less risky investment.

What's more, the law stopping foreigners from purchasing land in Bulgaria without setting up a company is in the process of being abolished. However, it won't be until 2012 that it is fully deregulated.

WHERE TO BUY

Bulgaria has three very distinct markets, all of which possess their own characteristics and qualities.

Black Sea coast

Bulgaria's Black Sea coastline has developed fast, and in many instances, you may have already missed the boat. Prices have been rising out of control in areas such as Sunny Beach and Golden Sands, and early investors are the ones who reaped the benefits here, seeing appreciation rates of 47%. Development still continues, with 22,500 holiday apartments built last year and a growth of 37% in property prices from August 2005 to August 2006.

It is important to be aware that the market in this area is in a state of flux and rather than being driven by demand, it's providing a wide-ranging supply of developments. There are currently reports that those looking to sell are being offered less for their property than they paid for it as the demand for sales is non-existent. As such, those who are buying today are advised to look outside of the traditional resort areas, and try the northern areas of the coastline. Instead, if you buy a good-quality apartment with golf, spa or hotel facilities, you may well be able to secure some rental income. Always look to buy as close as you can to the beach and amenities – those furthest away are more likely to be affected by the drop in prices. The crashing market is expected to be saved by the advent of budget flights – it's anticipated that Varna will see a 50% rise if these flights begin.

Varna and Balchik

The cosmopolitan city of Varna is one of Bulgaria's better-kept secrets. The country's third largest city, this verdant town is rapidly up and coming and has been put on the map thanks to direct BA flights into the city. Varna is popular with people either buying to let – generally to the locals – or many who are simply buying apartments in the city centre for themselves. Popular with expats, many of whom live in the surrounding villages, it is easy to integrate here thanks to the large retirement market. Being off the beaten track, you must make an effort to learn the language.

Just to the north of Varna is Balchik, an exciting new area which is seeing massive development thanks to the creation of three new golf courses and two new marinas – both golfing and sailing are major attractions in this area.

Despite the coastal location, you are not currently paying a premium due to the unknown nature of the area. Land prices are also lower than the rest of Bulgaria, around €850 per square metre for a four-star waterfront apartment, and rising to €1,200 for a luxury villa. This is a great area in which to pick up a bargain, whether an older property to renovate or a new build.

Ski resorts

A staggering 75% of Bulgaria is mountainous and it is among these towering peaks that the burgeoning property market lies. After Sofia, the ski resorts of Pamporovo, Borovets and Bansko represent the best investment opportunity in Bulgaria, especially with the new Perelik and Super Borovets residential developments.

When compared with ski property in areas such as France, Bulgaria offers great value for money. For between €25,000 and €30,000 you can purchase a studio apartment in Pamporovo, while prices in Bansko start at €25,000. Generally speaking, prices are steeper in Bansko due to higher demand, with costs varying from between €650 to €1,650 per square metre. In Borovets, prices start at €600 per square metre, rising to just under €1,600, and in Pamporovo from €640 and €1,550 per square metre.

Bankso represents 64% of the mountain resorts market with 8,000 units, although the whole ski market has grown by 152% since June 2005, with an increase in the number of holiday homes from 5,000 to 12,000 properties.

It's clear that better opportunities lie in the mountains than on the coast. Bansko is more likely to offer good rental opportunities, while the cheaper prospects of Pamporovo and Borovets mean better capital growth. Bulgaria may well host the 2014 Winter Olympics, and this will mean growth, publicity and heightened demand for skiing in these areas.

Sofia

Sofia is home to one tenth of Bulgaria's population and it's a city which has mushroomed in size in recent years. Despite being an ancient city – one of Europe's oldest, founded in 800BC – there are few remnants of its colourful Byzantine past, with more of the modern architecture of stucco-fronted buildings which post-date the communist years, and where most of the apartments can now be found.

Sofia is going up in the world. Popular with jet-to-let investors thanks to an influx of foreign investment – a number of multinationals have offices here now, including Porsche – property is currently selling at €800 to €1,300 per square metre, and selling fast. An apartment in central Sofia can secure you annual rentals return of 12%, mostly from long-term rentals. There are short-term lets to be had, although these are scarcer and less reliable. The most popular properties are newly-built developments.

The capital shoulders misconceptions of shabby communist tower blocks, but the reality – wide, leafy boulevards – is far from this. Currently undergoing something of a transformation, it's attracting many weekend breakers, international business people and diplomats, sending the tourist market into overdrive. All this makes Sofia a great place to buy at present. Currently, you can buy a one-bedroomed newly-built apartment close to Mount Vitosha for just £20,000, or a luxuriously finished apartment and all mod cons, such as fitted kitchens and all furnishings, for £50,000.

Rural areas

Prices are cheaper in the countryside. The medieval capital of Veliko Tarnovo and properties along the Danube River and around the major town of Ruse are becoming popular, especially with retirees. Looking for beautiful countryside? If so, check out the surrounding villages of the Stara Planina mountain range which stretches almost the entire width of the country. A picturesque town of narrow, cobbled streets, Veliko Tarnovo offers spacious four-bedroomed country properties for as little as £20,000.

WHAT TO BUY

There have been massive levels of development in the country over the last few years, and consequently most of the properties available in Bulgaria are newly-built development homes, along with increasing numbers of golf and spa complexes. Following in the Spanish model, golf is destined to become the next big thing in Bulgaria. There are currently only three golf courses in Bulgaria, but several more – all with leisure and country club facilities – are soon to be opened, such as the golf and spa resort of Dolna Bay, where a three-bedroomed villa is retailing at £95,000.

Bulgaria's rural properties are some of the cheapest in Europe, and for a meagre £8,000, rustic solitude is easily obtainable. Generally requiring renovation, traditional country houses often come with one or two large barns, and a substantial plot of land. A habitable rural property that requires minor modernisation can be acquired for between £12,000 to £15,000, which is an excellent price.

THE BUYING PROCESS

Despite all the coverage and press hype, Bulgaria is still an incredibly small market and has a long way to go before reaching her full potential – the Bulgarian Building and Construction Chamber envisages yearly construction growth of 15% over the next three years. Buying in Bulgaria is certainly not for the fainthearted and it is imperative to secure yourself a knowledgeable lawyer. Thanks to recent EU membership, the country is moving in the right direction for foreign investors, with mortgage rates dropping from 16% to 5.5%, and restrictions on the purchase of land soon to be abolished.

Stage 1: Restrictions on foreigners

As a foreigner buying in Bulgaria, there are restrictions on the purchase of land, but not on property. However, now that Bulgaria is part of the EU, legislation has been drawn up to abolish the restrictions on land purchase, although this is unlikely to be fully ratified until 2012. In order to buy land, you need to set up a limited company. This is a relatively straightforward process and a regular occurrence, and most agents are willing to organise this for you as part of the purchasing process.

In order to set up a company you are required to do the following:

- set up and register the property, including registration with the tax authorities. This costs £515;
- set up a bank account. To do this you will be required to make a minimum deposit of £1,700, although this will be refundable once the company has been official registered.

The registration process normally takes four weeks. Once the company is established, it can purchase any land, or a building with any land attached to it.

Stage 2: Funding your purchase

Mortgage rates have recently been slashed in Bulgaria, and it is only in the last couple of years that foreigners have been able to secure a Bulgarian mortgage through UK lenders. This is down to the recent admission of the country into the EU. Generally, the maximum loan will be 70% of the property's value, leaving the buyer to find a 30% deposit. Interest is normally levied at 6–7%. Consequently, a buyer may find it cheaper to secure equity from their first home and buy with cash.

Stage 3: Background checks and surveys

As with every purchase, you need to check the title deeds at the land registry office. Your checks need to ensure that you are buying the property you think you are, that it's available for sale, that the seller is the actual owner and therefore entitled to sell it and whether or not the property is sold with land – if it is, you will need to set up a company in order to purchase, (see Stage One above). Your lawyer should also check for any outstanding debts that may be attached to the property.

It is advisable that you get a survey carried out, especially if it is an older or resale property. As this is not standard procedure in Bulgaria, you should arrange for a full structural survey. This will cost you between £200 and £300.

Stage 4: Reservation and preliminary contracts

The first stage in the purchasing process is to pay a reservation fee in order to take the property off the market. Before committing to paying a reservation fee ensure that the property will actually be removed from the market, check whether the sale price is inclusive of VAT and what price will be declared on the final contract – the estimated or actual – as this will impact on the amount of tax you will have to pay.

Make sure you obtain a reservation receipt from your estate agent, which recognises payment of the fee. This should also contain an accurate description of the property and its location, and the amount you have paid in reservation, the duration the reservation period will last and whether or not the fee is deemed refundable should you pull out of buying.

Once the reservation fee has been paid, the preliminary sale contract should be drawn up within a couple of weeks. This will set out all the agreed details of the purchase and the amount of deposit to be paid, which is usually 10% of the sale price. You don't have to be present to sign the preliminary contract as you can arrange for your lawyer to sign it on your behalf by giving them power of attorney.

Off-plan property

When buying a newly-built home, the preliminary contract needs to include details and dates for the completion of the property, along with details of the construction materials and agreed payment options. Once construction is completed, you will then be required to sign a delivery acceptance record to show that you are happy the property meets the agreed standards. On signing the preliminary contract, your first payment will be due and you must ensure it is paid on time – otherwise you you could lose your property and deposit.

Stage 5: Completion

Once the preliminary contract has been agreed and the deposit paid, the final contract is then ready to be signed by both the buyer and the seller. This must be witnessed by a notary.

The whole purchasing process can often take less than a month and you will receive the title deeds proving your ownership of the house roughly two weeks following the date of final completion. While the originals will be in Bulgarian, you can – and should – request an English translation.

Be aware that the actual price paid for the property by the buyer and the price listed on the title deeds may differ. This is because in Bulgaria, property has both an estimated tax price and a separate purchase price. The tax estimation price is much lower than the actual purchase price, allowing Bulgarians to pay much lower rates of tax.

If the property is occupied at the time of completion, do not expect the buyers to move out straight away. In Bulgaria, it is normal for the sellers to be given one month following completion to vacate the property.

Stage 6: Additional costs

If you are buying an apartment off-plan then the estate agents' fees are usually paid during the signing of the preliminary contract, rather than on completion of the purchase, so you'll need to ensure that you have the funds available at an earlier stage.

As well as the cost of the property, there will also be additional fees and taxes to be paid before you can take ownership of your home. In Bulgaria you should budget for an extra 4–5% of the cost of the property for these charges. They may include:

- Transfer fees: 2–2.5%.

- Notary fees: 0.5–2%.

- Legal fees: 1–1.5%.

- Surveyor's fee (optional).

- Mortgage fees (if applicable).

- Foreign exchange costs (if applicable).

- Estate agents' fees 3–5%. Payable by both the buyer and seller.

- Registration fees: 0.15% of the price of the property.

- Maintenance fees usually in the region of €7 to €10 per sq m.

THE LETTINGS MARKET

Bulgaria has one of the most rapidly-growing tourist industries in the world, with visitor numbers reaching 4.4 million in 2006 and, while the outlook is healthy for investors, rewards won't be instantaneous.

With 386km of coastline, nine Blue Flag beaches, excellent skiing resorts and facilities, and a rapidly growing golf and spa market, along with 37,000km of walking paths in the Balkan Mountains, there are plenty of attractions for visitors. However, despite all these attractions, you should be aware that rental yields aren't astronomical, and despite parallels being drawn with the Spanish market, Bulgaria is not the new Spain in terms of rental yields. The Black Sea Coast does not enjoy the profits seen on the Costas, with prices on Sunny Beach beyond the means of many locals, a situation that is destined to adversely affect the area's rental market.

However, the major stumbling block is that 80–90% of the tourist market book their holiday through travel agents. Consequently, those who are looking to rent their property privately will find themselves competing with the larger developments and may struggle to secure bookings. You will also be hamstrung by the length of the tourist season, which is a mere four months on the coast. While this doesn't mean you can't make money – as long as you are careful what you buy and do your research it is possible to make a profit – it does mean you can't rely on making enough to cover all your outgoings.

The ski resorts probably offer the best rental opportunities. Still new on the scene and with ridiculously low prices for buyers, these resorts are easily comparable with those of France and Italy, while the cost of skiing is much lower. Bansko alone received 800,000 tourists in 2006 and earned the Daily Mail's award for Most Improved Ski Resort of 2006. Off the back of massive popularity and demand, First Choice announced that they are planning to increase their ski holidays to Bulgaria tenfold. Also, you can look at letting year round as, out of season, there are other attractions such as hiking and golf, which is a rapidly growing market in Bulgaria.

Rental income

Rental yields will always be higher for property located in complexes, as already mentioned, and these will also offer year-round property management and on-site facilities which will help to maximise your rental potential.

Rentals in Bulgaria are usually based on the number of people accommodated rather than on the size of the property, so a small one-bedroomed apartment with a sofa bed can potentially yield income from four people. There are also many new developments coming online which offer up to two years of guaranteed rental income. One such development offers property for £37,200 with a guaranteed return of 4% for two years, which equates to £1,488 per year.

Rental income yielded from letting your property will be liable to tax. UK residents have to pay a 15% withholding tax in Bulgaria but this is offset against UK income tax payable.

RENOVATING A PROPERTY

While building costs are comparatively low in Bulgaria compared with the rest of Europe, the cost of building and labour materials has gone up disproportionately in comparison with the overall cost of living in the country. The cost of building work varies greatly but, as a rule, it is generally one-third that of the UK, with the cost of building a new property between £150 and £250 per square metre.

On average, you should budget to spend up to 50% of the property's sale value on renovation works. While property repairs on Bulgarian property do not generally require planning permission, if you intend to buy a property to restore, make sure you secure building permission before you purchase. Many older properties in Bulgaria lack sufficient foundations, so get a thorough survey carried out before embarking on the project. You should also be aware that a lot of Bulgarian building is done in a traditional fashion, using techniques which differ greatly from the UK. This will only add value to the property at the end of the day.

LIVING IN BULGARIA

Daily life and people

Bulgarian people are friendly and welcoming, and are known for their Latin temperament and sense of humour, which tends to be self deprecating. A sociable bunch, they never cease to amaze expats with their ability to seamlessly combine work with an active social life. Despite their ebullient nature, those who are seeking a peaceful and quiet lifestyle will also find the calm they seek.

From 1946 until 1990, daily life in Bulgaria was dominated by the socialist political system. The communist party attempted to control every aspect of life, attempting to change they way the citizens behaved and thought. However, the Bulgarians managed to retain their traditional customs and beliefs, and ideals such as the importance of family still permeate the fabric of daily life. It's important to try to understand some typical Bulgarian customs prior to relocating to the country, especially the concept that Bulgarians shake their heads from side to side when they mean 'yes' and nod to say 'no'.

Despite being a rapidly westernising and developing country, many Bulgarians still incorporate traditional aspects of folklore and culture into their lives, especially in the form of festivals.

Visas and residency

Residents of the UK can stay in Bulgaria for up to 30 days within a six-month period without applying for a visa, and other members of the EU for up to 90 days. If you want to stay for longer than 30 days, you'll need to apply for a long-term, type D visa or a type C short-term visa which will allow you to stay for up to 90 days within a six-month period.

Two types of residence permit can be obtained by UK citizens; either a temporary permit for residency of up to a year, or a permanent one. To obtain a temporary residence permit you need to already have a type D visa, proof of National Insurance or social security status, and a minimum deposit of 3,000 leva (approximately £1,020) in a Bulgarian bank account. This will grant you a one-year visa which can be renewed annually, and a Bulgarian Identity Card.

To obtain permanent residence, you must have spent at least five years in Bulgaria on a temporary residence permit. More details on the visas, permits and the application process can be obtained from The Embassy of the Republic of Bulgaria in London, and you can download visa application forms from www.bulgarianembassy.org.uk.

Utilities

In Bulgaria, the voltage is 220 volts AC and two-pin continental plugs are used. Consequently you'll need to get an adaptor to use any UK electrical products there.

Gas is not in widespread usage outside of Sofia and so most central heating is electric, with wood-burning stoves used in rural areas. Billing for both gas and electricity is monthly, based on the amount you consume and there is no standing charge for utilities, apart from telephones. Payment can be made through your Bulgarian bank account, at the post office, via the internet or using a debit card.

If you need to connect to water and electricity, this can be organised through the municipal offices, as will any direct debit payment you may wish to set up. Water is drinkable in most areas, although in some rural regions it may be wise to buy bottled mineral water.

Telephone services are available throughout the country, although mobile phone reception can be poor in the rural areas. Bulgaria Telecom is the national telephone service provider and their website offers comprehensive details of their services. See www.btc.bg/en. There are public payphones throughout the country and also telephone offices within the post offices.

Email is also becoming more widely employed and the number of internet cafés is starting to grow. If you're looking to get internet at home, there are a number of service providers, but provision tends to be dial-up rather than broadband. However, this is starting to change.

Banking and currency

The national currency is the Bulgarian lev or leva when used in the plural. In official documents you may well see the currency leva written as BGN, but in most shops around the country it will be shortened to lv.

One lev consists of 100 stotinki (st). Banknotes are available in denominations of 1, 2, 5, 10, 20, 50 and 100 and stotinka in coins of 1, 2, 5, 10, 20 and 50. When paying for something in a shop, do not always expect the right change – the price is often rounded up to the nearest lev.

Between 2001 and 2004, 30 million counterfeit notes were confiscated, so in order to ensure you are receiving authentic currency, check that notes carry the Bulgarian Lion watermark. Credit cards aren't widely accepted in Bulgaria, except in hotels and restaurants that cater for foreign tourists, although cash machines are widespread.

There are restrictions on taking currency into Bulgaria. The maximum you can take into the country without declaring it is 5,000 leva (around £1,750), while in order to take in anything between 5,000 leva (£1,750) and 25,000 leva (£8,627) you will have to declare it at customs and produce a bank statement proving the origin of the funds.

It is recommended that you open a Bulgarian bank account (see the section on Buying a Property page 116), and to do so is fairly simple – all you are required to do is produce your passport and deposit some funds. Not all banks have English-speaking staff, although Raiffeisen Bank (http://www.rbb.bg) and Bulbank (http://www.bulbank.bg) offer English language services.

Taxes

Income tax is charged at between 15% and 29%. As Bulgaria has signed a double tax treaty agreement with the UK, foreign nationals will avoid double taxation on any income they pay tax on in Bulgaria.

According to Bulgarian taxation law, you are considered a tax resident if you have a permanent residence in Bulgaria or are a permanent resident: i.e. if you spend more than 183 days in Bulgaria in any year. If you aren't a permanent resident and are only working in the country temporarily, then tax is payable only on your income generated in Bulgaria. If you own a company, note that the rate of income tax for corporations was reduced to 15% in 2005.

The end of year for tax returns in Bulgaria is 31st December and tax returns must be filed by 31st March if you are a limited company, or 15th April for an individual.

Insurance

As always, ensure you get home and contents insurance for your Bulgarian property. There are plenty of policies to choose from. On average you can expect to pay between £70 and £150 per year depending on the location and type of property you own.

The following companies offer insurance policies in Bulgaria:

- Orel Insurance JSC, www.orel-insurance.com
- Bulsrad PLC, www.bulstrad.bg
- QBE, www.qbe-sofia.bg
- Grawe Bulgaria, www.grawe.bg
- Fidelitas Assistance Ltd, www.fidelitas-assistance.com
- AIG Bulgaria, www.aig.bg

Healthcare

With an EHIC card you will be able to get free emergency treatment in Bulgaria, should you need it. While facilities may be basic and hospitals under-funded, health care is of an acceptable level, although you may have trouble finding English-speakers. Consequently if you need some sort of specialised treatment, it's best to head for Sofia.

If you are relocating permanently then private health care is probably the best option. Most large towns and cities offer private medical care, with prices varying from £15 to £50 for a consultation.

As for over-the-counter medicines, pharmacies are well stocked and prices are much lower than in the UK.

Retiring

As with any retirement situation, if you are planning to retire to Bulgaria then be sensible about where you choose to live and make sure you won't be isolated or in particularly hilly or harsh terrain.

You will still be entitled to your UK pension and you can arrange for this to be paid into your Bulgarian bank account. However, there is no social security agreement in place between the two countries, so your pension will not rise with inflation; instead it will be frozen. However, now that Bulgaria has joined the EU this may well change, because if you choose to retire to another country in the European Economic Area (EEA), you might be liable to claim certain benefits that you would not normally get abroad, or a benefit which that country provides. For more details see www.dwp.gov.uk.

Education

The education system in Bulgaria is good and the Bulgarian people place strong emphasis on schooling. Compulsory education starts at the age of seven and ends at 16, although most Bulgarian children go on to further education. Schooling is divided into three stages: ages seven to ten, ten to 14 and then 14 to 18. Further education is also divided into three types: comprehensive (general studies), vocational (technical studies) and profile-oriented (specific studies).

Bulgaria has many excellent universities and institutes providing higher education and the country enjoys one of the highest proportions of university graduates, coming third in an EU poll with 21.1% of the population.

If you are relocating with your children, then you need to consider buying close to Sofia if you intend to send them to a private, English-speaking school.

- The American College of Sofia, www.acs.bg
- The Anglo-American School of Sofia, www.aas-sofia.org
- Prof. Vassil Zlatarski Private School, Sofia, www.zlatarskischool.org
- American College Arcus, www.ac-arcus.com

Driving

Despite being relatively traffic free and devoid of the tailbacks so common on UK motorways, Bulgaria's roads are not good. The World Bank recently condemned their condition, saying that only one third of the national road network was in good shape, with the majority of artery roads requiring upgrades to meet the EU road safety requirements. Road signs are written predominantly in Cyrillic, so you will need to invest in a road map which carries both Cyrillic and Latin place names. Bulgarians drive on the right-hand side of the road. Keep a look out for animals and horse-and-carts. During the winter, night driving is not advised as conditions get very bad. It is compulsory to carry a fire extinguisher and warning triangle, and to have – and use – headlamp converters when driving.

Speed limits are as follows:

- motorways: 120km/h (74mph);
- main highways: 90km/h (55mph);
- built-up areas: 50km/h (31mph).

You can drive in Bulgaria with your existing European licence, but if you intend to stay for more than six months, you will need to apply for a Bulgarian licence. Fuel is extremely cheap at around 50p per litre and diesel is also widely available.

Getting around

As with the road network, Bulgarian public transport has also suffered from a lack of investment. Train services have been most affected and outside of the major centres of Sofia, Varna and Burgas, they are irregular. Buying a ticket and negotiating the timetable will require the help of a Bulgarian speaker, although some details can be gleaned from www.bdz.bg.

Buses are much more reliable and link most major towns and villages, with services cheap and frequent. Longer journeys are run by private bus companies, and these are affordable and efficient – a three-hour journey from the coast to Veliko Tarnovo costs just £4.

Taxis are available in all major towns and fares are metered, with the average journey costing roughly 30p. However, it is a better idea to decide on a fare beforehand rather than using a meter. Taxis can often be an easier way of travelling if public transport is unreliable, but along the Black Sea coast fares can be vastly inflated.

Language

If you intend to relocate permanently to Bulgaria, it's recommended that you get to grips with the language. Bulgarian is a Slavic language, based on the Cyrillic alphabet. As such it is quite tricky to learn, and bears little resemblance to the Latin alphabet, with most letters being borrowed from Greek.

English is the most common second language spoken in Bulgaria and in many of the larger towns, cities and resorts, you'll find plenty of English-speaking Bulgarians. Many of the professionals you'll be dealing with during the property purchase are likely to speak English, but if you're looking to employ builders or cleaners, the chances are they won't.

Those looking to relocate to rural areas will have to be prepared to get a basic grasp of both spoken and written Bulgarian as there will be fewer English-speakers around.

Shopping

The cost of supplies in Bulgaria is extremely low and it's better to buy locally-produced goods than to pay for imported – or potentially fake – products. As already mentioned, there used to be a two-tiered pricing system, with higher charges for foreigners. As this is now illegal, look out for overcharging. Shops are open from 9am to 7pm, Monday to Friday. They're generally closed on Sundays.

For an international feel to your shopping, Sofia has the best boutiques and internationally recognised brands – including Bulgaria's first Marks & Spencer – and along the Black Sea Coast you'll be inundated with tourist shops selling trinkets, buckets and spades. Most towns tend to have a supermarket, such as Billa, Metro and Hit, and while customer service is improving, many shop assistants still aren't acquainted with the concept. You will find that when you buy, the price tends to be rounded up, for example, from seven leva and 17 stotinki to seven leva and 20 stotinki.

Post

The Bulgarian postal service has been slow to modernise, but is still quite efficient. Post offices offer all the services you'd expect in the UK, including letter and parcel postage, utility bill payments and telephone services; they also deal with banking services for the Bulgarian Postal Bank. Post offices tend to be open between 8.30am and 5.30pm from Monday to Saturday. For more details visit www.bgpost.bg.

Crime, corruption and the police

Unfortunately, Bulgaria does have a reputation for being plagued by corruption and it is a big problem, especially as the country is trying so hard to modernise. Now it is a member of the EU, pressure is being put on the government to resolve these problems and they are starting to make headway.

Most foreigners will not find themselves exposed to problems of corruption, although it is true that a few 'payments' here and there can make the purchase of land much swifter than the average four to five months you are generally looking at. If you ensure you employ a knowledgeable agent, then they will be able to grease the wheels for you.

Street crime and violent crime rates are very low compared with Western Europe, but this doesn't mean you can let your guard down – just make sure you take the kind of precautions you would back home. If you do need to call the police for any reason, dial 166.

Case study

Steve Harding describes himself as an optimist. Following a serious back injury which left him unable to work, Jan, his wife, was made redundant and their six-year-old daughter, Emma, fell seriously ill. It was when the family's life was at

129

it lowest ebb they came across a magazine which changed their lives forever, and their dream of living abroad became a reality.

'We wanted to sell our house and had been thinking of buying abroad for a while. We decided to buy in Bulgaria because we couldn't afford to buy anything except a one-bedroomed house in England. Coming across a magazine feature about buying in Bulgaria was just the catalyst we needed, and I immediately picked up the phone and rang estate agents, Bulgarian Gateway,' says Steve.

He first talked to Bulgarian Gateway in December, and by mid-January had made his way to Sofia. 'My first adventure was the seven-and-a-half-hour train journey to Bourgas, which was a magical experience and the best way to see the stunning countryside, which at this point was blanketed in snow.'

Steve's first impressions of Bulgaria were positive.

'The people here are warm, friendly and accommodating, and the scenery is breathtaking. While there is poverty here that the western eye might find unacceptable, Bulgaria is moving forward, and will only improve as investment levels increase.'

Steve's first purchase was an investment property in Melnica, 120km south of Bourgas and in a countryside location.

'This property was not intended for the family, but rather as a investment which we were looking at renting out to secure us some income. My main aim was to find a home for my family and I eventually came across a one-acre piece of land, which was going to be the plot for four houses.'

Thinking fast, Steve mentioned to the builder that he would be interested in buying the plot and building one property on it.

'The builder seemed keen, and in the end I purchased the land, on which we agreed to build a three-bedroomed bungalow. All of this has cost me just ⇔68,000, and the build was completed at the end of January 2007.'

Steve considers himself very lucky as throughout the purchasing process he had good guidance from his estate agents. However, he has had some reservations about purchasing an investment property in such a rural location, and advises anyone going out to Bulgaria to keep their wits about them.

'It was all very confusing when I first went to Bulgaria, and I do think maybe I should have thought through the location of our investment property slightly more thoroughly.'

While the process was fairly smooth, it did take Steve six months to get planning permission for his bungalow, especially as he purchased agricultural land and it had to be passed for building. However, he had a good solicitor and was helped by Ivan, MD of Bulgarian Gateway, who was Bulgarian and knew how the system worked.

Steve and his family will soon be relocating to Bulgaria permanently and they hope this will be the start of a new life for them.

'Opting to live in Bulgaria has been one of the most profound and fundamental decisions of our lives, and we can now look forward to an exciting new life. We intend to be self-sufficient and I am even thinking of having a wind turbine installed!' says Steve.

'My first priority – along with that of my wife and daughter – is to learn the language. I don't see the point in living in another country and not learning the language, although I think my daughter is slightly ahead of me!'

8
Croatia

Factfile
Population: 4.5 million
Population growth rate: −0.03%
Area: 22,839 sq miles
GDP growth rate: 4.3%
Inflation: 3.3%
Unemployment rate: 12.7%
Net migration: 1.58 per 1,000
Currency: kuna (KN)
Exchange rate: 1.00 GBP = Kn11.0135
EU status: Potential member in 2008/09
Number of foreign residents: 17.902 (0.46% of total population)
Time zone: CET (+1 GMT)
Capital: Zagreb

COUNTRY PROFILE

Described by George Bernard Shaw as the 'Pearl of the Adriatic', there are many reasons – not least the weather, low cost of living, high quality of education, low crime rates and good healthcare – to choose to buy in this stunningly beautiful country.

Did you know?
Croatia was the birthplace of the necktie, or cravat, originally worn by Croatian mercenaries back in the 17th century.

Why buy in Croatia?

With over 6,000km of beaches and 1,100 offshore islands, Croatia is a truly fascinating country. A few years ago it was tipped as being the next big property market and was soon labelled the 'new Tuscany'.

Proving increasingly popular with British buyers – over 300 properties were sold to Brits in 2004 – it's unlikely that Croatia will ever rival the popularity of the Bulgarian or Polish markets. Nevertheless, it can offer the investor appreciation rates of as much as 20–40% in some areas.

The country remains undeveloped, and this is something of a Croatian passion. One of the major attractions is that the Croatian government has pledged to protect the country and its natural beauty and coastline against over-development. With a stable government and prosperous economy, the country is more developed than many realise, with an effective infrastructure and many modern towns and cities.

There are no restrictions on foreign buyers, who enjoy the same rights as domestic/local buyers. With plenty of direct flights from the UK and a flight time of under three hours, reaching the country is also cheap and easy. Potential EU membership is only serving to increase the popularity and investment potential of Croatia as the usual price hikes are expected once membership occurs, probably in the next two years. Some estimate that prices could rise by as much as 300% by 2010.

Politics and economy

Historically, Croatia has always been a prosperous country, and following a period of war and recession, today it averages a GDP growth rate of between 3% and 4%. Croatia is a steady democracy that's well on track for joining the EU. The currency, the Kuna, is stable, having been shadowing first the Deutschmark and then the euro. Inflation is low but unemployment is relatively high, although this varies depending on the season. The Croat economy is a mixed one, with 30% attributable to industry, 7.9% to agriculture and 62.1% to services such as tourism.

Croatia became a parliamentary democracy back in 1991 and today is a democratic republic. The President is Stjepan Mesić and the Prime

133

Minister Ivo Sanader. The EU has pledged to invest €76 million to help Croatia meet the requirements set for membership of the EU, which demands that they strengthen their economic, social, political and democratic systems.

Geography and climate

Situated in the heart of Europe, its long, crescent-shape dominates the Adriatic coastline. As with many Eastern European countries, the geography is diverse. Travel away from the rugged coastline and you'll hit vast fertile plains, mountains, gorges, valleys and vineyards.

The country is divided into several different regions, the main ones being Istria in the north, Kvarner in the centre and Dalmatia to the south; all three are unique in both climate and appearance. Almost 10% of the country consists of eight national parks, including dense forests of oak, beech and black pine, which are home to lynx, bears and wolves. Thankfully, the country lacks any sort of heavy industry and so the natural beauty which has led to many parts of Croatia being listed as UNESCO World Heritage sites has remained unspoiled.

The most well-known part of Croatia is its 6,000km-long coastline, which runs from Istria in the north to Dubrovnik in the south. It's dominated by more than 1,100 islands and boasts a Mediterranean climate with mild winters and warm summers. Inland the climate turns colder, but the summers are hot. Zagreb, Croatia's administrative and cultural capital, is situated inland in the hilly region of Zagorije. The *lingua franca* here is English thanks to the presence of many multinational companies, a lot of which employ foreign staff.

History and culture

Following WWI, Croatia became part of the Kingdom of Yugoslavia, with Italy controlling much of northern Dalmatia up until 1943, and this is reflected in the Italianate influence seen in the area. Following the German invasion in 1941, Yugoslavia was ruled by the facist group, Ustasa. They attempted to ethnically cleanse the country by sending all the Serbs back to Serbia, and when attempts were made by the Germans to clamp down on their activities, Ustasa began an extermination programme, which left between 60,000 and 600,000 Serbs, Jews and Roma dead. What followed was a war which left around one million dead, as the Croats and Serbs united under Marshall Tito to expel Ustasa. At the end of the war, Croatia became one of five countries in the new communist Yugoslav Federation, ruled by Tito. However, Croatia – along with Slovenia – soon sought autonomy, feeling hamstrung by the less developed republics. In 1990, following a decade of economic crisis, Croatians voted for independence and freed themselves from communist rule. At the same time, the 600,000 Serbs living in Croatia also demanded independence, leading to the outbreak of war which lasted for six months and saw the deaths of 10,000 people. Fighting broke out again in 1993 and 1995 when the Croatians retook occupied territory, finally displacing the Serbian population. The country remained in a perilous state until 2000, when the Socialists gained political control and pledged a series of political and economic reforms which were designed to catapult Croatia into the European mainstream.

Culturally, Croatia has a long and colourful history, with many historic places and monuments, including six World Heritage sites and eight national parks. Among the most well-known Croatian sites is Dubrovnik, the old town of Hvar and the natural beauty of the town of Mljet.

Religion

Around 90% of the country is Catholic, with the remainder of the population a mix of Orthodox, Protestant and Muslim.

Tourism and getting there

Prior to conflict in the Balkans, more than half a million Brits used to holiday in Croatia each year. Today there are over 8.5 million foreign tourists visiting Croatia, making it the 18th most popular tourist destination in the world. Recently undergoing something of a revival, the country is once more attracting hordes of tourists and has reclaimed its reputation as being a playground of the rich and famous. Today tourism accounts for 22% of the country's GDP and given the vast swathes of unspoilt coastline, islands and cultural sites, it is easy to see why Croatia is such a popular destination. Once the country joins the EU – membership is set for 2009 – it is believed that the tourist industry will grow by almost 7% per annum.

Croatia is most famous for its sailing and hiking and has rapidly become one of Europe's most popular diving locations. All along the coast there are a string of natural parks including Risnjak and Palenica. Inland there are the elegant streets of Zagreb, while coastal Dubrovnik, Hvar and Rovinj are popular. While there is ample opportunity for rentals in Croatia, be aware that the hype that has been attached to the country – describing it as the new Spain and Tuscany rolled into one – is rather far-fetched.

Getting to Croatia is relatively easy, with both British Airways and Croatia Airlines offering regular flights from London to Zagreb. There are now also budget flights available with Ryanair flying into Pula in northern Croatia and easyJet serving Split and Rijeka.

Cost of living

Prices are slightly higher in Croatia when compared with many other Eastern European countries – whereas beer is £1 a pint, in Montenegro it is 33p. Be aware that prices do vary widely by region. An espresso in a rural district north of Zagreb could be 3.5kn (32p), jumping to 5kn (46p) on the coast. In general, living costs are lower than in Western Europe but may be higher than places like Serbia, Bulgaria and Romania. A meal for two with wine would cost you 150kn, (£14) while half a litre of local beer is 10kn (91p) in a bar, or 6kn (55p) in a shop. Eurodiesel is 6.91kn/L (63p) and petrol super 7.72kn/L (70.5p).

Food and drink

The Croatian diet focuses on homegrown vegetables and freshly made pizza and pasta, with local markets selling handmade bread and freshly-grown vegetables. On the coast, excellent locally-produced wines complement the flavoursome pasta, pizza and fish dishes, while pork is the most popular meat. There are many seasonal specialities, ranging from wild asparagus in April to world-famous truffles later in the year. In eastern Croatia, food is spicier, with paprika added to dishes such as pork *kulen*.

Wine can be bought for as little as £2 in the shop and there are a number of vineyards which produce some fantastic vintages. The Istrian region is known for its reds – Terans, Merlots and Cabernet Francs – while in Eastern Slavonia, some excellent whites are produced.

Beer ranges from local specialities through to international brands.

THE PROPERTY MARKET

Cheaper than France and Spain but more expensive than Turkey, the Croatian property market is much more established than many people think. Croatia's neighbours, most notably the Austrians, have been buying property in the country since the end of the Balkan war, as have the Germans and Italians. Croatia is regarded as a solid and safe investment, with a well-established tourist industry and a strong rental season.

Property prices in Croatia have increased by between 12% and 28% per annum over the last three years, although this isn't consistent throughout the country as prices vary dramatically depending on the area you buy in. Dubrovnik is already an expensive place to purchase, with certain properties reaching an unbelievable €6,000 per square metre, compared to Zagreb, which averages €2,300 per square metre. Despite recent price hikes – of up to 40% in some places – prices still remain an average of 30% to 40% lower than those of Spain and France. Generally speaking British buyers are choosing either entry-level apartments for an average of €100,000, small stone-built houses with pools for around €280,000, or large stone houses with pools for around €400,000.

Expected accession to the EU in 2009 means that the outlook for the Croatian property market is bright. Expectations are high as increasing numbers of foreign buyers will find it easier to purchase once the country becomes an EU member, with regulations set to become more flexible with regard to the financial packages available and registration of ownership. At the same time, more Croatian buyers are investing into their own market, which is making it more stable.

Slovenia is another state that emerged from the break-up of Yugoslavia and has gone on to become a success story. In the two years prior to its accession to the EU, Slovenia enjoyed price rises of 40% and given Croatia's track record, it is believed that she is on course to exceed these appreciation rates. However, before EU accession, the Croatian government is faced with reducing the backlog of civil cases involving questions of land tenure. They are making progress with the land registry office, as much of the process can now be conducted over the internet, thereby cutting out the previously slow bureaucracy.

Croatia is a different type of market compared with much of Eastern Europe as buyers tend to be well-heeled and affluent. Generally speaking, you shouldn't go to Croatia seeking a bargain. What Croatia does deliver is good-quality property and, while costing slightly more – a result of a shortage of property and affluence in the market – you are virtually guaranteed higher capital appreciation. Supply is destined to continue being restricted thanks to the geographical restraints on development – a result of Croatia's narrow coastal plain – and the choosy nature of the municipalities, which limit development in order to preserve the natural environment. The limited number of budget flights has also led to the establishment of a wealthy tourist industry. As a result of this, prices have been pushed up by the fact that the average buyer has more cash to spend.

Where to buy?

Prices vary drastically in Croatia depending on where and what you buy. A two-bedroomed apartment in Istria costs an average of € 100,000 to € 150,000. Prices are similar on the Dalmatian coast (including Split) whereas prices in Zagreb are around € 130,000 to € 170,000 rising to between € 140,000 and € 180,000 in Dubrovnik.

Istrian peninsula

The triangular county of Istria is situated in Croatia's north-west, bordering Slovenia and jutting into the northern Atlantic. Most foreign buyers in Croatia head for the Istrian Peninsula, an area where steady appreciation of between 20% and 30% has been predicted for the next couple of years. Remarkably untouched by the ravages of tourism and foreign property investment, this is a region with a rich blend of Italian, Slovenian and Croatian cultures and lifestyles. Croatia's most accessible area – thanks to the international airport at Pula – it is also the most popular with foreign tourists, with a total of 2.3 million visitors to the region between January and October 2006; Umag and Porec top the list of Croatia's most visited destinations.

There is a swathe of hotel developments and resorts along the coast, such as Porec and Pula, but they still maintain a certain Italian charm. Most foreigners come here to snap up the wealth of stone-built Istrian houses, causing prices to rise by 20% per annum. In the coastal town of Rovinj, prices are hitting £4,000 a square metre, which is a lot when you consider the local monthly wage sits at around £500 per month, and so many Croatians have been priced out of the market.

The most popular locations here are Rovinj, Pula, Vrsar, Porec and Novigrad – essentially the peninsula's west coast. Despite a massive rise in prices and interest over the last few years, there is still a large stock of property here and you can still find a bargain. For example, you can pick up a one-bedroomed new-build apartment, only 15 minutes from the sea, for €85,000. Looking for something a bit more historic? Stone ruins can be found for anything from €39,000 to €220,000. An average two-bedroomed house will set you back by €177,000 while for a newly-built villa you can pay anything between €240,000 and €300,000. Essentially, whatever you want to spend, there is something to suit your budget.

Dubrovnik

This ancient city is more than 1,300 years old and dates back to Roman times, with the city walls not only marking the beginnings of the old town, but some very decisive price bands, with inner city property being decidedly more expensive than that outside the city walls.

Dubrovnik is a city which comes with a hefty price tag thanks to the influx of the rich and famous into the area, which has guaranteed a steady rate of capital appreciation. It is also a very individual market that's different from the rest of the Dalmatian Coast. However, even the rich and famous can find it hard to obtain property here, with demand far outstripping supply.

Believe it or not, prices are comparable with London. Older, period properties are the most popular, but also the most limited in numbers. However, if you can afford to buy in the city, you're sure to make a safe investment as appreciation rates are extremely healthy and the rental market is year-round. If you're looking to purchase a two-bedroomed apartment, expect to pay €220,000 for a furnished property.

In the past, Dubrovnik has broken records, with parts of the city priced at a staggering €10,000 per square metre – that would mean paying €800,000 for an 80 square metre apartment. Within two miles of Dubrovnik you are looking at a more realistic – but still expensive – €3,000 per square metre.

Zagreb

Zagreb is a newly emerging market that offers a different kind of investment. Home to a quarter of the country's population, this city has been the cultural and political epicentre of Croatia since the Middle Ages. It oozes class and sophistication, and while on the surface this spotless centre is reminiscent of the chic cities of Western Europe, scratch the surface and you'll find a heady blend of cultures and peoples.

The property market here is diverse but generally fairly expensive. Look outside the capital and you can pick up a ruin for around the €30,000 mark and one-bedroomed apartments for between €70,000 and €80,000. In the city itself, most available property comes in the form of apartments, and if you want something central, you're looking at €135,000 for one bedroom; a period three-bedroomed apartment in the business district retails at around €375,000. With Zagreb experiencing a growing influx of multinationals and foreign businesses, demand has been growing for long-term rentals from international workers, providing a great opportunity for a healthy rental income.

The islands

With over 1,000 offshore islands to choose from, it's not surprising that you have the opportunity to buy one of your very own if you have the cash! Of the 1,185 Dalmatian Islands, only 50 are inhabited, but property on these is in high demand, with prices starting at € 130,000 for a newly-built two-bedroomed development.

The islands have experienced the usual 20% appreciation rates that have swept across Croatia and for an average one-bedroomed apartment, expect to pay around € 93,000, while for three bedrooms you're looking at roughly € 185,000.

The Dalmatian coastline

Stretching from Spilt in the north down to the Montenegrin border in the south, the breathtakingly beautiful Dalmatian region is not a place to find a bargain. However, if you do have the money to invest there, then you're guaranteed good, steady capital growth. The average price for a two- or three-bedroomed apartment is around € 200,000, with property costing an average of between € 2,500 and € 3,000 per square metre. Popular areas include Trogir and Makarska.

Because of the high costs of buying, one of the recommended locations to look at is the city of Split. This is a much overlooked city, and in places, it's incredibly beautiful. Located on the coast of southern Dalamatia, Split is Croatia's second city, being a bustling port and transport hub. A small, central, newly-built property here will cost around € 192,120, while there are also a number of renovation properties to be found. Such bargains are generally on the edge of the city in the post-communist tower blocks, but if you're looking for something for yourself, or to rent, it's recommended that you look at something with a more 'Western' feel. A two-bedroomed resale apartment located in the city centre can be yours for € 100,000. If you look to the old town then prices increase. A traditional, six-bedroomed period apartment with coastal views will cost around €600,000.

What to buy?

The recommendation in Croatia is not to go inland and buy something incredibly rural for a bargain price, as it simply won't make you money, either through capital appreciation or rentals. Unless you intend to live permanently in Croatia or you have a personal preference for resale houses, in order to secure the best returns for your investment, you should look to purchase a newly-built property. Generally, off-plan properties are more adapted to modern demands and living, the quality of construction is higher and it comes with the developer's guarantee. Newer properties also tend to be lower maintenance, especially apartments, and they offer better rental potential.

As seafront property sells at a premium due to the tough laws protecting the coastline, appreciation rates will be at their highest in these areas. Croatia is renowned for its quality properties and consequently agents recommend that you spend that little bit more to ensure you buy into a market where demand is high, supply limited and you have the option to let out your home – either long-term in cities such as Zagreb, Spilt and Dubrovnik, or short term along the Istrian or Dalmatian coast.

THE BUYING PROCESS

Given that the Austrians and Germans have been buying in Croatia in their droves since the late 1990s, the buying process here is well established. However, that doesn't make it easy and the bureaucracy can be slow and clunky to say the least – it has been known to take a year between commencing a property purchase to being named as the owner. Nevertheless, if you secure the right impartial advice and do your research, the process – while not lacking in frustration – should at least be hassle free.

Stage one: Restrictions on foreign buyers

Most EU buyers are free to purchase property and land in Croatia, with the only restrictions in place on agricultural or forestry land. However, before purchasing, you will need to seek the permission of the government to do so and this can take anything up to a year to secure. This is a mere formality on the part of the government, but it can still lead to significant hold-ups, unless you purchase as a Croatian registered company.

Stage two: Financing your purchase

Foreigners are unable to secure a mortgage in Croatia. British banks are also reluctant to lend money to fund a Croatian home purchase, and so most investors resort to releasing equity from their UK home. Some of the bigger banks in both Croatia and the UK are starting to look at the possibilities of lending and the situation is beginning to change, although most UK lenders are generally only dealing with those who have set up a company.

Stage 3: Surveys and background checks

Surveys are not as common in Croatia as they are in the UK and there are fewer building surveyors around. Although there is a formal qualification for a land surveyor, known locally as a *geodet*, there is no specific qualification for a building surveyor, unlike the UK; most building surveyors are qualified as architects.

It is not uncommon for Croatian agents to complain that getting a survey carried out will hold up the sale. Nevertheless, it is recommended that you do have one, especially if you are going to be buying an older, resale property. For a newly-built home, it is not as necessary to have a survey, especially if the property is protected by a guarantee for a couple of years.

As with many Eastern European countries, the transition from communism to capitalism has left behind many question marks over land ownership, with some instances of displaced Serbs returning to reclaim their land. While these incidents are few and far between, it is essential that you check the land registry status of the property before buying. Ensure that the cadastral (which records the provenance of the property) and the land registry (which states the owner's name) match. If they don't, walk away. Also check that the property was not built contrary to planning permission and that there are no debts registered against it. As the Croatian land registry is available to search online, get your agent to print you off a copy of the Certificate of Title (*Vlasnicki List*) on any property in which you are interested.

If you are buying an apartment, always check that it possesses a Division Document (*etager*). Without this, all that you are buying is a share of the building. For example, if there are eight apartments for sale, without an *etager* you will only own an eighth of your apartment and a eighth of everyone else's. Also, should you wish to modernise or change your apartment in any way, you will need the permission of all the residents in the development.

Stage 4: Deciding on your ownership

If you are reluctant to wait for the Croatian government to grant you approval to buy, you can bypass this by setting up a Croatian company. This is the fastest and most common way to purchase, but you need to be aware that setting up as a company will result in you incurring additional costs, such as paying an accountant to produce company accounts, and the payment of corporation tax on any profits made, such as rental income. You also need to decide on whether or not to register for PDV (VAT). This decision rests on the purpose of your company. If you are simply buying to let, it will probably not be a worthwhile exercise. It is best to discuss this in detail with your lawyer.

Setting up a company is a simple process that requires you to open a bank account which contains at least Kn20,000 (£1,827), and visit a notary, who will need to take your personal details – such as a passport number, address, full name and so on – and the list of activities in which the company will be participating. The process generally takes between two to three weeks and is inexpensive.

Ownership choice	Pros	Cons
Individual	Limited paperwork following transaction	Takes longer
Company	Quick and easy Can claim back PDV	Regular paperwork to be submitted Incurs costs

Stage 5: The contract

The first stage is to arrange for a reservation contract to take the property off the market. Generally speaking, this will cost you €200 and gives you a bit of breathing space until you can organise to have the deposit in place for the signing of the preliminary contract – this is generally between 5% and 10% of the total cost of the property. Make sure that you get your lawyer to have a look through the details of the preliminary contract as it will generally be written by the estate agent who is acting on behalf of the seller. It is normal to get it written into the contract that if the vendor withdraws from the sale you will have your deposit returned.

Once all the paperwork is completed and signed, the final stage is to get the contract notarised. You will need to have the remaining fee ready to pay on the signing of the final contract. Once it's signed, if buying as an individual, you will need to apply to the government for approval before you can get your name entered in the land registry. Generally, this is a standard procedure and you are unlikely to be turned down. The major problem is the time-consuming nature of the process. Once your lawyer has the confirmation certificate from the ministry, it can be passed on to the land registry office and you are recognised as the official owner of the property. If you are buying as a business you do not need to seek the permission in order to purchase a property.

Stage 6: Additional costs

When working out your budget, make sure you take all additional costs into consideration, as well as the price of the property. Agents in Croatia charge buyers a commission ranging from 2% to 3%, while legal fees will cost around 1% of the purchase price, with an additional 0.5% to be entered in the land registry. You'll also have to pay property transfer tax of 5% once the property is registered. If you buy newly-built property, this 5% will be levied only on the cost of the land, as opposed to it being levied on the entire property for a resale.

There may be PDV (VAT) on a newly-built property of 22% to allow for. Sometimes this is included in the overall price of the property, but ensure you check. A survey will cost between £300 and £400, while notary fees and translation costs are roughly £50.

THE LETTINGS MARKET

Currently, Croatia is not the location for buy-to-let investors or those seeking to cover their costs through rentals – you simply won't make your money back on the same scale as you would in Turkey or Tallin. That's not to say there isn't demand – the rentals market is just not keeping pace with the burgeoning property market, especially in areas such as Dubrovnik, where property prices are four times higher than northern Istria, yet rental values are only 1.5 times higher. The rental season is also shorter than in countries such as Italy and Turkey.

Renting an apartment in a place like Zagreb is relatively expensive thanks to the large numbers of UN personnel who have populated the capital, causing rents to rocket, particularly for city centre apartments. The cost of renting on the coast is dependent on the time of year, although you can expect to secure an average rental income of 7% per annum.

Despite all this the market is constantly growing. An article in *The Sunday Times* recently highlighted the shortage of villas that are available for rent in Istria when compared to the huge demand in the area.

While the opportunities for long-term lets are limited in the coastal areas, the potential for short-term lets is growing fast, as media and tourist interest continues to expand. The season has begun to extend and the future for year-round lets will continue to improve once the many golf course projects are completed. Istria is ideal for winter golf, and could soon be home to up to 21 courses and residential complexes.

An apartment represents a more lucrative investment than a house due to better rental potential and lower maintenance costs. Expected annual rental income is €4,000 to €6,000 in Istria, €3,000 to €5,000 in Dalmatia, and €4,500 to €7,000 in Dubrovnik. Zagreb is not suitable for holiday rentals but long-term rental income can yield anything from €400 to €600 per month.

RENOVATING A PROPERTY

You shouldn't have too many problems finding a builder who is willing and able to renovate your property, although they may be harder to find in the summer when many are employed in the tourist industry. An architect should be able to advise you on the renovations and put you in touch with reliable builders and you won't need to secure planning permission to carry out minor renovations. However, the bureaucracy in Croatia can make the process very unreliable, so make sure you triple check the requirements for building construction or renovation before applying for planning permission.

While the cost of materials is about the same as that in the rest of Western Europe, wage levels are around a third of their UK and Irish equivalents, meaning the labour costs are lower.

LIVING IN CROATIA

Daily life and people

As with the UK, you will find a significant north-south divide between the Istrians and Dalmatians. The northern Croatians are extremely well organised and much more teutonic in nature, something they have inherited from their Germanic neighbours. In contrast, the Dalmatians are very spirited and passionate people – local boy and tennis player Goran Ivanesevic typifies this spirit, as does the strength and courage of their people, as shown during the various wars and sieges the country endured.

The Croatian people are extremely friendly and welcoming to foreigners, regardless of your intentions in their country. Although there has been some upset over foreigners purchasing property, this seems to be more focused towards the resulting rise in the cost of living which has priced many locals out of the market.

A typical working day in Croatia lasts from 8am until 4pm, Monday to Friday, with a lunch break of an hour or less. Public services, shops and banks tend to be open all day from 8am until 7pm from Monday to Friday and from 8am until 12pm on Saturday.

Visas and residency

UK and Irish citizens don't require a visa to visit Croatia, although if you plan to stay for longer than 90 days you will have to apply for a residency permit. Temporary permits are issued for 12 months and can be renewed. You will need to apply at your local Croatian Embassy and will have to supply two photographs, a photocopy of a valid passport, proof of sufficient funds to support yourself and your birth certificate.

Permanent residence can be granted to a foreigner who has:

* stayed in Croatia with a temporary residence/work permit for a period of five years continuously;

* a temporary residence/work permit and who has been married to a Croatian citizen for at least three years;

* held a temporary residence/work permit and who is married to a foreigner with a permanent residence permit for at least three years.

Visit www.croatia.embassyhomepage.com for more details and an application form.

Utilities

Once you buy a property, it's unlikely that you will be able to register for utilities until the land registry has processed your details and you are officially named as the owner of the property.

Electricity is 220V, 50Hz. Croatia uses the standard European two-pin plugs so if you are visiting from the UK, buy an adaptor. The main electricity company is Hrvatska Elektroprivreda (www.hep.hr), which is state run. Electricity prices have risen in Croatia in recent years, but generally remain about 10% lower than in the UK. Generally speaking, most central heating is oil run, but some larger cities do have gas connections.

The internet is becoming increasingly available in Croatia and broadband can be installed in some areas. The main telecommunications company is Croatian Telecom (www.t.ht.hr). There are two million landlines in Croatia and 2.8 million mobile phone users. The main mobile operators are T-Mobile Croatia, VIPnet and Tele2. The international country code is +385.

Banking and currency

The Croatians use the kuna, which is available in 1, 2, 5, 10, 20 and 50 lipa coins, 1, 2, 5, 25 kn coins and 5, 10, 20, 50, 100, 200, 500 and 1,000 kn banknotes. There are 100 lipa in 1 kuna.

Setting up a bank account is straightforward and can be done in either foreign or local currency – all you need to do is produce your passport. If you want to set up a standing order for your utilities, you will need to produce the relevant documentation. You will be able to use all major credit cards and ATMs are widely available.

Taxes

There's a double taxation treaty in place with the UK, which means that if you pay tax locally, you shouldn't have to pay it in Britain as well. Capital gains tax is waived in Croatia if you own property for more than three years, although if you haven't, it is charged at the same rate as income tax, which is charged at a progressive rate of between 15% and 45%. The equivalent of council tax is vastly lower than in the UK. Corporate tax is charged at 20% on profits.

Insurance

Insurance is readily available through a variety of companies, including the international insurance company Allianz (www.allianz.com). Always get house and contents insurance (which is much cheaper than in the UK). You can also get pet, medical and life insurance.

Healthcare

Thanks to the EHIC arrangement, EU residents are entitled to free healthcare and emergency treatment in Croatia, although it is recommended that you secure private insurance. Healthcare standards in Croatia are high, with dental care good and inexpensive. There is no shortage of private hospitals and clinics, and hygiene and health standards are very high.

Retirement

There are no restrictions on UK residents retiring to Croatia, although ensure you have all the relevant documentation in place – for more details, see the above section on visas and residency. You are entitled to receive your UK pension in Croatia as you would in the UK and it is not subject to additional taxation.

Should you gain employment in Croatia, you will pay social security as you would in the UK. Residents from other EU states should check their situation with their local Croatian embassy.

Your UK will is recognised in Croatia as there is a reciprocal agreement in place between the two countries.

Education

The Croatian education system is regarded as being good, although there has been a limited amount of investment in it since the war. English is widely taught in Croatian schools, and so if your child is young enough, you may consider sending them to a state school. Private schools have only recently been legalised by the Croatian government so their numbers are limited. Two of these that teach in English are:

- American International School of Zagreb, www.aisz.hr
- Matija Gubec Primary School, www.os-mgubec.hr

Driving

While your national driving licence or International Driving Permit will be recognised and useable in Croatia, if you intend to stay for more than six months, you will need to apply for a Croatian licence. To secure a Croatian licence you will be required to undergo a medical examination and a theory test, as well as handing over your original licence to the relevant authorities.

Croatians are notorious for their reckless driving, so be prepared. You should also be aware that it is illegal to overtake military convoys, there is zero tolerance on drink driving and you must always have your headlights on, even during the day. Speed limits are as follows:

- motorways: 130km/h (80mph);
- main highways: 80km/h (50mph);
- built-up areas: 50km/h (31mph).

The roads in Croatia are not of a particularly high standard, with the only decent stretch running between Zagreb and Karlovac and Zagreb and the Hungarian border. However, things are looking up. Currently there is a motorway being built that runs from Slovakia right down through Croatia and on to Greece. This is expected to revolutionise the Croatian infrastructure and help open the country up to greater travel and tourism.

Getting around

There are internal flights available in Croatia and these are provided by Croatian Airlines (www.croatiaairlines.hr). The train network is still developing and is far from extensive – it was introduced back in the 19th century and Dubrovnik appears to have been left off the network altogether! Zagreb is the central hub from which most services depart. Trains are slower and less frequent than buses, but are roughly 15% cheaper. However, there are no trains running along the coast and only a few coastal cities are linked to Zagreb. Croatian Railways offer details of their services and fares at www.hznet.hr.

In contrast, bus services within Croatia are excellent and the express buses run everywhere, picking up passengers at many stops along the way. Prices are reasonable, with passengers charged by the kilometre. The following are some of the operators:

- AK Karlovac
- APP (www.app.hr)
- Autotrans (www.autotrans.hr)
- Brioni (www.brioni.hr)
- Croatia Bus (www.croatiabus.hr)
- Contus (www.contus.hr)
- Panturist (www.panturist.hr)
- Promet Split (www.promet-split.hr).

The mainland is connected to the larger islands by local ferries. The following offer services between the mainland and the islands:

- Jadrolinija (www.jadrolinija.hr)
- SEM Marina (www.splittours.hr)
- Rapska Plovidba (www.rapska-plovidba.hr)
- Mediteranska Plovidba (www.medplov.hr)
- Losinjska Plovidba (www.losinjska-plovidba.hr).

Learning the language

As with most Eastern European languages, Croatian is not easy to learn – in fact, in one language poll it was listed as the second hardest after Greek. Written in Latin script and using the Roman alphabet, Croatian is part of the Western group of South Slavic languages which is used

The House of the Blackheads, Rīga, Latvia

Rīga presidential castle, Latvia

Castle by the lake, in Trakai, Lithuania

Tallinn Old Town, Estonia

Glacial lake in Pirin National Park, Bulgaria

Old Town Dubrovnik and beach, Croatia

Prague Castle, Czech Republic

Traditional village house in Hungary

4

© 2007 scubabartek/iStock

Hungarian Parliament across the River Danube in Budapest

© 2006 Alexander Maksimenko/iStock

Old city in Budva, Montenegro

Gdansk with Hanseatic-style buildings reflected in the River Motlawa, Poland

View towards the Tatras Mountains, Poland

© 2006 Falk Kienas/iStock

A hay cart, Apuseni Mountains, Western Carpathians, Romania

© 2007 Mira Janacek/iStock

Old Slovakian houses

© 2003 iStock

Bridge Tromostovje in centre of Ljubljana, Slovenia

© 2007 Amar Cudic/iStock

Sultanahmet or Blue Mosque and Aghia Sophia sunset, Istanbul, Turkey

primarily by the Croats. It's closely related to Bosnian, Serbian and Slovene.

For Westerners, it is a difficult language to learn due to the stresses and pronunciation. Europeans are not used to some of the Croatian letters and sounds the language employs. Generally, problems tend to surround the grouping of consonants together in certain words, such as *Hrvatska*, the Croatian for Croatia, and also the complicated sentence structure.

Pronunciation

Croatian words are pronounced exactly how they are spelt. All letters and syllables in words are pronounced and there are no silent letters.

As a general rule of thumb, Croatian vowels are short. Note that there is no q, w, x or y in the Croatian alphabet.

Letter	Pronunciation
c	like ts in lets
č (hard)	like ch in church
ć (soft)	like ch in cheese
dž	similar to J in June
đ	like j in jam
g	like g in game
h	like h in ham
j	like y in yacht
lj	like l in lure
nj	like Spanish ñ

r	trilled
š	like sh in sheep
ž	like s in measure
a	like a in sofa
e	like e in met
i	like ee in feet
o	like o in dog
u	like oo in boot

Courtesy of www.visit-croatia.co.uk/croatianfortravellers

Post

As with many European countries, post boxes in Croatia are yellow. HPT Hrvatska is the Croatian postal service, and post offices can be recognised by their red, white and blue signs. Services include everything from selling stamps and telephone cards to sending faxes and offering call facilities. To avoid a trip to the post office, you can buy stamps, (*pismo*), from newsagents (*tisak*). In larger cities and towns post offices are open from 7am to 7pm Monday to Friday and 7am to 1pm on Saturday, while in smaller towns they're open from 7am to 2pm, and sometimes on Saturday mornings. The Croatian post office website is extremely helpful and details all the financial transactions that can be made, such as cash transfers and money exchanges. Visit www.posta.hr.

Crime, corruption and the police

The Croatian crime rate is low, and it is common to leave your house and car unlocked. As for organised crime, there have been many instances of corruption in the past and it is still a problem today. However, increasing EU pressure has forced the government to take a stand and, since 2004, penalties have become harsher and instances have fallen. Foreigners shouldn't suffer at the hands of mafia influences and although bribery can affect businesses, it is unlike to affect property purchases.

9

The Czech Republic

COUNTRY PROFILE

Despite having only existed for 11 years following the dissolution of Czechoslovakia, the Czech Republic is one of the most established and stable of the Eastern European countries, both politically and economically. Consequently, it offers one of the safest investments for foreign buyers.

> **Did you know?**
>
> - Charles University in Prague is the oldest university in central Europe. It was opened on April 7th, 1348, and today is attended by 42,000 students.
> - The Czech Republic is the birthplace of beer. In 2005, 19 million hectolitres (1 hectolitres = 100 litres) of the beverage were produced, with 40% of the three million hectolitres intended for export going to Germany.
> - The first radioactive spa in the world was opened in 1906 in Jáchymov.
> - The very first fair in the world took place in August 1754 in Veltrusy.

Why buy in the Czech Republic?

Well established in terms of tourism thanks to the allure of its capital, Prague, the Czech Republic has experienced something of a tourism glut in the last decade and could almost be labelled as overdeveloped by some. Nevertheless, the country still represents an attractive investment proposition, although many have already made their money and moved on to pastures new. However, for the less adventurous out there, the Czech Republic is a safe investment and an excellent buy-to-let proposition.

A member of the EU since 2004, the country is economically very healthy, with a hefty GDP growth rate of 6.1% and planned euro adoption in 2012, which is set to pave the way for increasing economic growth. Outside of Prague, property is priced at a mere 20% of that in many Western European countries, while the high standard of living and attractive countryside the country has to offer make it a good lifestyle choice as well.

The Czech Republic also has one of the most welcoming attitudes towards foreign investors and workers, with job opportunities among the best in Eastern Europe for foreigners, thanks to Prague's expansive employment market. What's more, it's unlikely that the Czech government will clamp down on foreign ownership of property, a threat which could apply to some other Eastern European countries.

Ease of access into the Czech Republic, thanks to regular budget flights with easyJet and Ryanair, means that not only is it possible to jet off to your second home for a long weekend at very little expense, but it also maximises the rental income you can gain from letting your property.

The diverse landscape offers everything from the rolling hills and forests of lush Bohemia, with its medieval towns, to the central mountain regions, home to High Tatras and Spindleruv Mlyn, the Czech Republic's foremost ski resort. These areas outside of Prague are becoming increasingly popular with second-home buyers.

Culturally, the country has no shortage of historical sites, the most notable being the city of Prague, but there are also 11 other UNESCO World Heritage sites to be explored. Peppered with fairytale castles and Renaissance chateaux, the Czech Republic is also the birthplace of beer, and there is no shortage of taverns at which to sample its yeasty goodness. The country is also a hotspot for walkers, a popular pastime with the locals as well, with the numerous forests and mountains making for fascinating treking.

Politics and economy

Foreign direct investment and EU exports have helped make the Czech Republic one of the most successful economies in Europe, despite experiencing recession in the late 1990s following independence in 1993. The Czech Republic has a growing economy driven largely by its industrial exports – particularly car production – and also its tourist market. GDP and economic growth have continued to increase, at a rate of 6% in 2006, and according to a survey carried out by financial experts Ernst & Young, the Czech Republic is the world's seventh most attractive country for investors.

With the lowest interest rate in Europe – 2.5% – low inflation and continually strong economic growth, you're unlikely to find such favourable economic and investment conditions anywhere else in Europe. However, on 1st January 2008, VAT is set to rise from 5% to 19%. Consequently, investors will be keen to purchase before the 14% hike, but it is expected that this will lead to many developers cutting corners in an attempt to complete and sell property before the cut-off point.

The government is a parliamentary democracy headed by Vaclav Klaus, while each of the Czech Republic's 13 regions has its own Regional Assembly and city council. In April 2003, the Czech Republic signed the Accession Treaty for the EU, and following a positive 80% vote from the population, the country became a fully-fledged member of the EU in 2004. The Czech Republic is now on course to assume usage of the euro currency. The government are keen to see this done by 2010, but the likelihood is that it will be nearer to 2012 before it is introduced.

Geography and climate

A landlocked country located more in central than Eastern Europe, the Czech Republic is bordered by Poland, Germany, Slovakia and Austria. Split into two regions, Bohmeia and Moravia, the country covers 78,866 square kilometres. This is a land of spectacular scenery, home to the Tatras Mountains and one of Europe's finest cultural centres, Prague. You can choose to relocate to anywhere from ski resort to traditional village or cosmopolitan centre.

As with most of Western Europe, in the Czech Republic the coldest month is January and the warmest, July. The climate is diverse, although generally it can be called continental, with hot summers and cold, cloudy winters in which it generally snows. Summers are when the rains are at their worst and temperatures vary depending on your altitude. In Prague, the average temperature is 10°C, while at Snezka, the country's highest peak, the average sits at –0.4°C; in Brno it is 8°C.

History and culture

Ruled by its larger neighbours until gaining independence in 1993, the Republic of Czechoslovakia was created in 1918 after the collapse of the Austro-Hungarian Empire following WWI. In 1945, after six years of Nazi rule, Czechoslovakia fell under the communist sphere of influence. Communism collapsed in January 1992 when the 'Velvet Divorce' saw the political union between the Czech Republic and Slovakia come to an end.

Culturally, the Czech Republic's hotspot is Prague, which boasts six centuries of architecture. Despite the hardships the country has suffered over the years and the numerous occupations – by the Hapsburgs and Nazi Germany to name only two – the country has remained virtually unblemished, with many cultural centres as pristine as ever. Prague manages to blend the country's mix of German, Austrian and Bohemian culture with contemporary life, and is now one of the leading centres for stag and hen parties. Outside of the capital, the country is dotted with towering stone-built castles and wooden churches, most of which are tucked away in small villages.

Religion

As a nation, the Czechs are massively uninterested in the church and religion. A survey carried out in 2001 cited 27% of Czechs as being Catholic and 59% as atheist, while 2% are of Protestant denominations. The second largest religious group – 12% – is that of the Hussite church.

Tourism and getting there

The best-established tourist industry in Eastern Europe, the Czech economy relies heavily on tourism to bolster its economy. In 2001, the total earnings from tourism reached 118.13 billion CZK (£2.86 billion) making up 5.5% of GNP and 9.3% of overall export earnings. The industry employs more than 110,000 people – 1% of the population – with Prague being the main tourist centre. In the third quarter of 2006 alone, 2.2 million foreigners visited the country, an increase of 4.3% on the same quarter for 2005, while annually, 17 million tourists stay in the Czech Republic.

There are many other tourist centres in the country, but after Prague it is the spa towns that attract significant numbers. These include Karlovy Vary and Mariánské Lázně. Other popular tourist sites are the many castles and chateaux, such as those at Karlštejn, Konopiště and Český Krumlov. Away from the towns, areas such as Český Ráj, Šumava and the Krkonoše Mountains attract visitors seeking outdoor pursuits.

In terms of reaching the Czech Republic, it is quick and cheap to fly, with British Airways, Czech Airways, easyJet, Air Lingus, Ryanair and SkyEurope all flying into the country. The increase in budget airlines has, as with most Eastern European destinations, helped open the country up to increasing numbers of tourists and second-home buyers, as well as helping to fuel the investment market.

Cost of living

The cost of living in the Czech Republic is significantly lower than elsewhere in Europe, but is relatively high and continuing to rise when compared with much of Eastern Europe. Despite the fact that Prague is the most expensive place to live in the country, the cost of living is still significantly lower than in most European cities. Outside of Prague prices decrease dramatically.

If you consider a meal for two with wine in Italy would set you back an average of € 80, in Prague you would be looking at € 40, while outside of the capital, the average would be € 25. On average, the cost of renting a two-bedroomed apartment in Prague would be around € 500 a month, including the cost of utilities. Outside of Prague, this would fall to € 350. In contrast, across the border in Germany, you would be looking at € 900.

Food and drink

It is a well-known fact – and a major tourist draw – that the Czech Republic is the birthplace of beer, or *pivo* as it is called in Czech. Home to both Pilsner and Budweiser, the Czechs consume the most beer per capita in the world; surprising when you consider that most Moravians prefer wine. The majority of Czech wine is produced in the South Moravia vineyards, and while it costs less than £1 a bottle, it is drinkable. For the best tipple, go for the whites – thanks to the cool climate, the grapes are harvested late and produce an excellent and affordable vintage.

Food and drink in the Czech Republic is cheap, although prices tend to be twice as high in Prague when compared to the rest of the country.

While the diet may lack imagination, there is plenty of international fare on offer in the larger cities. Meals are generally quite heavy, consisting of meat (generally pork or beef) served with dumplings and potatoes or rice. A traditional meal consists of a hot soup starter and a main course of pork, cabbage (or sauerkraut) and gravy, washed down with a glass of *pivo*. Despite the importance of meat in the diet, if you are a vegetarian there are a number of dishes that are vegetable based, such as breaded cauliflower and mushrooms or *nedliky s vejci* – diced dumplings fried with beaten eggs and served with pickles.

THE PROPERTY MARKET

Thanks to the economic and political stability the country offers, the Czech property market has continued to thrive. EU membership, strong GDP growth, a central location and high demand versus low supply have all helped to strengthen the market and resulted in constant price rises year-on-year ever since 1991. Nevertheless, prices are still much lower than in Western Europe, although the likelihood is that the gap will continue to shrink as the Czech Republic continues on its path to Westernisation and becomes a wealthier nation.

Foreign direct investment into the country is huge, reaching a peak in 2002 when € 9,012.4 million was invested. Foreigners still only represent between 1–2% of the buying activity though, and have little direct influence on the property market, especially when you look outside of Prague.

Apartments in the centre of Prague are the most sought after commodity – especially as the Czech people become more consumer driven. Prices for modern apartments increased by 30% in the capital in 2006, while investors can easily expect to secure gains of between 10% and 20%, and rental yields of more than 7%. Outside of Prague, price rises have been cited as hitting between 10% and 25% – with an overall average of 10% – as new markets open up, further fuelled by the growth in budget flights and improvements in the country's infrastructure, as well as spiralling prices and living costs in Prague, and a lack of available property.

It has also become increasingly easy to obtain a mortgage in the Czech Republic, with loans of 100% now available, adding to the pressure on the already undersupplied market. Also, Czech residents are starting to view property as an investment, a new development which has heaped additional pressure on the market.

Tourism continues to fuel growth and as tourist figures have increased – they currently sit at 17 million – so has foreign investment in property. Currently, 90% of tourism into the Czech Republic is directed at Prague, but as awareness and interest in the country continues to increase, new markets are constantly opened up and foreign purchase of property is set to rise.

Adopting the euro

The biggest influence on the property market at present is the anticipated adoption of the euro, scheduled for between 2010 and 2013 depending on when the Czech Republic can meet the criteria laid down in the Maastricht Treaty. There is much anticipation as to the impact this will have on prices. Trends seen in other countries imply that euro adoption will result in immediate price gains, although, the country has already seen vast price increases in recent years. It's anticipated that euro adoption will only encourage the price rises already predicted, which will continue until house prices in the Czech Republic reflect those of other European countries.

With the exchange rate set to change from 28CZK per euro (68p) to 26/25CZK (63p/60p) on the eve of adoption, it's anticipated that purchasers could experience appreciation of 7% over the next three years, based on the oscillating exchange rate alone.

Consequently, 2007 is expected to be a year of continued growth at similar levels to 2006, with a possible slowing to come into effect in 2008, but continued sustainability in the market right up until euro adoption.

Where to buy

Prague

The hottest market with the highest appreciation rates, Prague is an intriguing city and one of the most attractive and historical in Europe. Back in November 2006, the daily newspaper *Hospodarske Noviny* reported that flat prices had increased by 20% to 30% in the capital. There is high demand for apartments in Prague, and consequently prices have continued to rise at a rapid rate as supply has failed to meet demand. Ease of access has encouraged market growth – today, over 20 UK airports offer flights into Prague.

Located on the banks of the Vltava River, buyers are drawn to the city thanks to its fabulous cultural and historical attractions, cosmopolitan air and vibrant lifestyle, with numerous clubs, bars and restaurants.

Prices vary dramatically within the city, and despite seeing price hikes of 35% between 2000 and 2004, a studio apartment on the city's outskirts requiring renovation can be picked up for as little as €50,000. However, if you are looking for two bedrooms closer to the city centre then the average rises to €223,000. With appreciation rates set to grow at roughly 10% per annum and rental returns sitting at upwards of 7%, Prague still represents a good investment and looks set for continuing price appreciation, despite having already seen massive growth since 2000.

Brno

Rapidly emerging as an investment centre, largely thanks to the numbers of expatriates and professionals relocating to the city, Brno has become a European business hub. Ryanair began flying into Brno's international airport at the end of March 2005 and this has also helped to put it on the map as a property hotspot.

The country's second largest city, prices here are roughly one-third of those in Prague, but as with the capital, newly-built and modern apartments are the popular choice. Surrounded by forests, with the Moravian vineyards lying to the south and the protected Moravian Karst to the north, there are many country lodges and ski chalets to be purchased outside the city.

There are numerous attractions in this cosmopolitan metropolis, such as theatres, museums, cinemas and clubs, and the city won the competition for European City of the Future in both 2004/2005 and 2005/06. With rapid economic growth, averaging more than 9% during the last decade, Brno has been compared to Prague 10 years ago, and as such represents an excellent investment. Rental income sits at roughly 8%, although it can get into double figures.

A new motorway development that will link Moravia with Poland will see completion in 2008, making it an attractive area for Polish investors, which is anticipated to bolster the market. Currently, you can buy a studio apartment for 1,200,000 to 1,450,000CZK (£29,085 to £35,160), which it's estimated will make you 8,000 to 9,000CZK in rentals per month (£193 to £218); a two-bedroomed flat priced at 1,850,000 to 2,200,000CZK (£44,860 to £53,347), will generate 12,000 to 13,000CZK (£290 to £315) and for three bedrooms you would be looking to pay 3,000,000CZK (£72,633), with a rental return of 18,000 to 20,000CZK (£435 to £484). (Figures courtesy of www.czechpoint101.com).

Ski resorts

The Czech Republic's ski resorts may not be as developed as those of neighbouring Slovakia, but they have experienced a steady market and capital growth of 10% over recent years, and seen increased interest and demand from foreign buyers.

Spindleruv Mlyn is the Czech Republic's foremost resort and a recent host of the Women's World Cup. Although the mountains don't reach the heights of Slovenia, they enjoy 150 centimetres of snow in mid-December, as well as good seasonal skiing, with the numerous summer activities creating a year-round demand for rentals. What's more, ski pass prices are half that of France.

Representing a good long-term investment, typical properties include newly-built apartments of 60 square metres for 4,500,000CZK

(£108,000), or a ski cottage with land for only 2,600,000CZK (£62,500). With budget flights extending into Brno and Ostrava improving accessibility, these are destined to be new hotspots. Another excellent area which has seen little investment is the Beskydy Mountain range. While it has smaller mountains than the north, it's very cheap and offers year-round recreational activities.

What to buy

Predominantly, property which experiences the most demand and generates the best rental returns are apartments. Many are located in partitioned period buildings built in a Haussman style. Property built during the communist era tends to be poorly constructed and unattractive – think 1960s towerblocks. There are a number of newly-built developments springing up in Prague and Brno, but outside of these centres, property generally tends to be rural village houses or ski resorts, and many of these require renovation. Nevertheless, there is no shortage of property types to choose from, although for the best appreciation rates and rental returns, you need to chose a property that is easily accessible and close to tourist hotspots and amenities.

For those with money to burn, there are a number of dream properties for sale in the Czech Republic, including a 17th century castle for £912,000, a historic château in Moravia for £1,000,000 and a palace with 19 bedrooms, perched beside a 62 hectare lake for £3,000,000.

BUYING A PROPERTY

More advanced than many of their neighbours, the Czech Republic offers a comprehensive and straightforward purchasing system. However, for foreigners, there are restrictions on how you buy, and on ownership.

Stage 1: Restrictions on foreign buyers

Unless you hold a residency permit in the Czech Republic then you will not be able to purchase property as an individual. Instead, you will be required to set up a Czech Limited Company or an SRO. Just when this restriction is likely to be lifted remains unclear, but what is clear is that even if you do have residency you will not be allowed to purchase agricultural or forestry land.

If you do not have residency then setting up an SRO is a straightforward and inexpensive procedure, with the total costs panning out at between £1,000 and £1,600. Forming a Czech limited-liability corporation, is the fastest, most convenient and cost-effective way for a foreign citizen to establish themselves as a resident in the Czech Republic with all the required visas, a tax base, health insurance, and the many benefits of being a legitimate resident. Some 'favoured nations' also have special agreements with the Czech Republic which allows their citizens to buy land as individuals. This applies to countries such as Switzerland, Norway and the USA.

Stage 2: Funding the purchase

Most buyers will be looking to raise the funds for a property purchase through a mortgage, and in the Czech Republic there are plenty of local lenders who are not only willing to lend to foreign buyers, but do not discriminate between local and foreign investors. There are different mortgages open to you depending on whether you are buying as an individual or as an SRO. The maximum you will be lent as an SRO is 75% of the price of the property, leaving 25% to be paid, with the borrower obliged to invest at least 15–20% of their own funds into the purchase. As an individual buyer, it's now possible to get a mortgage for 100% of the value of the property.

Typically, when buying with a residency permit, the bank will allow a deposit of 15 to 20% and sometimes less. With an SRO, it is rarely under 25%. The maximum lending period rarely exceeds 15 years, although some banks are beginning to offer 20, and interest rates range from 4–6% per annum, with the rate being fixed for a maximum of five years before recalculation.

Stage 3: The survey and background checks

It is recommended that you carry out a survey before signing the preliminary contract, even though this is not a common occurrence. You also need to ensure you carry out all the necessary background checks. In some cases, the property you are looking to buy will be protected by general Czech law and contractual provisions, but this will not safeguard against the possibility of the seller disappearing and leaving you with a house that may carry financial or structural damages. Consequently, you should get some form of survey carried out.

Title services

Your lawyer is responsible for researching the history of the title with the property registry in order to ensure it is free of third-party rights – in other words that there is not collective ownership of the property and no debts attached to the title. A major issue to be aware of is that if you buy a plot of land with buildings on it, the buildings and land may have separate titles and even separate ownership. Note that it's possible to obtain title insurance for added security.

Stage 4: Ownership

There are two main ways to own property in the Czech Republic and you'll find them on real estate listings as OV (*osobní vlastnictví*) or private ownership, and DV (*družstevní vlastnictví*) or cooperative ownership.

In the Czech Republic there is no leasehold system as exists in the UK – although occasionally you may come across a cottage where the town or state owns the land and the owner leases the land from them.

Private ownership most commonly applies to stand alone homes, but is now becoming more and more common in apartment buildings. Newly-built apartment buildings are almost always owned as OV.

The benefit of buying OV is that both SRO and individuals can purchase them, and banks are willing to offer mortgages on them because they have collateral for money being lent. Consequently, these properties are slightly higher in price than DV properties because they are easier to finance.

Cooperative ownership (DV) has members who have bought the rights to be a member and use a particular flat. The land registry doesn't record the particular flat that the member lives in, just that they reside in the building. This type of ownership is virtually impossible for a foreigner to buy into. The memorandum of association (*notarsky zapis*) usually stipulates that membership is only available to Czech citizens. Often SROs and companies aren't even allowed to become members.

These flats are usually a little cheaper than OV flats because banks are less eager to lend to prospective DV owners.

The benefit of buying into a cooperative is that there's no waiting period for becoming the official owner of the flat, whereas when purchasing a privately-owned flat, the process of becoming the recognised owner in the eyes of the land registry can take up to six months.

There is the possibility of changing a DV flat to an OV, but it requires the cooperation and willingness of all members in the cooperative. Naturally, this process can be a painstakingly slow one. If even one member disagrees, it can cause real problems and drag out the process even longer.

Stage 5: The contract

As already mentioned, the Czech property registration system is well developed and has the correct searches and safeguards in place to allow you to obtain a clean property title. The process is divided into three stages, the first being the signing of a reservation contract which takes the property off the market and ensures it is not sold to anyone else. At this point a reservation fee of 0.5% of the property's sale value must be handed over to the estate agent.

Second is the preliminary or future contract. This binds both parties to the sale and the buyer can use this in the mortgage application process.

Signing this document is equivalent to an exchange of contracts in the UK. Once this has been signed, a deposit of between 10% and 20% needs to be paid.

Last of all, there's the final purchase contract. Once all other stages have been completed – i.e. when the property is finalised, has the relevant occupancy permit and the buyer has raised all the necessary funding – then the buyer and seller should proceed with the signing of the purchase contract in the presence of a notary. This is the equivalent of completion of a sale in the UK. Once the final contract has been signed, the remaining funds need to be paid in order to finalise the sale. However, despite the contract being signed and funds exchanged, you are not technically the legal owner of the property. Following completion, all the necessary paperwork needs to be submitted to the land registry to be processed; this can take several months. It is only once the land registry has acknowledged the sale and lodged you as the new owner on the registry records that the sale is technically complete.

Stage 6: Completing the sale

As stated earlier, officially you are not the owner of your property until you obtain the title deeds following registration of all the necessary documentation with the land registry. Consequently, it is essential that you deposit the final funds with a neutral party – preferably the notary – until you receive the final registration documents.

Registering a change of ownership is quicker if you buy in Prague – from four to six weeks compared with up to 24 weeks outside of the capital. Obviously you don't want to be left kicking your heels until registration comes through before you can move in, and so it's common in Prague to release some of the purchase price to the seller in exchange for the keys to the property. However, you will still only legally become owner of the property when the land registry records the change and not when the purchase agreements are signed.

Stage 7: Additional costs and taxes

On the completion of a sale, the seller will be required to pay property transfer tax of 3%. The buyer will be the guarantor of this payment and should the seller fail to pay, you could be asked to cover the cost instead. You can safeguard yourself against such an occurrence by arranging with the notary – who will be holding all the funds – to only release the sum equivalent to the payment of the property tax once the seller has made the payment.

The buyer will also be liable to pay property taxes and VAT. VAT on newly-built apartments is currently 5%, while for a parking space – which would be sold separately – VAT is 19%. Property taxes are minimal and the amount charged depends on the type, size and location of property purchased. Typically, you would be looking to pay £50 per year for a one-bedroomed apartment in Prague. There is a distinction made between property and land when it comes to taxes, and so you will also be subject to a land tax.

You will be liable for other costs too, and in total you should allow up to 8% of the price of the property for these. They include legal expenses which can be up to €2,000 if you have to set up a limited company, as well as paying the lawyer for the drawing up of the contract and background checks. Next come the notary's fees, roughly €300–€400, and finally the estate agents' fees of between 3–6% of the property price.

THE LETTINGS MARKET

The Czech Republic has long been regarded as a good investment, but what is critical to remember is that while the jet-to-let option is viable in other countries, it's not necessarily applicable to the Czech Republic. The problem with the Czech market is that its rental system is riddled with problems and there's very little legislation in place to control it. Rentals are dominated by the black market, with common practice being for property to be sublet by a tenant; it is very unlikely that the occupier will be renting from the owner of the property. Added to these complications is the issue of rent controls. In place to protect the locals from rent inflation, rent control means that the owner is unable to charge market rates for rent, and in fact is forced to charge rents averaging out at about a fifth of market rates. Tenants under rent control are also nearly impossible to evict and generally speaking there is very little a landlord can do if a tenant decides not to pay.

As an absentee or foreign landlord, be aware that you are likely to be the target of attempted overcharging for maintenance of a property, and property management companies often place problem tenants into foreign-owned property.

The relationship between property prices and rent continues to be favourable in most parts of the country. Rental returns obviously vary depending on where and what you buy, but you can expect to generate in the region of 6–15% without too much trouble. Rental returns in Prague have slowed since the boom during the 90s, and while the capital has only seen a small increase in rents, property prices have jumped substantially.

In comparison, Brno has seen the development of a much more stable lettings market, thanks to the influx of newcomers, which has caused a substantial growth in house values and allowed rentals to keep pace with rising property prices. Yields sit at between 6 to 8% per annum.

For more lucrative returns, expect to take a greater risk. Certain properties, such as ski chalets and family homes, can potentially generate higher rental returns but are not guaranteed the sorts of appreciation rates associated with newly-built city apartments.

Finding a buy-to-let property

If you intend to buy a property to let then make sure you carefully research the market. If letting to locals or looking at long-term lets, be aware of the rental restrictions and also the fact that the spending power of the Czech people is relatively low, so you need to be realistic about how much you'll be able to charge.

The main demand for rentals comes from expats and young Czech couples. For a one-bedroomed flat within Prague, you can expect to generate £465 a month – sometimes you'll be looking at more than you'd pay in London for a similar property – and up to £193 per month in towns outside of the capital. Foreigners will generally pay more, and on average you can expect to generate a gross rental yield of around 5 to 7% in Prague, and 6 to 8% in Brno.

When looking to rent somewhere for yourself, be aware that agencies will typically charge two months' rent, with three months rent expected to be paid up front, prior to moving in. Consequently you can end up paying 25,000CZK (£606) before you even move into your apartment – and be aware that the money will not be returned should you discover all is not as promised.

RENOVATING A PROPERTY

There is no shortage of property to renovate in the Czech Republic, whether it's a run-down country house in a rural area or a communist tower block in the centre of a city. If you renovate a property and then turn it into a hotel or B&B then all associated business expenses, plus repairs and improvements, are directly deductible from any income derived from the business, thus reducing your potential income tax.

As always, prior to buying, ensure you have planning permission for your modifications and any renovation work you intend to carry out.

LIVING IN THE CZECH REPUBLIC

Daily life and people

Boasting a sense of humour and down-to-earth mentality, the Czech people are diligent and open-minded. As with most Eastern European countries, family is central to daily life, which has resulted from many generations of cohabitation.

What may come as a bit of a shock is the Czech daily schedule. 'The early bird catches the worm' is a popular proverb among the Czechs, and many people get up at six and start work at seven. However, the working day does accommodate this, with people generally finishing work between 4pm and 5pm.

The man to blame for this is Austro-Hungarian Emperor Franz Josef I. Ruling from 1848 until 1916, Franz Josef was an early starter and held audiences around 6am or 7am. This habit trickled down into the populous and has become the daily routine ever since. Some are beginning to question the logic of starting work when most Europeans are still in bed, but many still choose to stick to the old routine – so don't forget your alarm clock!

Socialising also differs. The night starts early, at 6pm and most people go home around 11pm, so if you want to socialize with the Czechs you'll have to adapt to this schedule. As with everything, things are slowly beginning to change as a more western lifestyle is adopted by the younger generation.

Business hours:

- Offices: 8am to 4pm, Monday to Friday.
- Banks: 8am to 6pm, Monday to Friday. Some close early on Fridays.
- Shops: 8am/9am to 5pm/6pm, Monday to Friday, plus Saturday mornings.
- Shopping centres: 8am to 10pm, seven days a week.

Visas and residency

British citizens don't need a visa to gain entry to the Czech Republic and are permitted to stay up to 180 days without one. However, your passport must be valid for at least six months before entry and not due to expire during your stay.

EU citizens may apply for a temporary residence permit to allow them to stay in the Czech Republic, and will need to do so if they intend to stay longer than three months. Although a residency permit is not a mandatory requirement for EU citizens looking to live and work here, it is recommended that you acquire one, especially as it makes the purchasing process so much easier and allows you to purchase as an individual.

In order to secure a permit, you'll be required to produce a copy of your passport, two passport photographs, a document certifying the purpose of your stay, a health insurance policy, an accommodation contract and a sworn statement that you won't claim social benefits during your stay unless you are in the country on business or are actively employed there. The application process could take as long as six months if you apply from a UK embassy, but this time can be halved if you apply at a foreign police office in the Czech Republic.

Following a period of temporary residency, you're entitled to apply for permanent residency, provided you can demonstrate that you intend to seek employment in the country.

Utilities

The country is currently in the process of privatising the banking, energy and telecom sectors. Whether or not you have to pay your utility bills directly depends on your rental agreement. Those who own a property will obviously be faced with connecting supplies and paying for them, but if you rent then your rental agreement may have a utilities fee included in the price, in which case your landlord will handle payments.

Setting up your utilities is something that should ideally be done before you move into your property, as it can take days – and in some cases weeks – to get connected. To connect to gas and electricity, it's necessary to register with the regional distributor. The following documents will be required to start an account:

- Personal identification, or power of attorney.
- If you're renting, the written consent of the owner of your property.
- Proof of your right to inhabit the property, i.e. your rental or sale contract.
- Your bank information.

With gas and electricity, the government sets the price for household consumption and payments consist of regular deposits (*záloha*) which are paid every month. These are based on the size of your home and number of inhabitants. Quarterly statements will then be provided detailing the rate of gas/electric consumption and if more payments are required. If the bill has been overpaid then the surplus payments will be subtracted from the next bill.

As for water and sewage, property owners need to register with the relevant local water and sewage company for their district.

If you intend to live in Prague, www.spoluproprahu.cz offers comprehensive advice and information about setting up your utilities and paying the bills. If you ever suspect there is a gas leak, call 1239 straight away.

Banking and currency

The Czech currency is the Czech koruna (CZK), which has been in use since February 8th 1993, when Czechoslovakia was dissolved. It comes in denominations of 50 haléř, 1, 2, 5, 10, 20, 50 CKZ coins and 50, 100, 200, 500, 1,000, 2,000, 5,000 CKZ banknotes.

Opening a bank account is a fairly simple process which requires the production of a passport and one other form of ID. In some cases you may also need to produce proof of address.

A deposit will also be required in order to create an account, although this isn't much, varying between 200 and 2,000 CKZ (£4 and £48).

There are a number of good banks and many international branches to choose from, especially in Prague. One of the biggest banks is Ceska Sporitelna (www.csas.cz) which has a centre specifically for expats. Although bank charges can be hefty they vary from bank to bank. Others include Zivnostenska Banka (www1.zivnobanka.cz) whose bank charges are extremely low, as are HVB's (www.hvb.cz). To get more detailed information, see www.expats.cz/prague/article/money/bank-comparisons.

Always try to open an account which offers you telephone or internet banking as this will make it easier to manage payments and transfers,

175

especially if you have a limited grasp of Czech. Ask your bank to issue you a *platební karta* (payment card), which is similar to a debit card. Cash is generally the best way to pay for things in restaurants and shops, although some places are happy to arrange for payment by card. ATMs are located throughout the country.

Taxes

In order to ascertain how much income tax you pay, the first thing to establish is whether or not you are classed as a resident for tax purposes. You will be classed as a resident if you reside in the country for 183 days or more per calendar year. If you do, you will be charged on your worldwide income; if not, then you are only taxed on income generated in the Czech Republic. As the UK has a double taxation treaty with the Czech Republic, this means you will not be taxed twice on income earned in the Czech Republic. However, always secure the assistance of a tax expert when trying to assess your tax situation.

Income tax is charged at a progressive rate:

Tax Base (CZK)	Tax
0 to 121,200	12%
121,201 to 218,400	19% of base exceeding 121,200 (£2,938 to £5,294)
218,401 to 331,200	25% of base exceeding 218,400 (£5,290 to £8,022)
331,201 and over	32% of base exceeding 331,200 (£8,022+)

Corporation tax is charged at a rate of 24% and is levied against Czech businesses and corporations. Capital gains are taxed as income for both companies and individuals at a rate of between 12% and 32%, as with income tax. However, if you have purchased as an SRO then you will instead be charged at the flat rate of corporation tax at 24%.

If you buy as an individual and hold the property for more than five years, you will not pay capital gains on the sale of the property.

Insurance

It's always recommended that you get health insurance in the Czech Republic. VZP (www.vzp.cz) is the largest provider of general health insurance and their partner company, Pojistovna VZP (www.pvzp.cz), provides health insurance specifically for foreigners.

As for house insurance, those living in rented accommodation will still need contents insurance, even though security issues are taken care of by your landlord. It is possible to have the contents of your property insured from the UK by companies such as John Wason Insurance Brokers (www.johnwason.co.uk). Alternatively, there are Czech firms such as Insia (www.insia.cz), who will insure your house, contents and car.

Bringing or owning your own car in the Czech Republic can involve a lot of paperwork, and if you wish to obtain long-term insurance, the car must be registered and its owner must have third party liability insurance – as in the UK – known locally as *povinné ručení*. Full cover is not essential, but is the safest option.

Healthcare

The standard of health care in the Czech Republic does vary, and it should come as no surprise that Prague offers some excellent facilities. As a resident of the EU, British citizens are entitled to the same standard and conditions of health care as the Czechs. However, you must ensure that you carry an EHIC (European Health Insurance Card) in order secure any medical treatment required, and as payment may be necessary, it's also strongly recommended that you secure private health insurance.

EU nationals living in the Czech Republic who enjoy temporary residence (*přechodný pobyt*) have similar rights to Czechs, because of the principle of common healthcare provision across the European Union. If you are employed by a Czech firm, then payments will be made from your salary directly to a public health insurance company. If you are self employed then you will need to set up health insurance. Once you are registered, you will be issued with a health card by your insurance company, which should be kept with you at all times.

Retirement

As the Czech Republic is part of the European Economic Area (EEA), you could well be eligible for certain benefits. Those employed by a Czech company will pay social security contributions from their salary which will entitle them to various benefits. These payments, coupled with healthcare contributions, amount to 12.5%.

As a UK citizen living in the Czech Republic, you will be entitled to your UK pension, which can be paid into your UK bank account and then transferred to the Czech Republic. Thanks to the double taxation treaty, you shouldn't be taxed on your pension in the Czech Republic if it's taxed in the UK.

If you own assets in the Czech Republic, such as your property, it is recommended that you write a Czech will to avoid any discrepancy over inheritance should you die.

Education

If granted temporary or permanent residency, or even short-term residency for up 90 days, foreigners are entitled to study in Czech schools at either primary, secondary or higher vocational level.

As would be expected, outside of Prague there are few international schools, so the only option may be to send your children to a Czech-speaking school.

Brno has a good international university and business school, offering a degree course in medicine in English as well as numerous electronic and economic degrees. The foreign student population in Prague is significant and in Brno it's estimated at well over a thousand, making both markets good for buy-to-let investors. The total student population in the Czech Republic is well over 20,000.

- British International School of Prague, www.bisp.cz
- The English College in Prague, www.englishcollege.cz
- Riverside School Prague, www.riversideschool.cz

- The International School of Prague, www.isp.cz
- The International School of Olomouc (TISOL), www.tisol.cz

Driving

Unfortunately, the Czech Republic has one of the highest rates of traffic accidents in central Europe. You're required to hold a valid EU driving licence which can be used throughout the EU, but foreign drivers must be at least 18 years old and at least 21 in order to rent a car. A certificate of insurance, or 'Green Card', is also necessary and this is valid for three months and indicates that you have comprehensive insurance coverage.

The Czech Republic employs a zero tolerance policy towards alcoholic consumption when driving and a law brought in during July 2006 states that drivers must have their headlights switched on at all times.

Speed limits are as follows:

- motorways: 130km/h (80mph);
- main highways: 90km/h (55mph);
- built-up areas: 50km/h (31mph).

The maximum speed for motorcycles is 90 km/hr.

In order to drive on the motorway you will have to pay, but as there are no toll booths you'll need to buy a window sticker. For a year's sticker, it costs from 900 CKZ (£22).

In terms of fuel, petrol and diesel are readily available throughout the country.

Getting around

Buses are the best means of getting around and, as well as being cheaper than trains, they are also quicker and less likely to be delayed. Most major cities are linked by buses (Prague, Brno, Plzeň and Liberec), while there are also domestic flights in operation by CSA Czech Airlines (www.czechairlines.com) between Prague, Brno and Ostrava. The IDOS website is an excellent resource for information on travelling around the country (www.idos.cz).

The trains, while temperamental, do serve every corner of the country and, unlike the buses, they also operate regularly during off-peak hours. However, outside of the main routes, the standard of travel does decline, with trains dating back to the 1970s and journeys being very time-consuming, especially if you're trying to reach provincial towns or villages. Train stations can be very old fashioned and prices for tickets vary depending on which type of train you decide to take.

As the main tourist centre, Prague offers an excellent public transport network, and the cheapest and easiest way to travel around the capital is by tram. For more details visit www.czech.cz, which is an excellent resource.

Learning the language

If you're going to be relocating or living in the Czech Republic for any length of time then you need to get a grasp of the language. Czech – or *Česky* – is the official language of the Czech Republic and is one of the West Slavic languages. There are over 12 million native speakers worldwide. Although it is unlikely that you'll become fluent, your efforts at attempting the language will be appreciated by the Czech people.

While pronounciation may seem impossible, Czech is very much said as it is written and few letters are silent within a word.

Shopping

In Prague there is no shortage of stores and shops and you can find a number of foreign goods. Outside of Prague, while awareness of the consumer market is growing and the choice of products widening, customer service can leave a lot to desired, so be prepared. Shops are generally open from 8am/9am to 5pm/6pm, Monday to Friday, plus Saturday mornings, while shopping centres are open from 8am to 10pm, seven days a week. Expect shops to close in the middle of the day for lunch.

Post

Generally labelled as slow and unreliable, things are improving and the postal service can be effective. However, it can be a little daunting to navigate your way around a Czech post office. As with the UK, they do a great deal more than just send letters, offering services such as the payment of utility bills and donations to charity. When paying a bill or sending a parcel, you will be required to fill out a rather complicated form, so it's best to take a Czech speaker with you as few postal workers speak English. Be aware that in smaller towns the post offices close early.

Crime, corruption and the police

If you need to reach the police in emergency, dial 158. Per capita, the crime rate stands at 6.16 per 1,000 people, making the Czech Republic a fairly average country in terms of criminal offences.

Corruption is a big problem in the Czech Republic and while it is on the decline, the country is still one of the worst in the EU. The average home buyer probably won't feel the effects of this unless they try to secure a renovation permit or deal with municipal offices; this seems to be where the corruption mainly lies. In many cases, you may well be faced with an official who wants a bribe and will make life difficult for you until it is received.

Foreigners may also suffer for being foreign – that is, be charged higher prices for a property and goods simply because they are not a Czech. In one instance, a buyer was quoted 30 million CZK (£728,305) for a castle that was for sale, when it was only actually listed at 3 million CZK (£72,778). Be aware that inflated prices for foreigners is a common problem in the Czech Republic .

While judges insist there is very little corruption within the courts, taking a dispute to court is usually a three-year process, although this is something that is supposed to be improving thanks to EU pressure.

Case study
Corruption

Research is the key to security when it comes to property purchases, and you must ensure that you find a reliable estate agent and lawyer to deal with. Cyril Fitzgerald encountered many problems, and nearly lost everything. 'I went in to the purchase with no experience or knowledge of the market whatsoever, only knowing what type of property I wanted to purchase. I guessed things would go in a straightforward manner,' he reveals.

'I encountered a number of problems during the purchase, the first being that the estate agents I was dealing with simply wanted me to do the deal at all costs, no matter what. Changing their minds seemed commonplace and they tried to sell me absolutely everything and anything.' Cyril found that they repeatedly tried to talk their way out of the problems that Cyril came up against, 'They simply want the deal, and that's that.' He was charged hidden costs, such as fees for the purchase which the seller should have been paying, while for Cyril, the most daunting element was the bureaucracy. 'The less efficient the structures, the more time wasting and draining the whole procedure seemed.'

Cyril's inexperience meant he didn't find a reliable agent, and it may have cost him as much as ⇔3,000. 'More importantly,' he said, 'had I not found someone I could trust, I could have lost everything.'

Thankfully, Cyril came across established agent Czech Point 101, www.czechpoint101.com. 'My thanks to them for setting the record straight with their experience and knowledge. I wish I had had their advice from the start, but, knowing me, I had to find out for myself.'

10
Hungary

Factfile

Population: 10.1million
Population growth rate: −0.25%
Area: 93,030 sq km
Capital city: Budapest (population 2 million)
Inflation: 5.9%
GDP growth rate: 4.1%
Unemployment rate: 7.3%
Net migration: 0.86 migrant(s)/1,000 population
Currency: forint (HUF)
Exchange rate: £1 = ft380
EU status: New member as of January 2004
Number of foreign residents: 294,000
Time zone: CET (GMT +1 hour)

COUNTRY PROFILE

When compared with some Eastern European markets, Hungary is remarkably untouched, with most attention focused on the capital, Budapest, and with increasing interest around Lake Balaton in the country's southwest.

Did you know?

53.6% of the Hungarian population buy milk in a plastic bag. Milk in a carton is purchased by 47.1% and is preferred by those with a higher salary.

Why buy in Hungary?

Another beneficiary of EU membership, since May 2004 the country has blossomed economically, entering the 21st century successfully with a GDP growth rate of 4.1% for 2005, and *The Economist* predicting a 4.2% growth rate for 2007. The recent political and economic turmoil, which culminated in riots in the capital back in September 2006, doesn't seem to have damaged the rapidly expanding foreign investment market, although buyers have tended to be more watchful.

Hungary has one of the highest foreign direct investment levels in Eastern Europe and tourism is a massive industry, with nearly 14 million people visiting the country annually, and the holiday market having the distinct advantage of being year-round. Interest is being further bolstered by the increasing regularity of budget flights serving Budapest, with Ryanair also offering flights into Lake Balaton. With a legal system and land registry which is straightforward, well organised and efficiently run, foreigners can also be assured that they will enjoy a relatively trouble free purchase.

Hungary has one of Europe's strongest folk traditions, producing excellent examples of embroidery, pottery and wall paintings, and with a rich musical heritage, especially of Gypsy and folk songs. Despite the fact that 63% of the population lives in urban areas, the Hungarians have strong ties with the land and more than 50% of the population still indulge in part-time farming – in some rural areas, it seems as if time has stood still.

A stunningly beautiful country, the geography of Hungary is lush and varied, with two-thirds being covered by flatlands, juxtaposed with the verdant forests to the north. Of the hundreds of thousands of plains, the vast Great Plain in the southeast is undoubtedly the most famous, and the largest, covering 52,000 square kilometres. Hungary is dissected by the Danube, and one of the river's most picturesque stretches – the Danube Bend – is situated just outside of Budapest. This capital city is arguably one of Europe's finest and most cultured. Home to hundreds of restaurants, cafés and bars and numerous museums, the opera house, art galleries, and a zoo with some fine art nouveau animal houses, it is unsurprising that so many westerners are choosing to buy here.

Eighty kilometres southwest of the capital is Lake Balaton, one of Europe's largest lakes, covering a surface area of 592 square kilometres, and now one of Hungary's most popular second home destinations.

With 11 national parks and a number of UNESCO World Heritage sites, such as the ancient village of Hollókő, Hungary also boasts plenty of wildlife, from the more common European species to endangered animals such as wild cats and lake bats, and an extraordinary array of waterfowl. There are also numerous castles and fortresses to visit, while you can choose from over 130 Turkish baths. With more than 1,000 thermal springs scattered throughout Hungary, the country has a strong spa culture.

With a rich history, some fine wines – the vinification industry has undergone something of a Renaissance in the past 15 years – and hearty foods, Hungary is an enticing country, not least of all because its people are incredibly welcoming and friendly. As one of the post-communist bloc's most forward-thinking countries, there is a bright future ahead.

Politics and the economy

Economic chaos?

The Hungarian economy has always suffered as the government has attempted to reconcile the demands of its electorate with the rigorous constraints of running a market economy. Post communist years saw the standard of living drop for many, and the gap between the rich and poor grow increasingly wide. However, even though wages have risen to an average of £399 a month, this comes at a cost, requiring the government to spend over half its budget every year on social security. This is an unsustainable amount and with a budget deficit of roughly 10.1% of annual GDP, (compared with 3.2% in the Czech Republic), this is more than three times the limit set for members of the euro. Consequently, question marks have been raised over the sustainability of investments in Hungary, especially after the violent riots of September 2006 which followed the admission by Prime Minister Ferenc Gyurcsany that his government had lied in order to win the last election. However, the riots were small scale and supported by the minority rather than the majority of Hungarian citizens. Nevertheless, there is evident discontent over the government's economic policy and following last year's trouble, the government is focusing its efforts on economic reforms and capping spending.

Generally speaking, Hungary has made the transition to a market economy comfortably, with a per capita income nearly two-thirds that of the EU-25 average. The country continues to demonstrate strong, stable economic development, despite 1995 and 2001 experiencing sluggish growth followed by a sharp decline in the level of house construction. Nevertheless, there are many reasons to be optimistic. Between 1996 and 2003, inflation fell from 30% to 6% and despite expected rises of up to 7–8% in 2007, from 3.7% in 2006, predictions suggest inflation will settle at 6% by the end of the year, with the best case scenario seeing falls of 3–4% by the end of 2008.

The private sector accounts for over 80–90% of GDP, with cumulative foreign direct investment totalling more than $60 billion since 1989. Currently, Tescos and Vodafone both have a presence in Hungary, with 90% of telecommunications and 66% of the manufacturing industry controlled by foreign companies. Exports have continued to grow since the 90s and today, 75% of the country's trade is carried out with the EU. Unemployment has persisted above 6% but wage rates are now on a par with western levels. All this translates into a healthy investment environment and while the 90s saw many problems, thanks to high levels of investment from America, Europe and Asia, Hungary is making progress, albeit at a slower rate than Poland and the Czech Republic.

Hungary is aiming to adopt the euro by 2010 although this date is seen as highly unrealistic given the current shape of the economy in relation to the Maastricht criteria. A date of 2013–2014 is more realistic and some believe that Romania and Bulgaria might beat Hungary to euro adoption.

Hungary is a parliamentary democracy and has been since the collapse of communism in 1989, when it became the Republic of Hungary. The current President, László Sólyom, was elected by parliament in June 2005. The Prime Minister is Ferenc Gyurcsány, who was elected in 2004.

Geography and climate

Although a landlocked country, Hungary is no less attractive as a result of the lack of coastline. Bordered by several countries – Montenegro, Croatia, Austria, Slovakia, Slovenia and Romania – Hungary is centrally positioned in Europe, lying in the flat Carpathian Basin. This beautiful country boasts vast tracts of flat plains, along with the rolling hills of the Transdanubia region, and the Mecsek, Villány and Carpathian Mountains. As well as the Danube, Hungary is also home to the Tisza and Dráva rivers, as well as Lake Balaton. Hungary also boasts the largest thermal lake in the world, Lake Hévíz (Hévíz Spa).

The Hungarian climate is continental and temperate, with July and August offering the warmest temperatures. Protected by the Alps in the west and the Carpathians to the north, east and southeast, the winters are not as severe as you might expect, although snowfall can be heavy. Spring and early summer are the wettest time of year with many thunderstorms, while winters are cold, with snow lying for between 30 and 40 days on average – longer during more extreme winters, when the Danube often freezes. The average monthly temperature varies from 27 to 35°C in summer and 0 to –15°C in winter. The average annual rainfall is approximately 600mm.

History and culture

Because of her position in the heart of Europe, Hungary witnessed many invasions and rulers. The original settlers of the country were the Magyars, and today Hungarians still cling tightly to their Magyar roots, referring to themselves as Magyars and speaking *magyar nyelv* – Hungarian. The Magyars originated in central Asia but invaded Hungary, founding the Country of the Magyars (Magyarország) in AD896. The Hungarian state was officially founded in AD1000 when Hungary's first king, King Stephen, was crowned.

In the 14th and 15th centuries, Hungary was a powerful kingdom and ruled much of Romania, Ukraine, Slovakia and Croatia, but in the 16th century, the Turks advanced and occupied the country. Ottoman rule lasted until the mid-17th century, when it was the turn of the Hapsburgs, whose rule continued until the collapse of the Austro-Hungarian Empire after WWI. While the end of the war saw Hungary become an independent republic, being on the losing side meant she lost much of her territory. On the side of Nazi Germany in WWII, Hungary was eventually occupied by her allies until 1945, when the Russians liberated it. What followed was communist rule, which lasted from 1947 to 1988. In the late 1980s, it was Hungary that led the movement to dissolve the Warsaw Pact, moving away from communism and towards democratic rule and a market economy, culminating in a declaration by Mátyás Szűrös on October 23rd 1989, of the Third Hungarian Republic. Hungary's first free elections were held in 1990.

Culturally, Hungary is awash with traditional arts, such as ballet, opera, symphonies and writing, as well as folk and gypsy music. The most famous of Hungary's composers is Franz Liszt (1811–1886), a world-renowned pianist and composer of the Romantic period. Hungarians are also justly proud of their many inventions, which include the noiseless match (János Irínyi), Rubik's cube (Ernő Rubik), the krypton electric bulb (Imre Bródy, 1891–1944), the ballpoint pen (invented by László József Bíró) and the theory of the hydrogen bomb. Zsa Zsa Gabor and Harry Houdini also rank among famous Hungarians.

Religion

The Hungarian people are predominantly Catholic, with two-thirds – 68% – practising Roman Catholics. Of the remaining population, 20% are Calvinist and 5% Lutheran, with a small minority of Jews among the remaining 7%.

Tourism and getting there

The tourist industry in Hungary is focused around Budapest, which is also the beating heart of the country's economy. Tourism doesn't play as big an economic role as in many other EU countries, but it is a growing industry, ranked as the 15th largest tourist destination worldwide, ahead of Portugal and Greece. Tourism generated an income of $10 million in 2006 and with GDP generated from tourism set to increase by 4.7% between 2007 and 2016 the healthy outlook spells good news for investors.

More importantly, the tourist industry is attracting many westerners who have a greater disposable income and are investing more into the country during their visits. With over 10 million visitors to the country in 2005, income from tourism represents 4.7% of the country's GDP, and Hungary is currently placed 40th of 124 countries in the World Economic Forum's Tourism Competitiveness survey.

Tourist hotspots include Lake Balaton, which is visited by more than one million people each year. However, most choose to visit or stay around Budapest. That said, significant income from short-term rentals should not be overestimated in the capital, as most rental demand in Budapest comes in the form of long-term lets.

Finally, budget flights have helped stimulate the tourist growth and today Hungary has one of the most established tourist markets in Eastern Europe, primarily based around Budapest. Currently, Air Berlin, easyJet, Wizz Air and Jet2 all fly to Budapest and, thanks to budget flights, 2004 saw Ferihegy airport become the third busiest airport in Central Europe after Vienna and Prague, with 6.5 million passengers registered, up 28% from 2003. After only one and a half years of operation, the budget airlines flying to Budapest accounted for over 15% of the total market share at Ferihegy airport and this improved accessibility of Hungary has undoubtedly contributed to the growing number of visitors.

The cost of living

The cost of living in Hungary is not as low as it once was, but it is still lower than the UK, with a three-course meal and wine setting you back by an average of £20, while a family of four can feed themselves on between £20 and £40 a week, depending on their eating habits.

Budapest is obviously the most expensive place to live in the country, and areas of Lake Balaton can also be quite costly. According to the *Mercer*

Cost of Living Survey for 2006, Budapest is the 65th most expensive city to live in, dropping from 24th place in 2005.

Food and drink

Cuisine is just as much a part of the cultural experience in Hungary as visiting the Vár (Buda Castle) on the Buda side of the Danube, and Hungarian food has always been hearty, with an interesting blend of influences from both the Magyar settlers and western neighbours. Traditional dishes include goulash, which is flavoured with paprika and includes potatoes and any meat currently to hand. Meat features heavily on any menu, as does fish stew, stuffed peppers and paprika chicken. Sour cream and cheese are commonly included in dishes, with sauerkraut and dumplings introduced by the various Austrian and Turkish invaders, along with sweet pastries.

Today Budapest is a foodie's dream, with restaurants serving everything from Italian, French and Greek to Japanese, Thai, Chinese and Indian cuisine. Prices can be steep and in some cases on a par with London restaurants, but if you look off the beaten track, it's possible to pay more reasonable and local prices. If you fancy trying some of the local cuisine, there are also a number of places to look – some of which even serve pike!

As for beverages, there are some fantastic local wines to sample and you can buy a decent bottle of Hungarian red for as little as £2, with some excellent white and sparkling varieties on offer too.

THE PROPERTY MARKET

When you consider that Hungary has one of the wealthiest and most stable economies in Eastern Europe, and one of the east's most mature and well-developed property markets, it's staggering to think that you can still purchase a newly-built luxury flat for as little as £28,000.

Since Hungary abandoned communism and began to look west, canny investors have benefited from unprecedented property price rises, with the Hungarian Central Statistical Office reporting increases of 63% across the country between 1999–2003. During the same period, property in Budapest alone appreciated by 60%, with the capital the focal point for foreign buyers. Recently, these unprecedented price hikes have slowed, with the years between 2003–05 reporting respectable growth rates of between 15–20%, and rental income continuing to boast a minimum yield of 6%, peaking at around 15%. Consequently, buyers mustn't think they've missed out, as the current combination of good rental yields and high capital appreciation makes the market the perfect environment for investment. Prices are expected to continue growing at an average of 10% until 2010, and as soon as Hungary adopts the euro, the market is expected to see an upturn in value.

However, the GKI Economic Research Company (www.gki.hu) have reported no real growth in the residential market between January 2006 and January 2007, with 63% of estate agents reporting oversupply in 2007, compared with 81% at the end of 2006. GKI believe that the market will continue to decline in 2007 before seeing any growth, although January 2007 has seen national price growth of 4.5%. While this may seem like a pessimistic picture, it seems that the relationship between supply and demand has yet to settle. Since 1995, the number of dwellings constructed has almost doubled from 24,718 to 41,084 in 2005, with the number of construction permits issued leaping from 39,053 to 51,490. However, while oversupply may currently be an issue, affordability isn't and you can certainly get more for your money than you can in the UK. Experts also agree that the sustainability of the market has been largely guaranteed by local demand, and thanks to government housing subsidies Hungary has one of the highest levels of home ownership in Europe at 95%. Also, increasing numbers of citizens are applying for mortgages, making for a healthy resale market.

Where to buy

Budapest

The charismatic and enchanting capital city of Budapest is country's economic and tourist hub. Housing one-fifth of the country's population and accounting for 60% of Hungary's commercial activity, it is no surprise that the majority of foreign direct investment is poured into the capital, meaning more expats and a high demand for Western-standard, long-term rental properties.

A lucrative place to invest, Budapest is currently experiencing price hikes of 15% per annum, and given the accessibility of the capital via budget flights and the fact that you can drive to any corner of Hungary from Budapest within two hours, it's central location makes it a popular choice.

Despite recent rises in property prices, Budapest is still an average of 30% cheaper than many other European cities and given that prices for newly-built apartments range from under £30,000 up to £500,000, there is something for every budget. Certain areas of the city can offer a capital gain of up to 40%, although this is becoming increasingly rare as the market has calmed over the last two to three years.

Apartments tend to be the most popular and also the safest investments in the city. The best location is central Budapest, close to all amenities, transport and attractions. Districts V, VI, VII, VIII and IX are extremely desirable, with districts VIII and IX offering cheaper prices and being the most up-and-coming areas of the city. The greater price appreciation tends to be taking place on the Pest side of the Danube, with Buda appealing to the buyer with the bigger budget, being more expensive.

Traditional properties tend to be decorative 19th-century buildings, which are often divided into flats. These tend to offer a range of architectural features, ranging from art deco to baroque or rococo in design, and these can be found in most of the central districts. Increasingly, there is also a trend for newly-built developments situated on the Danube.

Lake Balaton

Experiencing price increases of around 20% per annum, Lake Balaton is Hungary's hottest property market outside of Budapest. It has long been a popular holiday destination with central Europeans and locals who yearn for some R&R, offering excellent watersports facilities and outdoor activities. It has also been popular with German second-home buyers for a number of years.

A major wine region and number-one holiday destination in Hungary, lying 96 kilometres to the southwest of Budapest, Lake Balaton is becoming an increasingly popular destination. It doesn't offer the same security as the Budapest market, but there is still money to be made from holiday rentals, and thanks to regular Ryanair flights, it is becoming more established, with prices rapidly rising. The average property is selling for around £34,000, although if you buy on the waterfront, you are looking at closer to £136,000. The northern shore of the 50-mile-long lake represents the better investment long term, although it is also the most expensive area, with the southern shore providing the cheaper housing, but also being more brash and prone to nightclubs and 70s-style hotels.

For bargain prices you need to look away from the lakeside and further inland, where you can pick up a small villa for around £34,000. Currently, the choice of property is plentiful and typically you will find spacious villas and country houses. However, supply won't last forever, although new builds are springing up around the lake. Nevertheless, you will get much more for your money than for the equivalent price in Budapest.

Be aware that parts of the lake are declared national park and therefore not open to purchase by foreign buyers.

What to buy

The residential property market in Hungary generally consists of freehold properties and typically you are looking at either resale or newly-built homes.

Resales are readily available in the Budapest market, with characterful 19th-century buildings dominating sales. Most buildings in central Budapest date from the 19th century. Unfortunately, during the communist period, there was almost no investment in their upkeep and so the quality of apartment buildings varies widely. Consequently, they tend to be sold renovated and spilt into apartments, with period architecture and traditional features such as balconies and frescoes adorning many. Offering all mod cons and plush interiors, these are not only the most in demand property but also the best in terms of rental yields, as they tend to be centrally located. However, in Budapest, space issues mean properties aren't always the largest – in fact, living space has dropped from an average of 99 square metres in 1995 to 87 square metres in 2005.

As for newly-built properties, the majority are sold off-plan and most developments sell out before construction has even begun, with the quality varying depending on the target market.

On Lake Balaton, you will find properties have more bedrooms and living space and are also grander – country houses and villas are the norm. For £64,000, you can pick up a three-bedroomed modern home only 1,000 metres from the lakeshore.

THE BUYING PROCESS

Despite the fact that the conveyancing and land registry system in Hungary are well organised and established, there are still many questions marks over some building planning and property titles. It is therefore essential that you secure good and experienced legal representation in order to avoid any problems.

Stage 1: Restrictions of foreign buyers

As an EU citizen you will be faced with no restrictions on purchasing a property in Hungary and can purchase any type and number of houses you want to with the exception of agricultural land and protected natural territories. However, there is a rule that any non-resident Hungarian cannot purchase more than two properties as an individual, and so the best course of action should you decide to buy more than two houses is to set up a company. However, if you are looking to purchase only one or two properties, it is possible to do so as an individual. There are drawbacks to this method though, as the current law states that any non-Hungarian must apply for a permit to purchase property in Hungary, and this also applies to EU residents. This law will stay in effect for the next one to two years.

Stage 2: Financing your purchase

You can secure a mortgage with a Hungarian bank in either euros, pounds sterling or forints, but they will only offer an LTV of 70% of the value of the property over a period of 20 years. The number of Hungarian lenders is expected to rise and this will undoubtedly result in a drop in rates as competition becomes fiercer.

There are a number of UK firms that will offer mortgages on a Hungarian property, although terms will be similar to the Hungarian companies, with a 70% loan which needs to be repaid over 25 years. In both cases, loans of up to 80% are becoming increasing available, although these tend to be repayable over 15 years. While rates do vary and buyers should shop around, as you would in the UK, generally you can borrow approximately 40% of the purchase price at a 3.8% to 7.2% interest rate, depending on the currency in which the mortgage is given. Euro mortgages offer the best value, with a rate of 4.8%, compared with 7–8% for pound sterling and 12–13% for the forint.

Be aware that when buying through a company, it can be more difficult to secure a mortgage unless you have been operating for more than one year.

Stage 3: Background checks and surveys

As Hungary was once a communist country, there have been issues over property titles, with paperwork out of date or incomplete, so it's essential that you get your legal representative to dig around and ensure the title is clean. This is important as you need to ensure you are purchasing from the title holder and that there are no outstanding fees on the title.

It is important to get a survey carried out, especially if you are buying a resale or renovation property. Always ensure the survey is carried out before you sign the purchase contract, and if you intend to renovate, try to get as accurate a picture as possible of the potential cost of the renovations. A Hungarian chartered surveyor will be able to carry out the survey for you.

Stage 4: The contract

Once you have reserved your property, checked the title and carried out a survey, the next stage is to sign the preliminary or pre-purchase contract. Having already paid a reservation deposit of between £1,000 and £2,000, once you have signed the preliminary contract, you will be liable to pay the remainder of the 10% deposit within 7 to 10 days. The outstanding balance will be required 30 to 45 days later. Off-plan properties have an extended payment period that can include up to six payments; ensure the details are covered in the contract. Should the seller pull out of the sale then the payment of your initial deposit will be doubled and refunded.

Before signing the contract, you need to ensure it includes details on payment terms, the size, location and land registry details, the purchase price of the property, the completion date if a newly-built apartment, any consequences to be imposed on late payments, as well as floor plans and timetabling for the construction of a new property.

Following the signing of the contract, it is sent to the land registry in order for the title to be transferred to the buyer. This is a process that can take up to six months. During this time the final sale is completed with the signing of the final contract and the outstanding price of the property is paid. However, you will not become the official owner until the registration process is completed.

Purchasing as a company

Setting up a Hungarian company is a routine procedure that will cost you roughly €850 (£577) and comes with many benefits to the owner. The advantage of buying property through a company is that all expenses can be written off, such as legal and estate agents' fees, stamp duty, renovation costs, furniture, utilities and all other associated expenditure.

Corporation tax is incredibly low at 12% on net profits, as opposed to capital gains tax rates of 25%, while if you own a Hungarian company there is no need to obtain a residency permit, which can be a lengthy process. It also makes the property more attractive on resale as you can sell the company with the property and the buyer will avoid stamp duty charges. One disadvantage is the need to submit annual reports and accounts, which will require you to employ an accountant.

In order to set up a company you will need to do the following:

1. Sign the company's Articles of Association in the presence of a lawyer. The lawyer will need to be given details about the company, including its name and the directors' names.

2. The founding capital of the company must be ft3 million or £8,140 and this amount can be applied to the purchase of the property.

3. Proof of identity must be supplied. This is generally in the form of a passport that has been notarised either by a local notary or at the local Hungarian Embassy, e.g. in London.

4. After the Articles of Association have been prepared, specimens of signature need to be signed in front of a public notary, then a bank account must be opened.

5. All the paperwork – documents, forms, authorisations and invoices – must go to an accountant, preferably Hungarian, who will take care of all the administration and prepare the required reports.

Although you will need to be in Hungary to open a bank account, the process can take just a couple of days, as opposed to many months if buying as an individual.

Purchasing as an individual

In order to apply for a permit to purchase a property in Hungary you will need to visit the public notary and get certification of your identity in order to initiate the process of permit approval via the local authorities. A public notary can be found at any Hungarian embassy or consulate and the cost is approximately €250 (£170), with the approval process taking up to three months. Prior to applying for a permit, you will need to have found a property and paid your reservation fee.

Stage 5: Additional costs

Generally speaking, you should allow for between 8–10% of the price of the property for costs such as stamp duty, agents' fees, notary costs and taxes. Typically, costs are as follows:

- Legal fees: 1.5% of the purchase price.

- Purchase permit: £175.

- Cost of setting up a company: €850 (£576).

- **Stamp duty**
  Resale property:
  More than Ft4,000,000 (£11,043) = 6% of purchase
  Less than Ft4,000,000 (£11,043) = 2% of purchase price

  New-build property:
  More than Ft30,000,000 (£82,885) = 6% of purchase price
  Less than Ft30,000,000 (£82,885) = none
  Garage: 10% of the purchase price.

- Notary fees: 2% of the purchase price.

- Estate agents' fees: 3–5% on average.

- All fees are subject to 25% VAT.

- Property tax is levied at ft900 (£2.50) per square metre or 1.5% of the purchase price for buildings, and at ft200 (50p) per square metre for land (1.5% of the market price).

THE LETTINGS MARKET

The lettings market shouldn't be relied upon to cover your expenses in Hungary. As most Hungarians tend to own their own home, demand isn't massive for local rentals, and given that the Hungarian workforce is highly trained and educated, there is less expat demand than you might expect. However, as in many other popular locations, you can now also purchase property with a guaranteed rental income.

The market in Budapest is decidedly residential, with rents geared towards long-term lettings from foreign employees, students and Hungarian business people. The centrally located districts – V, VI, VII, VIII, IX, and XIII on the Pest side, and I, II, III, XI, and XII on the Buda side – offer the best returns and are the most popular with tenants. In contrast, Lake Balaton is a short-term holiday lets market with a rental season that runs from May to September.

In both instances, rental yields of between 6% and 8% are available, but be aware that you are looking at costs of 10% in management fees and a 20% tax on any income generated. You will be required to register with the National Tax office (see www.apeh.hu) and secure a tax ID. More realistic is a figure of 4–5% yield once you have paid any additional costs.

RENOVATIONS

Thanks to neglect during the communist era, many of Budapest's 19th-century art deco and baroque buildings have fallen into disrepair, and consequently, for those looking to buy a renovation project, there are many options open to you. Rather than being faced with the traditional western concept of buying a wreck and transforming it into your dream home, in Hungary's capital you are more likely to find a property that requires some modernisation and a face lift, rather than a complete overhaul.

Generally speaking, it is recommended that foreign buyers shy away from undertaking major structural work on some of Budapest's classical buildings, as renovations are fraught with complications and difficulties, and more importantly, huge costs. Thanks to the abundance of traditional architectural features – which make property attractive to rent or resell – the cost of renovation works can be as high as the original value paid for the property. No special permission is needed in order to carry out renovation work and prices can vary from £30 per square metre for a basic renovation to £250 for something more lavish.

Be aware that undertaking a renovation will generally require you to replace lead pipes with a new system, overhaul the wiring and electrical system, and introduce a heating system to the property as many are often communal and this means that it is not possible to control the temperature independently.

In order to undertake a renovation project, you should always:

- get more than one quote for the work you intend to undertake;

- get a thorough survey done and an estimate of the kind of work you'll be required to undertake, as well as the potential cost;

- appoint an architect to prepare the plans and a project manager/company to oversee the work if you don't intend to be in the country full time.

LIVING IN HUNGARY

Daily life and people

While Hungary has wholeheartedly embraced western culture and is a proud member of the EU, Hungarians are equally keen to maintain and promote their heritage as Magyars, the race who invaded from central Asia and founded the country back in the 9th century, and from whom most of the population are ethnically descended. However, due to their proximity to the western capitalist country of Austria, the Hungarian people have maintained a somewhat spilt personality. Consequently, you may well recognise distinct western and central European customs and practices blending freely with traditional Magyar tendencies, evidenced in Hungary's move to reform state socialism and adopt democracy long before the collapse of Soviet Russia.

Free-spirited and sociable, yet stubborn, the Hungarian people have a tendency towards pessimism, probably thanks to centuries of enduring defeat and invasion. Nevertheless, there are no people more hospitable and they will go to great pains to make you feel welcome in their fascinating country. Today there are 9.5 million Magyars in Hungary, 1.45 million in Romania, 520,500 in Slovakia, 293,000 in Serbia,

170,000 in Ukraine and Russia, 40,583 in Austria, 16,500 in Croatia, 14,600 in the Czech Republic and 10,000 in Slovenia, highlighting the warlike expansionist tendencies which saw this race conquer most of Europe and even reach Spain.

Visas and residency

Nationals of European Union member countries do not need a visa to enter Hungary for a stay of 90 days. You can enter using a valid national passport or your national ID card. For a stay longer than three months, you must apply for a European Economic Area citizen resident permit. If you want to apply for residency, be aware that this process can take up to six months to organise and you must apply within 15 days of entering the country. If you are the director of a Hungarian company then you do not need a residency permit. Visit www.huemblon.org.uk for more information.

Utilities

Now that government subsidies have been removed for gas and electricity, both utilities have become more expensive, costing almost – if not quite – as much as in the UK. Gas is mainly used for cooking and electricity for lighting and household appliances. The major electric utility is ELMU (www.elmu.hu/e). Bills are monthly estimates with meter readings taken only once a year and a bill sent out for any outstanding payments. The largest gas supplier is FOGAZ (http://english.fogaz.hu) and you can either apply to be connected online or by contacting your local customer services office; all these details can be found on the website.

Telephone services are offered by Magyar Telekom (www.magyartelekom.hu), who offer mobile phone and internet services, as well as residential landlines. The dialling code for the country is 0036. As telecommunications have been privatised, the services are efficient and the phone system mainly digital. The other main mobile phone companies include Vodafone, who have a Hungarian branch (www.vodafone.hu) and T-Mobile (www.westel900.net). If you have a GSM phone, you may be able to continue using your current mobile in Hungary. Visit www.gsmworld.com for more details. All your utility bills can be paid at the post office or through your bank.

Banking and currency

The official currency of Hungary is the forint (ft). You can get notes in denominations of 20,000, 10,000, 5,000, 1,000, 500 and 200 forints, while coins come in 100, 50, 20, 10, 5, 2 and 1 fillér. Visa, MasterCard and American Express are accepted in most places and in general, you will be able to use most internationally recognised credit cards at larger stores around the country, but not in more rural areas or smaller grocery stores and souvenir shops, which only accept cash.

Setting up a bank account is as easy as in any Western country. All that is required is for you to present your passport at your chosen branch and one other form of ID. You have the option of opening an account in euros, dollars or the forint – or even all three should you choose. A minimum deposit will be required – generally € 100 for a foreign currency account and ft100,000 (£277) for a forint account – and in order to get a credit or debit card, you'll probably be required to make a deposit of € 200. Regular pre-authorised bank transfers can easily be set up to pay bills.

Most banks provide e-banking and branch opening hours are generally 9am to 5pm Monday to Thursday and 9am to 3 or 4pm on Friday, being closed on Saturday and Sunday. The Hungarian National Bank website is www.mnb.hu, while CIB Bank (www.cib.hu), Citigroup (www.citibank.com) and Hungarian Foreign Trade Bank (www.mkb.hu) are popular with expats.

Taxes

Hungary has signed a double taxation treaty with the UK so you can rest assured you will not be paying tax in both countries. As a foreign national living and working in Hungary, you'll be considered a tax resident and have to register as a taxpayer. However, if you are only living and working there on a temporary basis, you will only be taxed on income and gains made in Hungary. If you own a property in Hungary, spend 183 days a year in the country, or if Hungary is the family place of residence, then you will be classed as a tax resident and liable to pay taxes there.

Income tax is levied at a progressive rate from 18–36%, with 36% payable on annual gross income of ft1,550,000 (approximately €5,960) and over. However, income is taxed at the reduced, flat rate of 25% if it is classed as capital gains or rental. Corporate tax in Hungary in 2006 was fixed at 16%.

Always seek independent advice on taxes, especially as things have recently been changed. Good websites to consult are PriceWaterhouseCoopers (www.pwc.com) which has a Hungary-specific website with publications free to download on tax; www.worldwide-tax.com is also useful.

Insurance

The Hungarian Association of Insurance companies can be viewed at www.mabisz.hu and offers a list of accredited companies. It is recommended that foreigners living in Hungary take out private medical insurance, while house insurance is also available from a number of firms, as well as UK based ones such as John Wason Insurance brokers (www.johnwason.co.uk).

Healthcare

Mostly state owned, there are also a number of private hospitals and clinics, although these are generally in Budapest. The government is planning to privatise some of the health service, although the best option for foreigners is to take out private health insurance.

If you do need to be treated by the state heath service, be aware that there will be costs involved. While first aid and ambulance services are free for citizens of the UK, Scandinavia and most Western European countries, if you are not an EU citizen, follow-up treatment must be paid for, with a consultation in a doctor's surgery (*orvosi rendelő*) starting at ft2,500 and a home visit from ft4,000. As an EU citizen, as long as you possess an EHIC card, you are entitled to the same level of healthcare provision as a Hungarian citizen, and it is free. However, insurance is still recommended as, while treatment is of a good standard, emergency facilities can be unreliable.

The state currently subsidises healthcare for Hungarian citizens, but a resident of the country has to pay social security insurance contributions for the right to be treated by the state-run system.

Retirement, benefits and social security

It is perfectly feasible for you to retire to Hungary as a resident although it is not a hugely popular country with expats – maybe because of the language barrier, severely cold winter weather and the cultural differences. However, should you choose to retire here you can do so by applying for residency. You will be able to claim your UK pension in Hungary and your retirement pension will not be liable to tax in the country, whether they are paid in Hungary or from abroad.

If you are living in Hungary you will be required to make social security payments if working and you'll be allowed any benefits that are a consequence of these payments. If you have been claiming job seekers' allowance prior to leaving the UK, you will still be entitled to it in Hungary – you simply need to secure an E303 form and take this to the Hungarian employment service on arrival. This form can be secured through your local Jobcentre in the UK.

Education

As with the UK, the private school system operates a school year which runs from September to June, but the local Hungarian schools adhere to their own system; consequently, the majority of expats send their children to private schools. All are situated in Budapest and offer a variety of different languages, but all are of a high standard. You can also attend university in Hungary and there are a number of English-language courses offered.

- American International School of Budapest (AISB) www.aisb.hu

- Greater Grace International School (GGIS) www.ggis.hu

- International Christian School of Budapest (ICSB)
  www.icsbudapest.org

- Britannica International School www.britannicaschool.hu

- The British International School of Budapest (BISB) www.bisb.hu

- SEK International School Budapest (SEK) www.sek.hu

- BME International Secondary Grammar School (founded by the
  Budapest University of Technology and Economics)
  www.bmegimnazium.hu / www.bme-intl.sulinet.hu

- International School of Budapest (ISB) www.isb.hu

- Lauder Javne Jewish Community School and Kindergarten
  www.lauder.hu

- Budapest French School (Lycée Gustave Eiffel)
  http://web.matavnet.hu/lfb

- Austrian-Hungarian European School (Österreichisch-Ungarische
  Europaschule) www.europaschule.hu

- Japanese School of Budapest (Japán Iskola) www.hoshuko.hu

Driving

Hungarians drive on the right and as Eastern European countries go, they
are fairly conscientious drivers and the roads are uncrowded. There are
various road categories, the main being the motorways, which are easy to
drive on. Be aware that rural and side roads are often poorly lit. Look out
for pedestrians, livestock and railway crossings – many don't have gates.
City driving can be perilous thanks to the buses and trams which you
need to watch out for.

Getting a driving licence in Hungary is fairly straightforward, but you
won't need one for a short relocation period as you can use your present
licence to hire a car or drive your own. For longer stays, you'll need a
valid international licence. There is zero tolerance for drink driving and

using a mobile phone while driving, and the speed limits are as follows:

- motorways 130km/h (80mph);
- open roads 90km/h (55mph);
- towns 50km/h (31mph).

Petrol stations are open Monday to Friday, 6am to 8pm, although most multinational stations are open 24 hours a day. Unleaded petrol and diesel are available everywhere, with diesel, oil and LPG also available, and credit cards are accepted everywhere.

Getting around

Budapest has a cheap and efficient public transport system, with a clean and regular metro service in operation and numerous trams and buses serving the city. Visit www.bkv.hu for all scheduling information.

The Hungarian railway system is fairly rapid and reliable, with little overcrowding and good quality carriages and track. MÁV (Hungarian State Railways) serve most major towns and cities throughout the country and details of their services and fares can be found at www.elvira.hu. There are several types of service, including Express ('Ex' on the timetable), which require a reservation; InterCity ('IC') which is slightly more expensive; *gyorsvonat* (fast trains); and *szemelyvonat* or passenger trains – these stop at every village and hamlet and take a long time to reach their destination.

Buses can be unreliable outside of Budapest and so taking the train is a better bet. Volán are the main servers throughout the country (www.volanbusz.hu) and outside of major towns, rural services can be limited to one or two a day.

Learning the language

The origins of Magyar remain a mystery and its unfamiliar construction make it one of the more difficult Eastern European languages to learn, although it is believed to belong to the Finno-Urgic linguistic group.

While many foreigners living and working in Hungary are able to master the language, the *lingua franca* by which Hungarians communicate with foreign tourists is German, while many Hungarians also speak English. However, trying to secure a grasp of the basics will prove helpful and will be welcomed by the locals.

Shopping

The general opening hours for shops are Monday to Friday 10am to 6pm, and 9am to 1pm on Saturdays. Some of the larger shopping centres are open on Sundays too. Outside of Budapest, you'll be hard pushed to find many imported products, although in the capital itself there are many international brands to be found.

Tesco and Ikea supply most general household items and can be found in shopping centres, generally open from 6am to 9pm. Mammut is located in District II and is Buda's biggest and most centrally-located shopping mall (www.mammut.hu) while there is also the Campona shopping centre in the XXII district, Lurdy Haz in the IX district, Pest's oldest Plaza, Duna Plaza in the IV district and the Polus Center in Eastern Pest's XV district (www.polus.com).

For some real bargains, check out the Nagy Vásárcsarnok (the Central Market Hall) in Budapest. The capital also offers some of Europe's finest flea markets such as the Budapest Flea Market (Bolhapiac) in Petofi Csarnok and the Ecseri Piac market, in the Xth district – a great place for folk costumes and communist relics.

Post

The postal service in Hungary is passable but fairly slow, although services are improving. As with most European post offices, you can also pay utility bills at the majority of branches, open a savings account or organise money transfers and arrange a subscription to a foreign newspaper. Most post offices are open from Monday to Friday between 9am and 6pm and more details can be found at www.posta.hu.

Crime, corruption and the police

Crime rates in Hungary are low compared with much of Eastern Europe, and Hungarians have a healthy respect for the law. Corruption is also fairly low compared with many neighbouring countries. Hungary holds a CPI corruption score of 5.2 (see www.transparency.org for more details). Countries are judged on a scale of 0–10 with 0 being highly corrupt and Hungary currently sits above the Czech Republic, Latvia, Lithuania, Italy and Greece. However, that doesn't mean foreigners aren't likely to come across corruption, so be sure you surround yourself with experienced lawyers and agents who know the terrain, and never order or agree to buy anything without first looking at the price tag.

11
Montenegro

COUNTRY PROFILE

Victim of much conflict over the years, today Montenegro is an independent Republic and one of Europe's smallest, being roughly the same size as Wales. Offering one of the best investment opportunities, Montenegro packs a punch when it comes to appreciation, with average annual growth rates of 25%.

Did you know?
- The name Montenegro means Black Mountain which was probably derived from the thick 'black' forests that in the medieval times covered Mount Lovcen.

- Montenegro has always been a problem for cartographers as it is almost impossible to write all the letters of its name into the small space it takes up on the map.
- During four centuries of Ottoman occupation of the Balkans, Montenegro was the only country that remained independent.

Why buy in Montenegro?

Montenegro burst onto the property scene back in 2004. While it's now politically back on its feet, there are still many question marks over the economic stability and levels of corruption, which Montenegro is working on rectifying in order to secure EU membership, estimated for between 2010 and 2015.

The tourism market is leading the country's renaissance. Prior to the Balkan conflict, Montenegro was a popular tourist destination with some serious gliterrati sunning themselves on the sandy beaches, Sofia Loren, Richard Burton and Elizabeth Taylor among them. With tourism predicted to increase by an average of 9.9% per annum between now and 2015, Montenegro is tipped to be the biggest growing tourist market in Europe – good news for its economy and any potential investors.

Affordability is a major plus in Montenegro, and despite mass media interest, prices start as low as €70,000, with the undeveloped Adriatic coastline still offering returns of between 20–30% on your investment. Since 2004 it is estimated that around 1,000 British and Irish investors have bought property in Montenegro and thanks to the burgeoning property market and huge levels of interest shown by foreign buyers, the tourist industry has experienced massive growth. It is believed that the high appreciation rates are set to continue, especially as the country is still in the very early stages of a property boom.

Investors are also attracted by the low rate of property tax, which is currently 2%. Rental returns are also promising as the country offers a year-round lettings market, especially as eco-tourism continues to blossom.

Now that the government have removed obstacles for foreign homebuyers looking to purchase a home, this has actively encouraged investment from overseas. Economic growth is also underway, with massive EU funding overhauling the antiquated infrastructure and economic growth sitting at a respectable 4.3%. However, this is not a market for the cautious as the property market is not fully legislated, and while a land registry exists, it is hard to track down a property title.

It's not just the investment opportunities that are worth writing home about. Montenegro is just as beautiful as its Croatian neighbour, and with a coastline of 293.5 km – 73km of which is beach – sapphire blue seas, fjords, alpine mountain ranges and sparse, arid plains, the diversity of this beautiful country is dizzying. This varied geography also supports a wide array of flora and fauna, while the country boasts the UNESCO World Heritage sites of Durmitor and Tara River Canyon – the second deepest canyon in the world – and the old city of Kotor, plus a plethora of historic and cultural towns and monuments.

Politics and economy

Defined as a 'democratic, welfare, and ecological state', following a referendum in May 2006, Montenegro voted overwhelmingly to become an independent Republic. Currently, the elected President is Filip Vujanović and the Prime Minister is Željko Šturanović.

The property market has responded well to independence despite fears that the economy may be weakened as a result. By resolving their political future it seems to have in fact strengthened the market, following years of economic failure under Milosevic. An economic boom is currently underway with legal, tax and banking regulations being tightened in anticipation of securing EU membership, while foreign investment into the property market and a healthy growth in tourist income is helping to bolster the economy. Despite using the euro Montenegro is not a member of the eurozone, but adoption of the currency has helped to stabilise the runaway inflation rates that were previously being experienced.

Large-scale foreign investment and EU funding are helping to rebuild and develop what is essentially a very small economy, with a GDP per capita of $3,800 (£1,930). With 50% of the economy privatised and the government aiming to diversify the economy into new markets, Montenegro introduced a series of reforms between 2002 to 2006, aiming to modernise the Montenegrin economy. These include the increase in economic freedom, the reform of public administration and reduction in corruption, as well as the protection of property rights. Consequently, there seems to be no reason to question Montenegro's ability to become the economic equal of Hungary and Poland.

Geography and climate

Montenegro is situated in the southern Adriatic and covers less than 14,000 square kilometres. Bordering Croatia, Serbia, Bosnia and Herzegovina, and Albania, the country runs from the mountainous peaks of its southern borders to its four-mile-wide coastal plain, which is abruptly interrupted by Mount Lovćen and Mount Orjen, before plunging into the Bay of Kotor.

The county boasts a number of notable geographical features, such as the eight-mile Velika Plaža Beach in Ulcinj; Lake Scutari, which has a surface area of 243 square kilometres; Kolac peak, which is 2,528 metres in height; and the Tara River Canyon, which plunges to a depth of 1,300 metres. Montenegro also has four national parks: Durmitor (390 square kilometres), Lovćen (64 square kilometres), Biogradska Gora (54 square kilometres) and Lake Scutari (400 square kilometres).

The Mediterranean climate ensures warm summers and an average of ten hours of sunshine a day, with temperatures sometimes reaching 30°C, while the winters are cool. Inland, the winters are colder and the summers warmer, while in the mountains, winter temperatures can get as low as –6°C.

History and culture

Montenegro was the only Balkan state that managed to ward off the Ottoman forces between the 14th and 18th centuries, and was instead ruled by the prince-bishop of Cetinje from 1482. Prior to WWI, two Balkan Wars occurred, starting in 1912 and resulting in Montenegro doubling the size of its lands, gaining much of the defeated Ottoman Empire. On the side of the allies during WWI, Montenegro was occupied by Austro-Hungarian forces, and following a vote in 1918, the country was united with Serbia. This resulted in a mass uprising by the pro-Independence party which was eventually crushed in 1924. The end of WWII saw the creation of the Socialist Federal Republic of Yugoslavia, comprising some six republics including Montenegro; this lasted from 1945 until 1992. The federation was dissolved in 1992 following the bitter Yugoslav wars of the 1990s, resulting in an alliance with Serbia which lasted from 1992 until 2006. Although Montenegro disassociated itself from Serbia during this period, it wasn't until May 2006 that it officially declared itself an independent state.

Culturally, Montenegro is a rich country. With UNESCO World Heritage sites and a number of historic towns from pre-Romanesque, gothic and baroque periods, Montenegro has been shaped by a variety of influences, such as that of the Orthodox Southern Slavs, Central Europeans, and seafaring Adriatic cultures, most notably the Italians.

There are a number of sites of significant interest in Montenegro, including the numerous religious monuments found along the Adriatic coastline, such as the Cathedral of Saint Tryphon, the 800-year-old basilica of St. Luke, Our Lady of the Rock and the Savina Monastery.

As with many Eastern European countries, there is also a strong folk culture, with traditional music and dance – such as the *Oro*, a circle dance – playing an important part in Montenegrin life. National costume was also worn daily and in battle until recent decades, but it is rarely seen today.

Religion

Montenegro is a real ethnic blend, and most religions coexist quite happily and with no signs of antagonism. The majority of Montenegrins are of a Serbian Orthodox religion (65%), but there are also a significant number of Roman Catholic and Islamic communities. Staggeringly, some churches actually have two altars with Serbian Orthodoxy and Catholicism celebrated simultaneously.

Travel and tourism

Montenegro has been listed as the fastest-growing tourist economy according to the World Trade and Tourism council, and 2005 saw tourist figures increase by 17%, with a 47% increase in international visitors. Before the war, the country was a tourism magnet with half a million foreigners visiting the country annually. While Montenegro is far from once more reaching these levels, it has still witnessed huge growth since 2004, with the average tourist figures hitting 150,000 per annum and many travel agents once more offering holidays to the country. Thanks to the huge levels of publicity the country has received from overseas investors, growth is guaranteed, especially as stability is again returning to the region. While the infrastructure far from caters for tourism, with few luxury hotels, this lack of development is in many ways a good thing, leaving the stunning beauty untouched. It is to be hoped that this will continue, especially as the government has committed to protecting the environment.

The infrastructure has been vastly improved thanks to EU funding, but there is still a long way to go, and while there are currently no budget flights to Montenegro, it is only a matter of time before they start up. The country has two internatonal airports, at Tivat and Podgorica, and there are regular flights from Montenegro Airlines (www.montenegro-airlines.cg.yu) and Yugoslav Airways (www.jatlondon.com) from May to September. Many airlines fly into Dubrovnik and a popular way to reach the country is to fly into Dubrovnik and then travel across the border into Montenegro.

The cost of living

The cost of living in Montenegro from January 2004 to November 2004 was 2.4% higher compared to the same period in 2003, with retail prices increasing by 3.3%. Clearly, it still remains lower than in Western

Europe, with a one litre bottle of water costing around €0.60, a bottle of wine from €2 to €5, and a bottle of beer merely 50 cents. A meal for two with wine can be as little as €20.

The Montenegrin Statistics Bureau reported that the cost of living rose by 6.7% during 2005, while the average net wage increased by 9% compared to 2004.

Food and drink

Reliant on meat and fish and heavily influenced by Mediterranean fare, dishes are full of flavour and most of the ingredients are organic, with fresh fruit and vegetables grown in most gardens. Bread is eaten with every meal and restaurants serve smoked meats and home-made cheeses. Much of the traditional fare mirrors that of the country's Balkan neighbours, with stews, soups and hearty meat dishes central to the diet. Popular vegetables include stuffed peppers, sauerkraut, onions and beans, with a Greek influence evident in the presence of stuffed vine leaves and kebabs.

Beer is ubiquitous and extremely popular – and cheap! – while the local red wine, Vranac, is extremely drinkable. As for liquors, the national drink is a plum and grape schnapps known as Rakija.

PROPERTY MARKET

Low prices, stunning surroundings and traditional stone-built properties are drawing many investors to Montenegrin shores and thanks to Montenegro's birth as a new country in 2006, the ensuing stability has helped to render this tiny country all the more attractive. Estate agents have reported that since the referendum there has been a huge upturn in interest from the British market, although Germans and Americans have been investing here since the 90s.

Dubbed the 'Jewel of the Adriatic' a better description would probably be to label it a rough diamond, as only the more adventurous buyer should consider buying here, given the nature of the legislation system and the lack of security in the market. With regular water shortages and power cuts, plus a limited expat community, it is easy to find yourself isolated in a country where the culture is decidedly different. The issue of access – most people have to fly into Dubrovnik and then drive into Montenegro – means this is not a destination for those looking for an easy weekend getaway.

Back in 2001 the property market experienced an explosion in interest from foreign buyers. While there has always been outside investment and demand for property, this had generally been from locals and affluent Montenegrins living overseas. During the last two years, price hikes of 20% per annum have occurred, with some areas seeing 100% rises in a single year. Off-plan developments have sold out before the ground has even been broken, although the biggest demand is centred around stone-built, traditional homes situated on the coast.

The current environment is ideal for adventurous buyers, with a growing economy, low inflation rates and a massive upturn in interest from foreign investment and tourists. Prices currently remain low and the market is cheaper than other Mediterranean destinations and coastal countries in Eastern Europe – prices are 40–60% cheaper than in neighbouring Croatia. Property prices have risen significantly in Croatia over the past few years, with prices per square metre almost three times as high as Montenegro, whose market is expected to follow in the footsteps of Croatia.

With average prices ranging from £80,000 for an apartment to £150,000 for three bedrooms, you can pick up a renovation property for as little as £20,000, while a newly-built apartment will cost around £45,000, although in the more popular Bay of Kotor areas you are looking at more like £80,000. The best future growth is anticipated in the southern mountainous areas where it is expected that the winter sports industry will soon expand. However, the north is currently experiencing the best appreciation rates, with demand far outstripping supply, a phenomenon that is unlikely to change due to the limited space for expansion. The future looks good for the investment market, especially as the tax, legal and political situation is being made increasingly attractive for foreigners. Waterfront properties are especially set to see price hikes, with renovation properties more popular than new builds.

Where to buy

The government has an ambitious strategy of development for each Montenegrin region, including new marinas and luxury golf resorts for coastal areas and the transformation of an old navy base at Tivat into the largest marina on the Adriatic. All of this means the immature property market is poised to explode over the next few years.

The Budva Riviera

The coastal areas are seeing growth of 30% to 50% a year, with the narrow nature of the four-mile coastal strip protecting it from over-development, so property is in high demand.

The Budva Riviera – home to the famous picture postcard island resort of Sveti Stefan – is the tourist capital of Montenegro, being only 40 minutes from Tivat international airport. However, prices are much cheaper than northern Kotor, with a two- to three-bedroomed house costing around £85,000. Properties close to Budva's 38km of sandy coastline – and around Becici, situated 2km from Budva – are expected to experience the best growth. Budva is regularly compared to Dubrovnik and this area has experienced the greatest development in Montenegro.

The Bay of Kotor

Well on its way to becoming a popular holiday destination, this is one of the more expensive areas in Montenegro. Situated in the country's north, this is the area that has traditionally attracted the most foreign interest and investment. Rents have more than doubled in the last two years and this is a good area in which to invest in order to generate income from short-term lets. A three-bedroomed property will set you back more than £136,110, much higher than the Montenegrin average, reflecting the intensity of demand. Prices have risen by 50% in the last couple of years, putting property prices on a par with neighbouring Croatia. Being the closest area to Dubrovnik has also made Kotor a favourable location, not to mention the stunning coastline and landscape, and the fact that it's a World Heritage site.

Herceg Novi is another popular resort where property can be picked up for around £80,000, while another future hotspot is the Lustica Peninsula, where historic Montenegrin renovation projects can be had for under £40,000.

Bar

Located right down on the south of Montenegro's coastline, this small port town is close to the capital, Podgorica, and it's becoming increasingly popular with foreign tourists. Prices are expected to rise significantly in the coming years, as the rentals market here is still in its infancy.

Currently you can pick up a two-bedroomed house for around £75,000 to £80,000, and this would let for around £306 a week during peak season.

Inland

Areas such as Lake Skadar – Montenegro's largest lake and a haven for fauna and flora – and the northern holiday resorts of Bjelasica and Durmitor offer prices 200% lower than along the Adriatic coastline. With 60% of the country being mountainous there are also opportunities cropping up for ski resorts and these southern mountainous areas are destined to experience the best capital appreciation. Currently, it is uncertain whether permission will be granted for new builds around Lake Skadar, but there are a number of resale properties available. Nearby, the 350-acre Lake Skadar Golf and Country Club provides an exclusive residential development around a 36-hole golf course, and this is attracting much interest.

What to buy

Previously an upmarket area for investors, the country is aiming to continue in this vein, although the highest levels of demand are focused on the renovation properties and the old ruins, which can be picked up for as little as £15,000–£20,000. While these will require a lot of work, they are also incredibly cheap.

However, the best bet for foreign investors is the newly-built development projects, many of which sell out before construction has even begun and which offer excellent appreciation rates and rental yields. Most newly-built developments are located along the Adriatic coast, with those in the closest proximity retailing at around € 1,000 per square metre, dropping to € 800 the further out you go. However, there were only a couple of decent developments last year, with more destined over the next couple of years, so you need to be quick.

There are also options for those looking to set up a business, with a number of bars, hotels and restaurants for sale, while further inland there are eco-tourism opportunities thanks to the fishing and skiing activities available.

THE BUYING PROCESS

As domestic and foreign buyers are treated equally when it comes to property purchase, this can be a good country for foreigners to buy in. The main problem you will encounter surrounds the property title and ensuring you are buying from someone who is entitled to sell.

Stage 1: Restrictions on foreign buyers

There are no restrictions on the purchase of property by a UK resident in Montenegro as there is a reciprocal agreement in place with the UK. Residents of other countries should check with the Montenegrin authorities. However, you cannot purchase land which is deemed of ecological or historical significance. This has created a problem as it is not always clear which areas these are, given that there are some unscrupulous characters who will try to sell property in these areas. Also, in order to register land in the land registry, you will have to set up a limited company in the country. Property purchases of a house or ruin which comes with up to 500 square metres of land are usually allowed to be registered by foreigners without the need to form a company.

Always ensure you get the proper legal support and carry out full checks, especially as it is not compulsory to register a property with the land registry, which can make it difficult to check its history.

Stage 2: Financing your purchase

While mortgages are beginning to become available in Montenegro, from 50% to 70% loan to value, the best option is still cash. Most buyers find the easiest path is to re-mortgage their UK home and then purchase in Montenegro with cash, particularly as many UK lenders are nervous of loaning money to fund a purchase in such an immature market.

Given that Montenegro uses the euro, this does simplify money transfers and issues of money exchange. You'll also find that if you do secure a euro mortgage, rates are currently lower than sterling and offer the best value.

Stage 3: Background checks and surveys

The actual process of purchasing a property in Montenegro is much the same as any other European country, and just as straightforward. As has been stressed earlier, the main problem is the land registry system and the ownership of land. While the registry system is computerised and very good, because it is not obligatory to register your property many have no record or history, making it difficult to establish whether you are purchasing from the actual owner, or if they are allowed to be selling the property. This is further complicated by the fact that many Montenegrin families are arguing among themselves about ownership, and that under Tito's government, much private land was confiscated. Consequently, many families are currently negotiating with the government to reclaim their lands. You need to avoid buying from a third party where there are currently claims from the actual owners on your land and property, and so you must ensure you secure the best legal advice and get detailed checks carried out.

Surveys are not carried out in Montenegro and there is not a culture of surveying in the country. However, you should get a survey carried out, especially as the majority of the properties for sale are old, traditional stone-built houses.

Stage 4: The contract

Once you have arranged funding and done all the meticulous background checks, the next step is to sign the contract. If you want to arrange for the property to be taken off the market while you carry out all the necessary checks, try to arrange for a reservation contract to be signed, rather than a preliminary contract, as this ties you to the sale.

The first stage of the sale is to sign the preliminary contract. At this stage a 10% deposit will be required and this is non-refundable. However, should the seller pull out, then they will be required to pay you 20% of the price of the property. Once the preliminary contract has been signed and you are happy that the property is safe to purchase, you move on to the signing of the final contract in the presence of a notary. The title deeds are then registered with the land registry to transfer the property legally over to you. As the land registry is an efficient body this should not take long to process.

Stage 5: Additional costs

Generally speaking, additional costs can be quite high in Montenegro, as you may find you will need more legal advice to buy here than you would in some other Eastern European countries, given the complications over land titles. These costs can be as high as an additional 10% of the property price.

Once the sale is completed, you will be required to pay a property tax of 2% for a resale house and 17% for a new build. The amount will be based on the valuation of the price of the property by the Montenegrin Inland Revenue, rather than what you actually paid for it.

Other costs include the payment of notary and legal fees, which are both usually 4% and 3–5% for the estate agents. You'll also have to pay council tax, although this is a minimal amount, and also a capital gains tax on profits made from a resale – 9% for a company and up to 23% on a scaled structure for individuals. You are also likely to have a bill for translation fees, which will be around €50.

THE LETTINGS MARKET

Thanks to the reinvigorated tourist industry and the fact that this is the country's main industry, there are opportunities to secure short-term lets in Montenegro, with a number of estate agents offering 'ready to let' property for sale. However, while the market is expanding, it is still very young and so lettings can be sporadic at best and you shouldn't rely on rental yields – weekly income is very low, with yields of around 2–3%.

The difficulty in reaching Montenegro, with only one direct flight during summer, means you generally have to fly into Croatia and negotiate the poor infrastructure to reach your destination. Consequently, if you do intend to secure some rentals, you need to be on the coastline, close to Kotor or Budva, and be somewhere accessible – while this is a small country, the difficulty of negotiating public transport or taking to the roads with the notoriously bad Montenegrin drivers can be off-putting for potential tenants.

There are very few property management companies in Montenegro at present, but this is beginning to change. While the tourist market is potentially year-round, you may find yourself competing with some of the newer developments which are offering guaranteed rentals to their buyers. One of the best prospects for rentals would be holiday complexes, as there would be a management infrastructure in place, rents would be guaranteed and you would be well placed to benefit from future appreciation rates. The general view is that if the tourist industry can recapture the 60s era when this was Europe's most exclusive destination, and if budget flights can be secured, then rentals will become an excellent generator of income. Consequently this is a market where you should look at any rental income as an added extra and buy something in which you would like to spend time.

RENOVATING A PROPERTY

Given that the most popular buys are stone-built traditional farmhouses, renovating is a popular pastime in Montenegro. While builders are affordable and generally do a good job, there may be issues over the finishing, with you holding a very different opinion of what a finished property is compared with the construction workers. The best thing to do is get a recommendation from someone who lives in the country and who knows a good architect or builder. Also, be aware that it can be a very difficult and costly process to renovate here. Planning permission can be difficult to gain if you intend to buy on the coastline, and despite the rumours circulating, you do need planning permission to build or renovate in most areas of Montenegro. While there was once a period when a few hundred euros would have 'avoided' the need to secure planning permission things have changed. However, if you build or renovate outside of an 'urbanised' area or around 3km from the coast, you'll probably find you don't require planning permission.

LIVING IN MONTENEGRO

Daily life and people

Montenegrins are dedicated to their colourful and rich traditions, morals, customs and history. Their social and cultural identity has historically been centred around clans and family groups, with a strong relationship exisiting between the average Montenegrin and their family. While they once dominated Montenegrin lifestyle, clan autonomy was ended with the creation of the Republic of Yugoslavia. However, clan influence has not been eradicated from Montenegrin society, with accusations of nepotism levelled at some government appointments. The warlike nature of the clans has permeated into Montenegrin characteristics, with the constant need to repel many invaders instilling the characteristics of strength and bravery (*cojstvo*) in its people.

As a nation, Montenegrins are communicative and hospitable people, and very welcoming. Unfortunately, you have to be aware that some

Montenegrins may try to manipulate foreigners for financial gain. However, this certainly does not mean that all Montenegrins are dishonest.

Visas and residency

UK residents with a valid passport can visit Montenegro for 90 days without having to apply for a visa. Should you want to stay for longer than 90 days then you must apply for a temporary residency permit from the Ministry of the Interior. All visitors entering the country for a holiday must be registered with the police or the local tourist office, unless you're staying in a hotel. You are only able to register for a work permit and residency from within Montenegro itself.

The following countries do not need a visa to enter Montenegro: Germany, France, Italy, Netherlands, Belgium, Luxembourg, Great Britain, Ireland, Spain, Portugal, Greece, Denmark, Sweden, Finland, Austria, Switzerland, Norway, Iceland, Monaco, Lichtenstein, The Vatican States, Andorra, San Marino, Israel, Cyprus, Malta, Czech Republic, Slovakia, Poland, Slovenia, Lithuania, Latvia, Estonia, Croatia, USA, Canada, Singapore, Republic of Korea, Australia and New Zealand. Citizens of other countries will be required to secure a visa. For more information, visit www.mfa.gov.yu.

Utilities

All utility companies are state run, apart from telecommunications. The utilities situation in Montenegro is not the best, with a lack of investment meaning there are regular power cuts and water shortages. EPCG are the main power company in Montenegro, and household bills have risen by around 20% in recent years, with a current average per month of €22.

The telecommunications service is, by contrast, modern and reliable. Telecom Montenegro is the main operator, with mobile phone services provided by ProMonte (www.promonte.com) and T-Mobile (www.t-mobile-cg.com).

Internet services are provided by Internet Crna Gora (www.t-comcg. com), owned by Telecom Montenegro, which offers ADSL and dial-up connections, but the service is not reliable – most connections are dial-up and broadband is uncommon. Currently, only 7.9% of the country has access to the internet.

Water is supplied by Vodovod Water Company (www.vodovod.com). Once well developed, services today have deteriorated, with regular shortgages, especially along coastal areas.

In order to connect your property, you'll be required to take your registration papers to each utility company in order to get the bills and account changed to your name. Direct debits are currently not set up in Montenegro so you'll have to organise monthly payment for all utility bills.

Banking and currency

Montenegro uses the euro, which replaced the Deutschmark back in 2002. Notes come in standard euro denominations of €5, €10, €20, €50, and coins of 1, 2, 5, 10, 20, 50 cents, and €1 and €2.

It is recommended that you set up a bank account if you are going to buy a Montenegrin property. Banks are open from Monday to Friday, 9am to 7pm and 8am to 3pm on Saturdays. When you open a bank account, be aware that many banks charge for withdrawals and bank transfers at a rate of between 0.5% and 1.5%. Some international transfers can take as long as 10 days to process and, while there are no restrictions on the amount of euros you can take into the country, there are restrictions on what you can take out, with proof of origin required. All international transfers into Montenegro have to go through an intermediary institution first.

Taxes

You will be classed as a tax resident if you have a permanent home in Montenegro or if you spend more than 183 days per calendar year in the country. If you are only living temporarily in Montenegro then you are regarded as a non-resident for tax purposes and are only taxed on your Montenegrin-sourced income, such as rental.

The UK does have a double-taxation treaty in place with Montenegro so you won't be taxed twice. Income taxes are levied at a progressive rate up to a maximum of 24%, and capital gains are also treated as income tax. If you have owned a property for longer than three years then you are exempt from paying capital gains. Inheritance tax and gift tax are levied at between 1 and 30%, while residents are liable for tax at 25% on rental income generated in Montenegro. Annual property taxes are charged at between 0.08% and 0.8%, which is calculated based on the market value of the property on 1st January each year. Corporate tax is charged at a progressive rate of between 15% and 20%.

Insurance

There are a handful of insurance companies in Montenegro which deal with English speaking residents. These include:

- DDOR Novi Sad, www.ddor.co.yu, which offers car, home, life, health and travel insurance;
- Dunav Insurance Company, www.dunav.com, which offers personal, property and car insurance.

Healthcare

There are an increasing number of private clinics in Montenegro that offer a good standard of health care, with many doctors speaking English. There is now a reciprocal healthcare agreement in place to allow UK residents to receive free emergency health care too. For all other treatment, you must ensure you have health insurance. The British Embassy in Podgorica (+381 (81) 205 460) can advise you of the best clinics for foreigners.

Retirement

Montenegro is an affordable and attractive destination for those seeking to retire and UK residents are fully entitled to retire to the country. Your UK state pension will be payable to you in Montenegro at the same rate as if you were still living in the UK.

Education

The Montenegrin education system is split into pre-school, elementary, secondary – this offers a choice between three strands of secondary education, from broad to specialist – and higher. Few attend pre-school, but elementary education is state run, free and compulsory for all children between the ages of seven and 15. Visit the Ministry of Science and Education at www.vlada.cg.yu for more details.

Most schools teach in Serbian, and so foreigners are recommended to enrol their children in one of the several private schools. The main school is the QSI International School of Montenegro (http://mtg.qsi.org).

Driving

If you want to drive in Montenegro, you can do so using your British driving licence, although it would be helpful to get an international licence if you intend to stay long term.

European Green Card vehicle insurance is valid in Montenegro, but make sure you carry your vehicle registration/ownership documents and proof of insurance with you. There are more than 5,000km of roads in the country, the two main ones being the Adriatic motorway which runs from Igalo to Ulcinj and the motorway running from Pertovac to Bijelo Polje via Podgorica and Kolasin. Montenegrins are not the best drivers and the roads can be difficult to negotiate outside of built up areas, with poor signposting in places. EU money should help to improve the infrastructure, though.

Vehicles drive on the right hand side of the road, seatbelts are compulsory and you can drive with 0.03% alcohol in your bloodstream. Speed limits are:

- motorways: 120km/h (75mph)

- main highways: 80km/h (50mph)

- built-up areas: 50km/h (31mph).

Limits can vary, but are signposted where appropriate.

You can get unleaded, super (98 octane), diesel and euro diesel petrol in Montenegro.

Getting around

Generally speaking, the best way to get around is by car, but even though Montenegro is a small country, travel can still be time consuming. There are no internal flights, but you can get around by train. Bar, Podgorica, Kolasin, Mojkovac and Bijelo Polje are all on the main railway line running from Montenegro into Serbia. For scheduling and timetables, visit the Railways of Montenegro website, at www.zeljeznica.cg.yu/eng.

Buses are infrequent, with the best services being in the capital. That said, travelling by taxi is probably the best way to get around Podgorica.

Learning the language

Montenegrins speak a dialect of Serbian, known colloquially as *Maternji Jezik* (mother language). With its roots in ancient Slavic, there are very few similarities between Montenegrin, Croatian, Bosnian and Serbian, even though they share the same roots. The main difference between the Serbian and Montenegrin is that the Montenegrin dialect has two extra letters. Writing is generally done in Latin script, but Cyrillic is also widely used; Albanian is also spoken in some areas.

As for learning the language, a lot of people along the coast do speak English, but as there is no large international community in Montenegro, it is worth getting a grasp of the language. Serbian is not easy to learn and it's made more complicated by the various dialects spoken within Montenegro, but the locals will appreciate any efforts you make and it will benefit your integration into the community.

Shopping

The larger towns and cities have supermarkets, although many shopping excursions will involve visiting more than one shop. There are a number of bakeries and grocers in smaller towns and there is an abundance of fresh produce on sale, such as organic juices. You will struggle to find any UK or imported produce, though.

Shopping hours are generally 8am to 7pm, Monday to Friday, and 8am to 3pm on Saturdays. You will find some 24/7 convenience and food shops, while in tourist centres during the summer season, many shops stay open until midnight.

Post

Postal services are reasonably good, but letters do take an average of a week to reach their destinations, whether internal or overseas.

Corruption, crime and the police

Generally safer than the UK, crime is limited in the country and tourists will feel safe wandering around after dark. A much bigger problem is corruption, which is rife in the government and is highlighted by the presence of many Russian money launderers and mafia in the country.

Corruption monitor Transparency International has yet to rate Montenegro as a separate country, but the combined state of Serbia and Montenegro received a score of 2.8 out of ten, placing it below Malawi and Mozambique, in a position of 97th out of 159 countries. The country is working towards sorting its problems out in an effort to join the EU, but there is a long way to go before the country is cleaned up. Foreign home buyers are more likely to suffer at the hands of corrupt individuals, rather than the government, but as long as you ensure you carry out the correct background checks and do your research, you should be able to negotiate the system successfully.

12
Poland

Factfile

Population: 38,536,869
Population growth rate: −0.05%
Area: 312,685 sq km
Capital city: Warsaw (population: 1,932,500)
Inflation: 1.3%
GDP growth rate: 5.3%
Unemployment rate: 14.9%
Net migration: −0.46 migrant(s)/1,000 population
Currency: złoty (PLN)
Exchange rate: £1 = 5.68PLN
EU status: Member as of May 2004
Time zone: CET (GMT +1 hour)

COUNTRY PROFILE

One of the biggest success stories in Eastern Europe, in next to no time Poland has turned itself around from being a communist, one-party, insular state into a democratic republic with a burgeoning western economy, complete with modern skyscrapers and a café culture.

Did you know?

- Augustus II, the Elector of Saxony and King of Poland, demonstrated his great physical strength by breaking horseshoes in two with his bare hands, a feat that earned him nicknames such as 'the strong', 'Saxon Hercules' and

'iron hand'. He was also believed to have a prodigious sexual appetite, fathering hundreds of illegitimate children during his lifetime.
- The world's first public library was opened in Warsaw in 1747.

Why buy in Poland?

Poland boasts one of the most dynamic and advanced of the Eastern European economies. Foreign investment exceeded $10 billion in 2006 alone and the country has successfully made the transition from a state-directed economy to a primarily privately owned market economy, which is now blossoming.

Ranked as one of the best investment opportunities in Europe, numerous budget airlines have bolstered the developing tourist industry, while the enthusiasm for investing in Poland has seen the property market perform beyond expectations. The burgeoning tourist market has contributed to the dramatic price rises, particularly in Kraków.

EU membership and the introduction of funds into the country have helped see it turn from being regarded as an eastern backwater to a leading European location, with the government actively pursuing adoption of the euro. The increased economic prosperity has helped to support and bolster the development of the property market.

Property prices continue to rise at a steady 10% per annum in the major cities, while a property shortage has created a healthy relationship between supply and demand. The local market is also performing well, with the level of home ownership rising steadily, increasing from 48% in 1998 to 55% in 2003. It has been estimated that €15 billion will be invested into Poland over the next five years, and combined with its strong economy and the anticipated adoption of the euro in the near future, Poland is the number one choice for many investors.

Politics and economy

Pursuing a policy of economic liberalisation since the 90s, the success of Poland's transitional economy has been mind-boggling. While growth rates slowed from 6.9% in 2004 to 4.9% in the first quarter of 2005, in the first quarter of 2006, GDP growth rates jumped to 5.3%, making the Polish economy one of the most dynamic in the European Union. Enjoying GDP growth today of 5.8%, a 16.7% leap in investment and a flourishing exports market, Poland now has a thriving private sector which has created more than 300,000 new jobs in 2006 alone. Since 2004, EU membership and access to EU structural funds have boosted the economy, with an inflow of $100 billion in foreign investment since 1990.

GDP per capita roughly equals that of all three Baltic States combined, but Poland still faces some mammoth tasks, such as reducing its budget deficit rate and high rate of unemployment, as well as meeting the strict criteria for adoption of the euro, predicted for somewhere between 2009 and 2013.

Poland's constitution dates back to 1997 when it formed a liberal democracy. Since the collapse of communism, politically the country has seen a series of weak governments, racked by instability and accusations of corruption. In September 2005 the right-wing Law and Justice party won the parliamentary elections, replacing the previous government – a union between the Democratic Left Alliance (SLD) and the Union of Labour. The current president is Lech Kaczyński, and his twin brother, Jarosław Kaczyński, is the Prime Minister. The new government has proceeded cautiously on economic matters, retaining the corporate income tax cuts while indicating their intention to reduce the top personal income tax rate.

Geography and climate

Situated in north central Europe, Poland is one of ten countries that joined the EU in 2004. Bordered by Belarus, the Czech Republic, Germany, Lithuania, Russia, Slovakia and the Ukraine, Poland is known for its shipbuilding and steel industries, but is far from an industrial country. Stunningly beautiful, the Tatras and Sudetes Mountains lie to the south, in contrast with the expansive agricultural plains of northern Poland. Inland, there are 9,300 glacial lakes, which are fed by the Vistula, Oder, Warta and Bug Rivers, many of them boast popular resorts. To the northeast you'll find the stunning Baltic beaches while the many national forests are dense, primeval places, inhabited by bears, wolves and eagles.

Poland enjoys a temperate climate, with the best of the weather between May and September. June, July and August see temperatures of 24°C but they also experience regular thunderstorms. Winter is a different story, with cold, cloudy weather, and the country is buffeted by Siberian winds and snow in the south.

History and culture

Poland has repeatedly seen itself in the hands of invaders, with its borders constantly shifted, leading to the country being populated by many different cultures – Slavic, Celtic, Germanic and Baltic being the most prominent. Eradicated from the map and with its territories divided between Russia, Prussia and Austria during the 18th century, the end of WWI saw the restitution of the Polish state and the creation of the Second Polish Republic. The country suffered greatly during WWII with Poland losing the highest percentage of citizens – more than six million Poles perished, half of whom were Jews. The end of WWII saw Poland reduced to 20% of its former size, with the Soviet Union enforcing communist rule on the country. Independence came with the installing of a president in 1990.

Culturally, Poland has weathered the storm of war and occupation, with influences from both the west and east evident in the art, literature, folklore and architecture. Famous Poles include pianist Frederic Chopin, scientist Marie Curie, film director Roman Polański and painter Jan Matejko.

Polish towns reflect the whole spectrum of European styles, with Kraków boasting some of the best-preserved Gothic and Renaissance architecture in Europe. There are a number of UNESCO World Heritage sites in the country, including the Wieliczka salt mine, Auschwitz concentration camp, Warsaw's historic centre, the old city of Zamosc, the Medieval town of Torun and the wooden churches of southern Poland, to name just a few. Teutonic castles and fine Polish mansions are to be found throughout the countryside, while the elegant cities of Warsaw, Kraków and Gdańsk are not to be missed.

Religion

Poland is predominantly Catholic, and the last Pope, John Paul II was born in Kraków. Roughly 98% of Poles are practising Catholics, but there are many other religious minorities, with 510,00 Eastern Orthodox, 120,000 Jehovah's Witnesses and various Protestant faiths. The previously predominant Jewish population was decimated in WWII.

Tourism and getting there

Poland's tourist industry has grown since EU accession in 2004 and is incredibly strong, being the eighth fastest growing in Europe. Outpacing more established markets such as Switzerland and Greece, most visitors are still from neighbouring countries – such as Belarus and Slovakia – with Americans and Western Europeans accounting for fewer than 1 million of the 15.2 million visitors in 2006. The 12th most frequently visited country in the world, today Poland is ranked 18th in terms of the tourism-related revenue it generates.

Thanks to the social and economic growth the country has experienced, and the westernisation of Poland's travel and tourism market, there has been a 50% growth in the number of Western European tourists, helped by the increased ease of access. With 40% of all foreign investment in Poland in the tourist market, it is expected that the industry will continue to grow strongly, offering excellent opportunities for investors, as well as high rental yields.

Air transportation is expected to continue to expand, with many international routes to be added. Ryanair (www.ryanair.com) flies into Kraków, Rzeszow, Wrocław, Łodź, Warsaw, Poznań, Gdańsk, Bydgoszcz and Szczecin, while easyJet (www.easyjet.com) flies into Warsaw and Kraków .

The cost of living

Poland offers a very high standard of living, but for a fraction of the price of a Western European lifestyle, with prices roughly 40% less than the equivalent of the UK. A one-litre bottle of water will set you back 34p, a loaf of bread 29p, while a bottle of Poland's legendary vodka costs just £7. You can enjoy a three-course meal with wine for a mere £11.

Prices have remained low, partly due to the high rates of unemployment, which have capped wage rises. Currently, the average Pole earns £471 a month.

Food and drink

Smoked meats, cheeses, sausages, fruit and vegetables are the most highly rated foodstuffs in Poland, although meals are more hearty than healthy, with meat, dumplings and potatoes featuring heavily. *Kielbasa*, or Polish sausage, is one of the most famous dishes, while stewed cabbage (*bigos*) and meat or potato stuffed dumplings (*pierogi*) and potato pancakes (*placki ziemnaczane*) are staple fare. There are numerous snack bars in the country, serving baguettes topped with melted cheese, fried mushrooms or grilled chicken, while hotdog stands serving fries and frankfurters are also common.

The most famous alcoholic product of Poland is its vodka. As the birthplace of the spirit, you will find some fantastic varieties on offer and it's impossible to visit the country without sampling some. However, be prepared, the Poles are seasoned vodka drinkers and it's not uncommon for three people to polish off half a bottle over lunch!

PROPERTY MARKET

Poland has been touted as one of Eastern Europe's most expansive markets, second only to Romania, and billed as one of the best locations for investors, with one of the healthiest buy-to-let markets in Europe – an investment of £100,000 is predicted to be worth £500,000 in less than a

decade. Touted as offering price growth of 393% over the next 10 years
– which may be rather unrealistic – PriceWaterhouseCoopers report that
Poland is likely to see the largest increase in residential sales across
Europe.

Poland's property prices grew rapidly in the lead up to EU accession,
with RICS reporting an average appreciation rate of 20% in 2002 and
2003 and 10% in 2004. Estate agents Knight Frank have forecast growth
of 12.5% for 2007.

Poland is one of Eastern Europe's most undervalued and fastest growing
markets, with property in some areas increasing by 30% per annum and
prices doubling in the last two years. Still in its infancy, and despite the
massive levels of growth, continued demand, economic development and
expansion of the tourist industry all mean the future is looking positive,
with appreciation rates of between 10–30% predicted. Despite all this,
prices remain much lower than in Western Europe, starting at £30,000 for
a renovation project, £140,000 for a city centre apartment and £200,000
for a large, country house.

There are some negatives in the Polish market, with many properties
being dark and pokey and some developments offering poor-quality
finishes. You'll also find many communist-era grey tower blocks, and
these should be avoided – while they are cheap, there will be no demand
from the local market, with affluence spreading and Poles seeking
higher-quality housing.

While there were some slight concerns over the relationship between
supply and demand a few years ago, if anything, Poland today is
suffering from a lack of property. In the 1990s, Poland had one of the
most severe property shortages in Eastern Europe, and currently there is
still an annual shortage of 40,000 properties per year. Despite
construction growing by 30% in 2005, with an average of 90,000
buildings per year being created, there is still an overall shortfall of 1.4
million homes, a situation exacerbated by the rise in home ownership
among locals leaping from 22% to 55% in less than a decade.
Consequently, market growth is seen as sustainable, with appreciation
rates at their highest in the larger cities where there has been a significant

growth in jobs and increased demand for longer term rents from Poland's expanding middle class and young professionals.

Poland has also experienced a mortgage boom, making it easier for people to buy, although taking out a złoty mortgage can end up being incredibly costly, so look for a euro or alternative currency mortgage. Today, mortgages can be secured for 90–100%.

Forecast for 2007

- GDP: 4.8%
- Average property market growth: 15%
- Warsaw: 15–20%
- Kraków: 18%
- Łodź: 20%
- Tri-city: 15–20%
- Katowice: 15%
- Poznań: 15%
- Wrocław: 15%

Where to buy

There are a number of fabulous cities in Poland, many of which offer low prices and excellent appreciation rates.

Kraków

Regarded as the hottest market in Poland, the UNESCO World Heritage centre of Kraków has seen price rises of as much as 58% in certain areas over the last couple of years, with this massive growth being largely attributed to the burgeoning tourism market – seven million tourists are visiting the city annually. A lucrative buy-to-let market, largely thanks to the demand from locals, as well as business people from overseas, a newly-built apartment can be picked up for as little as £80,000–£90,000. It can be very hard to get planning permission in Kraków, but that said the most in-demand and popular properties are newly-built apartments. There's a vast shortage in many areas and developments are selling out before construction has even begun.

Warsaw

While Kraków has been traditionally regarded as the epicentre of the Polish property market, Warsaw has in fact been outperforming the rest of the country. The economic powerhouse and capital of the country, GDP in Warsaw is four times that of the rest of Poland. Experiencing the biggest growth of all of Poland's cities, the market is still maturing yet offers the kind of security London buyers can expect. With 17,000 new apartments built in Warsaw per annum, 2006 has seen prices more than double in some areas, averaging between 10–15% in recent years. There is a solid investment base here, with a strong demand from the local professional market who are looking for property to rent, and so these figures are expected to double by 2010. You can expect to generate yields of around 6% in Warsaw. For £75,000, you can purchase a two-bedroomed apartment, with prices ranging between £1,000 and £2,000 per square metre.

Gdańsk

The dark horse in the market, there has been significant demand for rental property from the local market in Gdańsk, and during 2005 this was the strongest performing market in Poland, seeing the best appreciation rates. Situated on the Baltic coast and close to a string of beaches, Gdańsk has a historic Old Town that's very popular. Benefiting from the 'easyJet effect', with budget flights opening up the market in 2005, there is a significant shortage of accommodation for short-term holiday lets, meaning you can secure good rental yields. Prior to EU membership, prices rose sharply here, although the market has stabilised following a period of supply outstripping demand, yet it still experienced rises of 28% in 2005.

Poznań

Experiencing faster growth than any Polish city, this is a rapidly developing commercial centre and university town. Cheaper than areas such as Warsaw and Kraków, property costs an average of £650 per square metre compared with £1,000 in Warsaw. Now located on the budget flights route, residential properties are anticipated to grow by between 15–20% in 2007. While playing second fiddle to cities such as Warsaw in terms of publicity, Poznań still represents an excellent investment while remaining fairly unknown. This fast-growing town has high employment levels, a young, well-educated and affluent population and a shortage of newly-built, high-quality developments. With demand consistently rising, the future looks good for investment in Poznań, especially as the market remains significantly undervalued when compared to much of Poland.

Wrocław

The fourth-largest city in Poland and a bustling financial centre which is second only to Warsaw, Wrocław is well located, being central to the cities of Prague, Warsaw and Berlin. Served by a busy international airport, Wrocław is easy to get to, and once you're there, you'll also find that this is an excellent place to live. With over a million tourists visiting the city every year, Wrocław is Poland's third most popular destination. Demand for property is high, with the population currently sitting at around 640,000, but destined to grow to over a million within a decade.

Sopot

A popular destination with both Poles and international visitors, back in the 1920s and 30s this was a haunt of the international jetset. Still popular with tourists today, the seaside and spa resort of Sopot is part of the Tri-City area and has been voted one of Poland's best places to live. An interesting investment opportunity, Sopot is Poland's summer capital and is easy to reach, being located close to Gdańsk International Airport. Prices rose by a record 6.7% at the start of 2007, with the average price of property per square metre increasing to 6,396PLN (£1,125).

Zakopane and the ski resorts

Poland's ski facilities are well developed and the two main resorts in the country are Zakopane and Szcyrk, which have already played host to

World Cup skiing events. Offering great value for money, guaranteed snow and year-round facilities, tourist figures sit at over two million in Zakopane alone, with a ski chalet generating a rental income of around £450 per week. Demand is stimulated by regular budget flights into Kraków, only 100 kilometres from the resorts, and it's a journey that can be made in an hour and a half, thanks to the construction of new motorways.

Szklarska Poreba, a spa-ski resort, is touted as being the next big hotspot. There's plenty of property to chose from, cheaper prices than the more established resorts and an increasing number of tourists, all of which is having a positive effect on property market growth.

What to buy

With huge levels of construction taking place in Poland – although not enough to keep up with supply, a problem further exacerbated by a shortage of builders – newly-built properties are the most popular and in-demand style, being easy to rent and sell on. Agents advise that you either buy off plan or you buy an old, characterful property to restore. This is due to the extremely poor levels of construction that occurred during the 60s and 70s – the stereotypical communist tower blocks of which more than 60% require repair. Newly-built apartments or houses in the city suburbs offer the best investment, thanks to demand for rentals generated by the growing Polish middle class and professionals; these can generate yields of between 6–8%. Older properties can also be a good investment, especially if they are located close to the ski resorts of southeastern Poland. A country house with a living area of 270 square metres can be picked up for just £219,000, with apartments priced from £30,000 and chalets from £80,000.

THE BUYING PROCESS

Thanks to the accession of Poland to the EU and the position of the country as forward-thinking and economically well-developed, purchasing a property is straightforward.

Stage 1: Restrictions on foreign buyers

Before EU accession, foreign purchasers had to secure permission from the Ministry of Internal Affairs and Administration in order to buy a home, but thanks to Poland's EU membership, many of the obstacles have been removed for foreigners seeking to buy in Poland. However, buying land can still be tricky, although you can buy up to five properties, regardless of type, without any difficulty. Although most foreign investors buy as individuals when purchasing a residential home, if you are buying commercial real estate then the favoured approach is to do so via a Polish company.

Stage 2: Financing the purchase

All loans secured will require proof of income in Poland and your mortgage payment must not exceed 38% of your income. Polish banks are willing to lend to foreign buyers and can offer some of the best rates, although non-Polish nationals can only secure a mortgage if they have temporary or permanent residency. Loans can only be secured in euros, Swiss francs or US dollars. You can get a złoty mortgage, but these can end up being extremely costly. Polish banks are also offering buy-to-let mortgages for investment purposes. Today, many companies are offering mortgages of up to 80% or 90% LTV. There are few UK banks who are willing to lend you money to buy a Polish property, and so many people re-mortgage their UK home instead. However there are some specialist loan companies who will finance your purchase in Poland and it is worth talking to them before looking at re-mortgaging.

Stage 3: The contract

You have an option in Poland: you can either take the two-contract approach that is normal for most Eastern European countries, or – if you are ready to move quickly and have confidence in the property and the seller – you can opt for a one contract approach. This requires you to sign in the presence of a notary, having done all the usual title and background checks, but instead of signing a preliminary contract, you can jump right ahead to only signing the final contract.

The more standard approach is to utilise the two-contract approach. The first step is to enter into a pre-agreement arrangement by signing the preliminary contract in order to get the property taken off the market. Be aware that this is a legally binding contract signed in the presence of a notary and it commits both the buyer and the seller to the sale. At this time, a deposit of between 10% and 30% will have to be paid.

Before signing the preliminary contract, you should also ensure that if you are buying a property off-plan, all details of payment schedules and completion dates are included in it. Often, financial penalties are stipulated in case of either side failing to fulfil the requirements. There is usually a period of three months (maximum) between the signing of the preliminary contract and the final contract, and during this period you can modify any of the terms within the contract.

During this time your lawyer or notary should be checking the property title to ensure it is clean before the purchase is confirmed. The final contract will be signed once the details of the contract have been agreed and the title checked out. Signed in the presence of a notary, once the final contract is concluded, the remaining payments are made, contracts exchanged and the courts are instructed to transfer the ownership title into the buyer's name. Be aware that registration can take many months in Poland, with the registering system much slower than in many other parts of Eastern Europe.

Stage 4: The survey

As with most Eastern European countries in Poland a survey is not regarded as an essential part of the conveyancing process, with few local residents getting one carried out during the purchase of property. Consequently, you will find that there are no licensed surveyors in Poland and you'll need to commission a report from a local builder or architect which is less detailed than your typical UK survey.

Stage 5: Registering your property

As with most European countries, Poland has a dedicated land registry office which holds the title records for every Polish property. In order to complete the sale of your property and be officially recognised as the owner, you will be required to register the contracts with the land registry department.

It's essential to be careful when checking the background of a property title. Years of invasion and communist rule resulted in many lands being confiscated, especially from Poland's Jewish population. While there is little chance of finding your home reposessed by a displaced Pole, more caution should be exercised when buying a property in say, a block of flats. Always ensure the property has its own registry number and that one number does not apply to the entire building, otherwise you will be buying into a community-owned flat and will enjoy less protection from the law. At the end of the day, if you buy a property in good faith from the official owners named on the title, then you will be protected by law should any complications arise.

Fees typically work out at around 1.2% of the cost of the property, but the calculation is complicated and the average fee does vary.

Stage 6: Additional costs and taxes

Extra costs generally come to between 8% to 10% of the total value of the property. The breakdown of additional fees is as follows:

- Agents' fees: 1.5–3%
- Taxes: 5%
- VAT on newly-built properties: 7%
- Stamp duty/transfer tax: 2%
- Notary fees: 2–3%
- Legal fees: 1%
- Registrations fees: 2%
- Total costs: 8–10%

While capital gains tax of 10% is payable in Poland, if you have owned the property for more than five years, when you come to sell you will not be liable to pay capital gains on any income generated. The announcement that VAT on property is expected to increase from its current 7% to 22% in January 2008 will probably cause a rush of completions prior to this date, benefiting the early investors.

THE LETTINGS MARKET

As one of Europe's best jet-to-let markets, Poland offers plenty of opportunity for rentals. Although yields have dropped over the last five years, you can still expect returns of between 6% and 11% depending on where you buy. The best returns are centred around the expanding cities, such as Warsaw, Kraków and Poznań, where there is a growing demand for rentals as jobs continue to be available and the Polish middle class continues to grow. In Warsaw, there are a number of developments offering guaranteed two- to four-year rental returns of 5% (see www.letterstone.com).

Long-term rental potential offers the best returns, especially as the Polish are happier to rent than deal with mortgages, although this is changing. The best locations are central, close to offices, shops, entertainment districts and transport hubs. With the increasing numbers of corporations and companies relocating to Poland, there is also a massive market to rent to business people, generating around £450 a month for a two-bedroomed apartment. Many Polish towns also have a large student population, which is a rich rental vein to tap into, while out in the Tatras, resorts like Zakopane can offer year-round rentals, with weekly returns averaging £500 for a chalet.

RENOVATING A PROPERTY

There is a very limited market for renovation properties in Poland. While there are no shortages of old properties to modernise, the best options for investors are to buy renovation projects in the countryside, sticking to newly-built properties in the city centres – these are the most in-demand in terms of rentals and resale. However, as a developer, there are plenty of opportunities to buy dilapidated buildings in one of Poland's major cities, redeveloping them into flats which can then be sold on.

Renovating is no more difficult in Poland than in the UK, so long as you ensure you find decent builders, although costs will on average be six times less for builders and four times less for material than in the UK. Nevertheless, costs can still spiral, with the average expenditure being £200 per square metre.

LIVING IN POLAND

People and daily life

Exceptionally hospitable, friendly and helpful, the Poles are fiercely proud of their heritage and history, retaining a feeling of duty towards each other, their family and friends. Music is an everyday part of life in Poland, and each year numerous musical and cultural events are organised, including the International Festival of Mountain Folklore and the Festival of Classical Music.

Despite these evident traditions, Poles today are very forward thinking and strive towards westernisation and the establishment of a strong economy. Patience and resilience is another characteristic of the Polish persona.

Visas and residency

If you are going to be staying in Poland for less than 90 days, then as an American, Australian, Canadian, EU or New Zealand citizen, you are not required to secure a visa – a UK citizen can stay for six months without a visa.

For longer stays you will be required to secure a temporary residency permit (*Karta pobytu obywatela UE*), which will allow the holder to live and work in the country. A general duty fee of PLN 300 (£53) is charged for a residence permit for a specified period of time. If you have lived in

Poland for five years then you are entitled to apply for long-term residency, provided you have stable income and health insurance. Visit the Polish Ministry Of Foreign Affairs website (www.msz.gov.pl) or the Office for Repatriation and Aliens (www.uric.gov.pl) for more details.

Utilities

Once you've bought your new home, you'll be required to spend time transferring all utilities into your name, which will require you to visit all the relevant offices in person, along with the previous owner. You can't do this in writing, by the internet or over the phone: be prepared for long queues – this is a time-consuming process. Bills are normally paid on a monthly basis, whether at the post office or by direct debit. It is recommended that you talk to your lawyer or estate agent about the intricacies of organising your utilities.

Banking and currency

Poland uses the złoty, with coins available in 1, 2, 5, 10, 20, 50 groszy and 1, 2, 5 złoty denominations, with 10, 20, 50, 100, 200 złoty banknotes. Cash is used more often than credit cards in Poland, although all major cities now allow credit cards, with ATMs widely available.

Most Polish banks are foreign owned and so you will find it easy to choose a bank and open an account. You should open an account as soon as possible so you can easily and quickly transfer money for deposits and any other costs associated with buying a property. Banks are generally open from Monday to Friday, 8am to 5pm, with the larger branches opening on Saturday mornings. Online banking is also available.

The following offer services in English:

- PKO Bank Polski, www.pkobp.pl
- Bank Pekao SA, www.pekao.com.pl
- Citibank, www.citibank.pl
- Bank Zachodni WBK SA, http://english.bzwbk.pl

- Bank BPH, www.bph.pl
- National Bank of Poland, www.nbp.pl.

Taxes

Poland has a double taxation treaty with the UK so you won't be taxed twice for any tax that you pay in Poland. The current classification for a tax resident has recently changed, and under the new regulations you will be considered a tax resident if you have closer personal and economic ties with Poland than with any other country, or if you reside in Poland for more than 182 days in a tax year.

Poland is currently revising many of its tax laws, and income tax – while continuing at current progressive rates – will change in 2009, with the maximum rate of 40% being decreased to 32%. VAT on property is also due to change, being increased from 7% to 22% in January 2008.

Current taxes are as follows:

- Income tax:
  19% up to £6,544
  30% on income up to and including £13,098
  40% on income above £13,098.
- Capital gains tax: as of January 2007 the tax laws have changed, with capital gains now levied at 19% on the profit made from the sale, rather than 10%, unless you have owned the property for more than five years, in which case you pay nothing.
- Corporation tax: 19%.

Insurance

There are a number of companies in Poland which can offer you car, property, health and life insurance. As in the UK, you simply need to visit a broker and arrange for the relevant cover.

- Ergo Hestia, www.hestia.pl
- Warta, www.warta.pl

- Commercial Union, www.cu.com.pl.

Healthcare

While Polish healthcare is of a satisfactory level, it is nowhere near as good as that provided by Western European countries, with a lack of emergency services and facilities in many areas. There is a reciprocal agreement in place allowing EU citizens to be treated for free in an emergency, so long as you have an EHIC card. In all other cases you will have to pay for treatment – and in some cases up front – which has led to accusations of bribery and corruption against some hospitals. However, most doctors are well trained and experienced, with the younger staff speaking good English, but don't expect English to be widely spoken. It is recommended that you secure private medical insurance and there are a number of private clinics which can offer treatment, especially in the larger cities.

Retirement

It is possible to get your pension paid to you in Poland. The country is a long way from becoming a retirement centre, being much more of an investment hotspot, but it is straightforward to secure the relevant visas to allow you to retire here. You may be able to secure benefits while in Poland but each individual case is different, and so you'll have to talk to the relevant office, once in the country.

Education

There are a number of private schools in Poland, and while the state system is well developed, you may decide to choose to send your child to one of the English-language and curriculum-based facilities. You can also study at a Polish University where there are a number of English-language courses run.

The Polish education system is run by the Ministry of Education and Sport (www.men.home.pl) and schooling is compulsory between the ages of six and 18. Most of the international schools are situated in Krakow or Warsaw. Visit www.poland.pl/education/international.htm for all contact details.

Driving

The roads in Poland are varied, with few motorways, and it can be difficult to overtake. Be aware that in rural areas there may well be horses and carts on the road. EU citizens can drive in Poland with just their local driving licence but non-Europeans must carry an International Driving Permit. Seatbelts are compulsory, it is illegal to use a mobile phone while driving and you are not permitted to have an alcohol level above 0.2% in your bloodstream while behind the wheel. Be aware that the police are very hot on speeding. The speed limit is as follows:

- motorways: 130km/h (80mph);
- open roads: 90km/h (55mph) outside built-up areas;
- 110km/h (68mph) dual carriageway;
- 100km/h (62mph) single carriageway;
- towns: 50km/h (30mph)
  20km/h (12mph) in residential areas.

Getting around

Getting to Poland is now relatively straightforward thanks to the numerous budget flights on offer, which are available from throughout the UK. easyJet (www.easyjet.com), Ryanair (www.ryanair.com) LOT (www.lot.com) and British Airways (www.ba.com) all operate regular and affordable flights to Poland, with LOT also offering numerous internal flights between the major cities.

Public transport is cheap and efficient, although it can be overcrowded and very slow. The Polish State Railways company (www.pkp.com.pl) runs the train network, and if you are travelling long distances then this is the best option. There are various services available, with intercity and express trains operating between the main cities, and fast or normal trains serving the quieter areas. While services have been cut since communist times – especially to the more remote areas – fares are cheap and services are getting faster, especially on the mainline intercity and express services.

Buses are operated by PKS and PPKS, which offer reasonably cheap travel across the country, and there are many different regional operators. While sometimes slow, they do offer excellent coverage of the country.

In Poland's larger cities, trams are a cheap and effective way of travelling around, while Warsaw also has a metro system.

Learning the language

You may well encounter a language barrier in Poland, but the Polish people are more than happy to help you learn their language. English is a popular subject at school and given that 35% of Poles are under 25 years of age, the English-speaking population is growing. However, outside of the major conurbations, Russian and German are more commonly spoken, especially among the older population.

A difficult language to learn given the complex nature of the grammar, Polish is a phonetic language, making pronunciation easier. It uses the Latin-based alphabet rather than Cyrillic, and it has the second largest number of speakers among Slavic languages after Russian. Originating from several local Western Slavic dialects, Polish has close relations with Serbian.

Shopping

The Polish have certainly got a taste for Western European items, and so in the larger towns you will find many international brands and stores. Most grocery shops are open from 7am to 7pm; some are open on Saturdays but all are shut on Sundays. There are numerous supermarkets belonging to international chains, many of which are open 24/7. Modern shopping malls are becoming more frequent in the larger cities, such as Warsaw. Still, spare some time to tour the *bazary* (market places), which are usually located close to the main shopping centre, and where you can buy almost everything, most notably fresh fruit and vegetables.

Once outside the main cities you may find it harder to find certain imports. While shopping is cheaper in Poland at present, it is unlikely that prices will remain low as the country continues to develop economically.

Post

Post offices are generally open 7am–9pm, Monday–Friday; 8am–3pm, Saturday and are closed all day Sunday.

As with most European post offices, you have the option of paying your bills and opening a savings account. The Polish Post Office can be visited at www.poczta-polska.pl.

Corruption, crime and police

An inefficient commercial court system, a rigid labour code, bureaucratic red tape and persistent corruption keep the private sector from performing to its potential. The corruption rate of the country currently sits at 3.7 (the worst rating you can have is 0, the best is 10) and the country's reputation does suffer from the levels of bribery and corruption that occur – an unfortunate hangover from communist days. Foreigners will be exposed to this sort of problem when it comes to pricing – be aware of double standards, as you may well get charged a higher rate for goods than a local would. Also, be aware of unscrupulous developers who may try to sell you poor-quality property.

While the police hierarchy has been overhauled, removing the secret police elements, they are a dispirited lot, and while violent crime in the country is generally low, there has been a rise in instances of street crime.

13
Romania

COUNTRY PROFILE

A country of outstanding natural beauty and home to one of the world's most enduring myths – that of Dracula, based on the historical figure of Vlad the Impaler – Romania has reinvented itself as Europe's biggest investment opportunity.

Did you know?
While most people know that the mythical Dracula lived in Transylvania, many don't know that Bram Stoker's infamous count was based on the real-life figure of Vlad Ţepeş. Ţepeş intermittently ruled an area of the Balkans called

Wallachia in the 15th century, and was also known as Vlad III, Vlad Dracula and Vlad the Impaler. The word Ţepeş actually means 'impaler', and he was so named due to his penchant for killing his victims by impaling them on stakes. He is thought to have killed between 40,000 to 100,000 people in this fashion.

Why buy in Romania?

With a lack of available property, cheap prices and rising numbers of affluent Romanians, demand is growing for good-quality homes. Couple this with Romania's burgeoning economy and a rapidly-growing property market and you have a superb environment for investment.

The Romanian economy is growing fast, with GDP currently sitting at a massive 7.8%. Jobs are on the increase, wages are rising and thanks to the skilled labour force, foreign direct investment into the country is rising too – by the end of 2005, $13.6 billion had been invested here, with multinationals such as Avon, Wrigleys and Renault settling in the country.

Romania formally assumed EU membership as of 1st January 2007 and this has had, and will continue to have, a positive impact on the country's growth, with EU funding helping to reform the infrastructure and economy.

In terms of tourism, Romania is the fourth largest-growing economy, and between 2007–2016, it is believed the annual average rate of tourist growth will be 7.9%. As the tourist industry becomes better established, then this is destined to further fuel the property market.

Outside of the macroeconomic factors, Romania is an extremely beautiful and welcoming country. The scenery is stunning and unspoilt, the coastline is superb, stretching for 244 kilometres, and the summer climate is characteristic of Central Europe. There are a number of spas in the country, which provide various treatments, while there are also good, cheap skiing facilities. Other outdoor activities include bear and wolf tracking, trekking the Carpathians and bird watching on the Danube Delta.

Culturally, the country is extremely well developed, with numerous UNESCO World Heritage sites and some fabulous towns and cities – including Braşov, Timişoara, Sighişoara and Bucharest, to name but a few.

Politics and economy

Another of Eastern Europe's post communist countries, today Romania is a stable parliamentary democracy where executive functions are shared between the President and the Prime Minister. The current President is Traian Băsescu and the Prime Minister Călin Popescu-Tăriceanu. Currently, Romania is enjoying an atmosphere of stability and cohesion, and while economic recession and financial scandal have been rife since the fall of communism, the country is making great leaps towards becoming a free market economy. However, a certain amount of realism should be kept in mind. Romania is still one of Europe's poorest countries, even though it is hoped that EU accession and the consequent funds will help revitalise an economy left bankrupt from many years under the rule of the dictator Ceauşescu. Emerging from three years of recession in 2000, since then the government has been working on re-invigorating industry and has privatised a number of previously state-owned enterprises. With growing demand for Romanian exports and low unemployment, the future looks promising, with the property market and the level of foreign direct investment set to expand.

Geography and climate

Southeastern Europe's largest country, covering 238,391 square kilometres, Romania borders the Ukraine, Moldova, Hungary, Bulgaria, Serbia and Montenegro, with a coastline to the southeast which borders the Black Sea. The Danube flows along the southern border and its delta leads into the Black Sea to the north of the resort of Constanţa. The country is clearly split in two by the Transylvanian Alps and the Carpathian Mountains which sweep from the north to western Romania, clearly dividing the regions of Transylvania to the north and Wallachia in the south. Thanks to the varied topography, Romania's wild, mountainous landscape is tempered by the Black Sea beaches and Europe's largest delta, that of the Danube – also a biosphere reserve and World Heritage site – to the Parisian boulevards of Bucharest.

The Romanian climate can be very changeable and also severe, especially in the winter months when the landscape remains snow-clad for many weeks, with plummeting temperatures of between –15 and –20°C and icy winds from Russia. Spring is wet but pleasant, heralding a season of blue skies, but it isn't until May that the weather really warms up. The summer months are hot, with nine to ten hours of sunshine a day, particularly along the coast. The autumn months are cool, marking the start of the migration of the millions of birds on the delta.

History and culture

There is evidence that Romania has been inhabited since prehistoric times. In recent years, the country has experienced long periods of occupation at the hands of the Hapsburgs, Ottomans, Austro-Hungarians and Russians. It wasn't until 1859 that the modern state of Romania took form, with the merging of the principalities of Moldavia and Wallachia. On the side of the allies in WWI, Romania was conquered and occupied by the Austro-Hungarians and Russians, and at the war's end, Transylvania was returned to Romania by Hungary. However, on the side of Nazi Germany during WWII, Romania was taken by Russian forces during the Axis powers' defeat, and a communist regime was soon implemented, with the Russian forces maintaining *de facto* control until the 50s, forcing the abdication of the Romanian king. Following the retreat of communist troops in 1958, Romania became an independent state, and while maintaining a Stalinist policy throughout the 60s and early 70s, the country had a very open relationship with the world, cultivating close ties with Germany. Economic growth continued throughout this period, based on foreign loans and the increasing influence of international financial bodies such as the IMF – a policy which flew in the face of communist leader Nicolae Ceauşescu's policies and eventually resulted in a reimbursement of foreign loans which crippled and impoverished Romania's people and economy. In 1989

Romania revolted, overthrowing Ceauşescu which eventually resulted in the creation of a democratic republic.

A cultural hotbed, Romania's chequered past has developed a varied identity in the country. The Romans left a massive influence in the form of the Latin-based Romanian language and the architecture, with historic castles, traditional villages and colourful wood-built churches, while Romania is also home to the infamous Count Dracula. There are a number of UNESCO World Heritage sites, including the wooden churches of Maramureş, the citadel of Sighişoara, the painted churches of northern Moldavia, the Saxon fortified churches of Transylvania and the Dacian fortresses of the Orăştie Mountains. Bucharest is known as the 'Paris of the East' and offers elegant architecture and wide, leafy boulevards, while the region of Wallachia is home to a strong gypsy culture.

Religion

Christian Orthodoxy is Romania's leading religion, practised by 90% of the population, despite the fact that Romania is a secular state with no national religion. The remaining 10% consists of Roman Catholics (5%) and Protestants and Jews (5%).

Tourism and getting there

The tourist situation is comparable with that of the Czech Republic ten years ago. The fourth fastest-growing tourist economy in the world, while only six million people visit every year, the industry is predicted to grow by 7.9% per annum between 2007 and 2016. Tourism has a hugely important role to play in Romania's future economic and social development, with the 2006 tourism economy contributing 4.8% to Romania's GDP and accounting for 485,000 jobs, representing 5.8% of total employment. Over the next ten years, travel and tourism in the country is forecast to achieve annual growth of 6.7% in terms of GDP and 1.6% in terms of employment. This would take the share of GDP and employment to 5.8 and 6.9% respectively by 2016. While there is an increase in tourists from Western Europe, most come from neighbouring countries which are equally poor. If Romania is to develop economically, it is essential that the tourist economy is well marketed and developed in the west and also that budget flights are introduced into Bucharest.

There are currently four international airports in Romania, with the majority of international flights using Henry Coanda Bucharest airport. Considerable investment is needed to ensure that these airports are able to cope with more visitors and upgrading of Sibiu Airport is already under way, which will provide an important access point to Transylvania. Currently, Wizz Air (http://wizzair.com) offer flights from London Luton to Bucharest and British Airways (www.ba.com) fly to Bucharest, Timişoara and Targu Mures from Heathrow.

The cost of living

The cost of living in Romania is among the lowest in Europe, with services and products almost 50% cheaper than those of their Western European counterparts. In Bucharest, a loaf of bread costs as little as 9p, half a litre of beer from 10p to 40p, and a litre of milk 8p – and this is the most expensive city in the country! However, the cheap cost of living does reflect the living standards, with Romania not offering the quality of living of many of its other, more developed Eastern European counterparts.

Food and drink

Romanian fare is not designed to be *à la carte* but instead to be warm, filling and nutritious to help you cope with the cold, harsh climes. Pork dominates the menu, along with cabbage and potatoes. More traditional dishes include *sarmale* (cabbage leaves stuffed with rice, meat and herbs) and *mušchi poiana* (beef stuffed with mushrooms, bacon, pepper and paprika), with many Hungarian and Turkish influences evident in dishes such as moussaka and hotpots.

Romania offers some good wines, although beers tend to be imported.

257

The national beverage is a plum brandy known as *ţuică* and there are numerous coffee shops in which you can stop off and enjoy a pastry and a hot beverage – Romanians take their coffee black and sweet.

THE PROPERTY MARKET

On the cusp of a real estate market boom, Romania is tipped as the next big investment market. However, just because the country looks set to see an explosion in prices doesn't automatically mean you'll make a killing – you need to invest your money wisely and, more importantly, you need to be an adventurous buyer.

Prior to EU accession, prices had been rising at around 30% per annum, with the country enjoying extremely good economic prospects, foreign investment and a strengthening of the currency. A fast-moving market since 2003, the turnover of property was rapid as buyers clamoured to take advantage of the spiralling appreciation rates. Land has seen price growth of between 300% and 1,000% in the last six years, while in the summer of 2004, prices increased by an incredible 80%. Massive regeneration and infrastructure investment are expected to provide future investors with massive returns, while the low prices, growing market awareness and the relaxed regulations and property legislation have encouraged a frenzy of buyer activity.

Currently, property remains cheap by Western standards, with country houses in need of renovation on sale for a mere £5,000. In Bucharest, prices for newly-built apartments start at £40,000, rising to £300,000, while in other towns and cities you're looking at £45,000 to £150,000 for the same type of property. In rural areas, a three-bedroomed country house can be picked up for as little as £25,000. The average property price in Romania is £17,000.

Buyers tend to be buy-to-let investors, rather than permanent relocators. Permanent purchases are still predominantly focused around local buyers, with massive growth in the sales market in recent years. It's expected that property prices will continue rising strongly following EU accession. *A Place in the Sun* magazine predict that the next decade will see price rises of an astonishing 414%. Romania should see increases of 20–30% in 2007, with many new developments and apartments being introduced into the market. It is estimated that a property purchased today for €175,000 could be sold for as much as €750,000 after 10 years. Long-term, the forecast is for a growth in demand as well as supply, as developers begin a flurry of newly-built complexes. Most experts believe that because of EU accession, soon there will be no restrictions on foreign ownership.

Where to buy

Bucharest

Bucharest is known as the 'Paris of the East' thanks to its sophisticated air and rich cultural scene, and it's the biggest market for property investors. However, compared with Paris prices, Bucharest offers a whole lot more for your money. Close to the most attractive areas for tourists – the Black Sea coast and Brasov – Bucharest is still fairly isolated from the rest of the country, situated as it is down in Romania's southeast. The city is the major entry point into the country, and as of January 2007, Wizz Air fly there from London Luton.

The ideal location for purchase of Romanian property, foreigners will generally be looking at buying a newly-built apartment in a development in the Bucharest suburbs. Prices start at around £80,000 for a newly-built city centre property, although one-bedroomed apartments can be picked up for £34,000 in the surrounding areas. Current annual appreciation growth rates are up to 20% in certain areas, a rate set to be sustained or even increased between 2007 and 2010. Knight Frank report average returns of 12.5% for 2007. While there is substantial growth in the market, thanks largely to massive investment into the capital, you still need to assess the potential very carefully as it is early days.

Rental potential is growing thanks to the influx of businesses and the local population looking for better quality property. You can generate €500 a month for a one-bedroomed apartment and you can purchase a property with a two-year guaranteed rental yield of 7%.

Timişoara

Located on Romania's western boundary, Timişoara is known as 'Little Venice' and is the country's fourth largest city. Full of historic buildings, it is rapidly developing as a cultural centre, attracting increasing numbers of tourists. There has been an increased demand for property since 2001, with the last two years seeing prices growing from € 10 a square metre to € 30, with forecasts that this will rise to € 75 in 2007. A city which is labelled as being a safe bet for property investors, there is a lot of construction and development taking place due to the demand for better quality housing to replace the communist-style properties. The average price of a two-bedroomed property currently sits at less than € 50,000.

Brasov

Situated in the heart of Transylvania, Brasov offers the best return on investment in Romania as an international airport is currently being built, as is a motorway between Budapest and Bucharest, which will pass through the city. Industry is developing at a rapid rate. Well located, Brasov is only a few minutes' drive from Poiana Brasov, the main ski resort in Romania, and it's close to the 2007 European Capital of Culture, Sibiu, which is also attracting an increasing number of buyers. There is excellent rental potential with long-term demand from the local market and increasing numbers of tourists fuelling the short-term market. You can expect to generate yields of 7%. There is a mix of buyers, with both investors and holiday makers purchasing here, yet prices remain affordable – a one-bedroomed apartment can be picked up for € 40,000.

The Black Sea Coast

Running for 244 kilometres, the coast and its sandy beaches are popular with tourists, and this is the most well-known investment destination outside of Bucharest. Easily accessible, being close to the international airports of Bucharest and Constanta, Western Europeans have only just started discovering and investing in this area.

Prices here have risen by 100% in the last in the last few years, although you can still purchase a one-bedroomed apartment from € 35,000.

Generally, buyers are both investors and holiday makers, as this is an excellent location for family holidays, thanks to the gorgeous scenery and numerous activities on offer.

The main resorts are Mangalia; Mamaia, the coastline's oldest resort; Constanta, Romania's second largest city; and the spa town of Eforie Nord. While there is much interest from the local holiday market, there are still limited numbers of westerners renting here. Expect returns of 6% to be gained from the holiday let market.

Romanian countryside

The Romanian countryside offers some of Europe's lowest prices, although don't expect to experience the same level of price appreciation that you would in the towns and cities. Buyers will need to be prepared to spend some time renovating and bringing property in line with Western standards, but for €15,000 you can purchase a two-bedroomed house. Most buyers looking at these rural areas are doing so for relocation purposes.

What to buy

The best and safest investments in Romania are in the areas where there has been economic, commercial and tourist growth. These tend to offer the most market stability and also the least amount of corruption.

The most popular properties are those that offer the best chances for resale, and you can maximise your income by buying in a newly-built development. While there are plenty of renovation projects and older properties you can buy, there is limited demand for resale, and you will not be making as much money in terms of appreciation as you would for newly-built homes. Keep an eye on the construction market though, as if you buy a newly-built property, in order to maximise your income you will need to sell before demand and supply equalise.

While you will need to set up a company in order to buy land, there is money to be made by doing so, especially along the Black Sea Coast. This option will soon become more attractive as the legislation regarding land purchase is set to change within five years of EU accession, allowing foreigners to buy land as individuals.

THE BUYING PROCESS

While many restrictions upon foreign buyers have been removed, this is a very young market and there are still problems to be faced. However, now that Romania is a member of the EU, many of these obstacles are being removed.

Stage 1: Restrictions on foreign buyers

Foreigners who want to buy a property in Romania should be aware that they do not enjoy the same level of freedom as local buyers. In order to purchase land, you will need to set up a limited Romanian company. This is likely to be phased out within five years of EU accession, but for now it is a requirement. It's a mere technicality and will only set you back by £300, but make sure you employ an English-speaking lawyer based in Romania to take you through the process. While you could complete this within one day, it is more likely that it will take between two to three months to process. There are no restrictions on buying property.

Stage 2: Financing your purchase

In 2006, the Romanian mortgage market was changed to allow foreigners to secure a mortgage in the country. However, while this may be possible in theory, in practice it is still early days and some banks may be rather reluctant. If you're buying land, you may also have problems persuading a bank to lend to a company with no credit history.

Consequently, it is recommended that you secure your mortgage through a specialist mortgage company or by raising the money through re-mortgaging your UK home. It is possible to secure a mortgage in a variety of currencies and typically; you'll be looking at 75% LTV.

Stage 3: Surveys

Many of the older Romanian buildings are structurally unsound and although getting a survey carried out isn't something that is typically part of the conveyancing process, it is well worth doing.

Stage 4: The buying process

Before signing anything, ensure you have secured the best legal advice possible, especially as Romanian property titles can be defective. You also need to secure the services of your own lawyer as the notary in Romania is a neutral party.

Once you have found a property you like, the first step is to reserve it through a reservation contract. Once you have reserved the property, you can sign the preliminary contract. This binds both the buyer and the seller to the sale, so ensure that the property title has been checked and is clean before you do so. Should either side pull out, it will result in court action, which can be a costly and lengthy procedure.

Once the preliminary contract has been signed, you will need to pay a 10–20% deposit and then begin a thorough round of background checks on the property and secure all outstanding funds required to complete the conveyancing purchase.

Stage 5: Titles

Romania is a country fraught with problems when it comes to real estate titles. Under the dictatorship of Ceauşescu, land and property were confiscated and since his downfall, previous owners have been entitled to reclaim it – many cases are still in court. Consequently, potential buyers must ensure they do their homework and avoid buying a property with a defective title or with ownership which is under dispute. Employ a lawyer and get them to check everything from the property being in an earthquake zone to having more than one owner named or any outstanding fees against the title.

Checking the property's background has been made difficult due to the poor health of the land registry system. While the government is striving to clean up the entire process, progress is painfully slow. Once you have completed the sale, the contract will be sent to the land registry office to transfer the property into your name.

Stage 6: Completing the sale

Once you are assured that your lawyer has exhausted the background checks on the property title and secured all the necessary paperwork – including either your company registration documents or your permission to buy – you can go ahead and sign the final contract in the presence of a notary. Once signed, you will need to pay the remainder of the balance of the property price.

Stage 7: Additional costs

Purchasing costs are lower than in many other Eastern European countries, roughly around 3–4% of the price of the property. Stamp duty is around 2% of the property price, estate agents' fees between 2–6% and legal fees between 2–10%. Notary fees usually come in at around £200.

THE LETTINGS MARKET

In Romania there are no legal differences between buying a property to let and buying a property for personal use, but you will need to pay a tax of 16% on your profit. While this may be an attractive proposition to investors, the rentals market has yet to take off, being very immature and yielding roughly 6–7% per annum. This is further exacerbated by the fact that Romanian citizens prefer to own rather than rent homes.

While the tourist industry is rapidly expanding, it is still very limited, with most tourists coming from Eastern Europe and having very limited budgets, meaning you cannot expect a significant income from short-term lets. In the long term, the larger towns and cities are generating increasing levels of interest as more companies relocate to Romania, creating a demand from their employees.

If you are aiming to let short term, you may be better off looking to the cities or ski resorts, as the summer season is very limited and the latter locations can offer a year-round season.

The market is definitely strengthening, with yields growing over the last few years, but don't expect to cover your costs or make a quick buck – the market needs to be given time to mature before you can start making a healthy profit. On average, you can expect to generate around £300 a week in Bucharest; outside the capital, you can probably generate this level of income in a month.

RENOVATING A PROPERTY

There are a number of properties that require renovation or are structurally unsound in Romania, meaning that if you are looking for a DIY project then you're in the right country. However, while Romanian labour is cheap and their standards high, organising a renovation can be difficult, especially due to the language barrier you will undoubtedly encounter. You will also need to look at getting clearance from the local mayor's office, which can be time consuming and tricky, requiring you to grease a few wheels along the way. If you are seeking to buy a historic property then ensure you check its classification, as foreigners are restricted from buying property which is of national value.

Finally, be aware that if you are buying to renovate, this should be a personal project as there is a very limited market for traditional renovated homes, especially in rural areas. Always get the right advice and support as renovating will be a tricky project.

LIVING IN ROMANIA

Daily life and people

With Romanians able to trace their ancestry back to the days of the Romans, they also claim similar character traits, being lively, sociable and warm people who live life to the full. Embracing EU accession with open arms, the Romanians are reportedly keen to be part of a greater Europe, especially the younger generation who have an incredibly optimistic outlook.

Family values are hugely important in Romania, as they are in many other Eastern European countries, with art and music also central to life and reflecting the strong folklore roots.

Visas, permits and residency

UK, USA and EU residents do not require a visa to enter Romania for a period of up to 90 days, but if you intend to stay for longer, you must register for a temporary residency permit at the local passport office within 15 days of first entering the country. Once you are registered, you will be issued with a residency permit that is valid for one year and can be renewed at the end of this period for between three and six years. Once the temporary permit has expired and depending on your individual situation, you will be able to apply for permanent residency.

Utilities

In order to get connected to utilities, you first need to register for them. This can be a lengthy process that's likely to take a few weeks. You will first be required to secure a document from the land registry stating that you are the new owner of the property, but instead of then attempting to connect to utilities yourself, unless you speak Romanian, it is recommended that you organise for your estate agent to sort this out for you.

Most utility companies are state owned. Gas is available from local gas stations, while water and sewage are organised by the local government. Electricity is generally supplied by Electrica (www.electrica.ro). Bills tend to be cheap, but not all utilties are available depending on how isolated the area is. As you may well be required to pay in advance for your heating or electricity – Romania is still very much a cash-only country – you should contact the Ministry of Industry and Trade for details on the county you are looking to buy in.

Mobile phones are owned by 20% of Romanians, and Orange have a mobile phone company operating in Romania (www.orange.ro) as do Alcatel Romania (www.alcatel-lucent.ro), who also offer broadband services.

Banking and currency

The Romanian currency is the leu, with one leu subdivided into 100 bani. Coins can be acquired in denominations of 5, 10, 50 bani and banknotes in 1, 5, 10, 50, 100, 200, 500 lei. Romania is expected to adopt the euro in 2014.

In order to open a bank account, you only need your passport and there is a choice of opening a euro, Romania leu or pound sterling account, with a £35 deposit. There are a number of banks which offer services in English:

- Alpha Bank, www.alphabank.ro
- BRD – Groupe Société Générale, www.brd.ro
- Citibank, www.citibank.com
- HVB Banca Tiriac, www.unicredit-tiriac.ro
- National Bank of Romania, www.bnro.ro
- ING Romania, www.ingromania.ro.

Opening hours are usually 9am to 1pm, Monday to Friday.

Taxes

As with all countries, taxes apply depending on whether or not you are classed as a tax resident in Romania. You are classed as a tax resident if you reside in the country on a permanent basis, or spend at least 183 days a year there. Companies are classed as tax residents if the management of the company is based in Romania. As a tax resident you will be taxed on your Romanian and worldwide income, but as there is a double taxation treaty in place with the UK, you will not be taxed twice. Non-residents will only be taxed on income generated in Romania, such as rental income.

Income tax and corporation tax are levied at a flat rate of 16%, as is capital gains tax for both individuals and companies. However, if you have owned a property for two years, this rate drops to 10% with no capital gains payable if you sell the property after three years of ownership. VAT is usually levied at 19%.

Insurance

It is recommended that you take out private medical insurance in Romania. There are many companies that offer insurance for your car and home and you should have few problems finding an English speaker, as many of these firms are part of international corporations:

AIG, www.aiglife.ro

BT Asigurări, www.bta.ro

The Generali Group, www.generali.com

Omniasig, www.omniasig.ro

Healthcare

Healthcare standards in Romania are very poor, so foreigners must ensure they get private medical insurance to cover any treatment they may need. While doctors are well trained, facilities are poor and English is not widely spoken, especially outside of the larger hospitals.

As Romania is now part of the EU, all EU residents are entitled to free medical treatment on the production of an EHIC card. Visit the Department of Health website, www.dh.gov.uk, for more details. However you may be expected to pay cash upfront for any additional treatment in a state hospital, or just to ensure you get the best treatment possible.

Retirement

It is still early days in the Romanian property market and consequently most buyers tend to be investors rather than permanent relocators, with no expat community existing there yet. As such, anyone thinking of retiring to Romania needs to be prepared for a big culture shock, and to have a real sense of adventure!

Education

The education system in Romania underwent a major overhaul following the collapse of communism in 1989. Education in Romania is not up to the standards of Western Europe and so if you are looking to relocate with your family, it is recommended that you educate your children in an international school.

- Fundatia International British School of Bucharest, www.cobisec.org
- American International School of Bucharest, www.aisb.ro
- The International School of Budapest, www.isb.ro
- Cernavoda International School (tel. +40 241 239 090)
- International Computer High School of Constantza, www.ichc.ro
- Acorns British Style Nursery, www.acorns.ro.

Should you look at enrolling your child in a Romanian school, while you are entitled to education, be aware that all applications are vetted by the International Relations Department within the Ministry of Education.

Driving

While the Romanian driving laws are strict, Romanian drivers often flout or disregard them. The standard of roads varies dramatically throughout the country, with the main roads and one motorway – Pitesti to Bucharest – being in good condition, while rural roads are full of potholes. Romanian roads tend to be traffic free outside of the larger towns and cities, and they are also often very scenic – driving is possibly the best way to see the country.

Romanians drive on the right and your British driving licence is valid so long as it carries a photo; otherwise, an international driving licence is required. The speed limits are as follows:

- motorways: 130km/h (80mph);
- open roads: 90km/h (55mph);
- towns: 50km/h (31mph).

Be aware that in rural and mountainous areas, roads can be perilous and there is the possibility of meeting horse-drawn carts, pedestrians and animals.

Getting around

There are some domestic flights in operation in Romania, with Tarom (www.tarom.ro) serving several Romanian cities from Bucharest. If you are looking to travel by bus be prepared for some confusion, as they are fairly sporadic, and bus stops are not clearly marked. There are several operators in the country, with one of the largest being Autogari (www.autogari.ro), which connects most of Romania's major towns and cities. Eurolines (www.eurolines.ro) also offer services between Romanian cities, as well as international services.

While facilities can be very basic, the Romanian railways serve every nook and cranny of this scenic country, with prices being amazingly cheap and the service prompt. The Romanian Railway is run by CFR (www.cfr.ro). In Bucharest you can get about by tram, trolley bus, metro or bus – www.romaniatourism.com has full details on transport in the city.

Learning the language

Unlike its Eastern European counterparts, Romanian is a Romance language, descended from Latin and being part of the French, Spanish and Italian group. While English is increasingly spoken among students, there are still many people who only speak Romanian and so it is recommended that you get to grips with some basic phrases and employ the services of a local – either your lawyer or estate agent – to help you get settled in the country. A smattering of German is spoken in some areas, and Hungarian in Transylvania. While Russian was once widely spoken and is still well known, Romanians are reluctant to speak it.

Romanian has a distinctive eastern influence, with a number of words adopted from Turkish and Greek. However, those with knowledge of a Romance language will find it easier to learn Romanian than many other Eastern European languages, and many words are instantly recognisable.

Shopping

Shops are normally open from 9am to 6pm. While there are hordes of Dracula T-shirts and the usual tourist tat, there are also a number of attractive handmade items on sale in Romania, plus some excellent flea and antique markets.

Imported goods are extremely expensive in comparison with local products, such as Romanian wine, which is excellent and only costs around £2 a bottle. However, even Bucharest isn't the destination for a long weekend of shopping, with only the World Trade Plaza (www.wtcb.ro) and Unirea Shopping Centre (www.unireashop.ro) offering a good selection of upmarket products.

There are a number of supermarkets and hypermarkets where you can buy all the produce you need, such as the Metro chain, Billa supermarkets (www.billa.ro) and Penny Market, with Tesco looking to launch into the market in the future.

Post

Post offices tend to be open from 7am to 8pm, Monday to Friday. As in the UK, post boxes are red, and they are clearly labelled *Poştă*, as are all Post Offices. It normally takes around five days for a letter to reach the UK from Romania and two weeks to Australia or America. Visit www.posta-romana.ro for more details.

Crime, corruption and the police

Romania does suffer from corruption, with legislation changing regularly and a weak enforcement of property laws. Agents insist that while bribery was rife five to ten years ago, today things are much safer. However, you need to be careful about who you buy from and to make sure you avoid being charged more than a local purchaser.

If there is an emergency, dial 112 or 955 for the police.

14
Slovakia

Factfile
Population: 5.4 million
Population growth rate: 0.15%
Area: 49,037 km²
Capital city: Bratislava (population 450,000)
Inflation: 3.7%
GDP growth rate: 6.0%
Unemployment rate: 16%
Net migration: 0.3 migrants per 1,000
Currency: Slovak Crown (Koruna)
Exchange rate: £1=49SKK
EU status: Member as of May 2004
Time zone: CET (GMT +1 hour)

COUNTRY PROFILE

Experiencing market growth similar to that of the Baltic States and described as being the next Hong Kong, Slovakia has been labelled an investment paradise.

Did you know?
- Famous Slovakian's include Eugen Andrew Cernan, who was of Slovakian origin, and the second American to walk on the moon; Jozef Murgaš, a Roman Catholic priest, who contributed to the invention of radiotelegraphy, a feat which earned him the nickname the Radio Priest; Štefan Bani ,

inventor of the first military parachute and BASE jumping – he based the design on the principle of the umbrella; and Maximilián Hell, the first astronomer to measure the distance between the Earth and the Sun.

- The hill known as Krahule, near the town Kremnica, is the geographical centre of Europe.
- In 2007, the Slovakian automotive industry is estimated to produce 950,000–1 million cars, giving the country the highest per capita car production in the world.

Why buy in Slovakia?

Budget flights regularly fly into Bratislava, helping to stimulate the already healthy tourism market, while recent reforms of the political and social system and the introduction of a flat tax rate of 19% have transformed Slovakia into Europe's tax haven. Set to adopt the euro in 2009 and with annual GDP growth of 6% – expected to rise to 7% in 2007 and beyond – Slovakia offers some excellent incentives to investors.

Following a period of stability in the market, supply is now outstripping demand quite significantly, especially in the capital Bratislava, and so prices are set to rise for the foreseeable future. Prosperity in the country is leading to a local desire to see the poor-quality housing replaced by new developments, there has been a growth in both construction and the mortgage market, and if the euro really is adopted in 2009 then this is going to lead to a boom in prices and investment.

Despite modernising and following a westernised economic model, Slovakia hasn't been overcome by the negative attributes of western commercialism and remains very much an unspoilt country. For those seeking to buy in a place which offers beach resorts and bars, this isn't it. Thanks to Slovakia's many attractions and the numerous activities which can be enjoyed – such as skiing, caving, and walking – this really is a location for the more sophisticated buyer. What's more, rental yields are currently between 8% to 10% meaning that you can look at generating a subsidiary income while watching your investment appreciate at a rapid rate.

Politics and economy

Slovakia is a parliamentary republic and has been since 1993 when the state of Czechoslovakia was dissolved. Part of NATO and an EU member since 2004, the country hopes to be using the euro by 2009. The current President is Ivan Gašparovič and the Prime Minister – who holds the most power – is Robert Fico.

Economically, Slovakia is in the process of transition, moving towards a more western-style economy which relies on services and away from the traditional industry-heavy economy. The former Prime Minister, Mikuláš Dzurinda, initiated a series of reforms that overhauled the labour, tax, pensions and healthcare systems and helped fast track Slovakia to the position as Europe's fastest growing country economically. Annual GDP growth has been averaging 6% per annum since 2004, with 2007 expected to see this rise to 7%. Since 1999, foreign direct investment has quintupled and in 2004 the World Bank labelled Slovakia as having the fastest improving environment for investors. This is largely thanks to Slovakia's flat tax system of 19%, which allowed the government to abandon stamp duty.

With affluence on the rise and wage growth outperforming that of the Baltics at 7%, the government managed to reduce the budget deficit from 7.2% to 3.6% in just two years. When compared to many of its Eastern European counterparts, Slovakia is clearly head and shoulders above the rest when it comes to economic dynamism and investment opportunities.

Geography and climate

Situated more in central than Eastern Europe, Slovakia is well located in terms of accessibility, lying in Europe's heartland. Covering just over 49,000 square kilometres, the country borders Hungary, Austria, the Czech Republic, the Ukraine and Poland.

Around 40% of the country is forested, with most of central and northern Slovakia covered by the Carpathian Mountains, which are home to some stunning lakes, valleys and caves, and prime skiing territory. To the south is the capital, Bratislava, while to the east of the city are the Slovakian lowlands and the Danube basin.

With bitterly cold winters and hot, wet summers, spring sees an explosion of blooms and boasts sunny but chilly days, perfect for exploring the country. There is an average of 135 days of snow per year in the mountainous areas, while the lowlands enjoy a more temperate climate.

History and culture

Invaded by the Celts in 450BC, the Slovakian people have occupied their country since the 5th century. Slovakia has spent most of its history under Hungarian or Austro-Hungarian rule, a situation which prevailed from the 11th century until the collapse of the Austro-Hungarian Empire at the end of WWI. Following the end of the war, Czechoslovakia was formed, which was subjected to communist rule from the end of WWII until 1989. On 1st January 1993, the Czechs and Slovaks agreed to dissolve Czechoslovakia and go their separate ways as two independent states.

Boasting some stunning ecclesiastical history – centred around the towns of Trnava and Nitra – and peppered with a huge number of traditional wooden churches, Slovakia doesn't seem to have been ravaged by its years under communism. Bratislava has seen its old town restored and while there is evidence of communist tower blocks, for the most part your interest is captured by the baroque architecture and broad, tree-lined boulevards. Dotted with picturesque medieval towns, the country is a haven for hikers and nature lovers. The Tatra National Park boasts some stunning walks, while the Tatras mountains are home to eagles, wolves, bears and otters, and there are plenty of skiing opportunities available. There are numerous opportunities for spelunking (cave exploration), a strong spa culture with over 1,000 springs dotted around the country, and sightseers will have their hands full trying to get round the 200 castles and fortifications the country boasts.

Slovakia enjoys a mix of nationalities, with the largest group – around 10% – being Hungarian. You will find that many road signs are written in Magyar as well as Slovakian. There is also a large Roma population, which makes up around 1.7% of the total population.

Religion

A religiously tolerant country, the largest group are the Roman Catholics, accounting for almost 70% of the population. The second largest denomination are Protestant (9%), with 13% following no religion.

Tourism and getting there

The tourist industry is rapidly growing in Slovakia, with over 30 million people visiting the country in 2006. Visitors weren't allowed to enter the country during the communist era, but since the 90s, Slovakia has been receiving more than 500,000 tourists each year. Thanks to the spas, skiing, caving, culture and beautiful landscape, the country is destined to continue attracting visitors, especially as the affluence and economy continue to develop.

There are numerous budget flights into Slovakia, with Ryanair (www.ryanair.com) flying into Bratislava and Sky Europe (www1.skyeurope.com) flying into Bratislava, Kosice and Poprad-Tatry from London.

Cost of living

Slovakia is still an affordable country to live in and visit, although imported goods can be costly. A meal out can cost around £7 per person – obviously being more expensive in Bratislava – while the average weekly shopping bill is around £20. Even though Bratislava sits above Prague in the *Mercer Cost of Living Survey*, outside of the capital costs are much lower – whereas a meal may cost SKK1,000 (£20) in Bratislava, you are looking at closer to SKK650 (£14) elsewhere.

Food and drink

Given the ties between the two countries, there are many similarities between Slovak and Czech cuisine. However, Slovakian recipes have a hint of Hungarian spice, thanks to the many years under Magyar rule; goulash is a popular dish here.

Thanks to the cold climes that Slovaks have to endure, meals are loaded with carbohydrates, with lots of thick soups and potatoes. The heartiest meal of the day is dinner, which usually consists of warming soups and a meat-laden main course. Typical fare includes *kapustnica* (a hearty, sour cabbage soup with smoked pork sausage), while potato gnocchi with sheep's cheese and bacon is the national dish.

The main wine-producing region is situated down towards the Hungarian border, although Slovakia isn't renowned for its varieties. Beer is the main drink here, with domestic brands such as Golden Pheasant, Topvar and Corgon the favoured tipple. Other beverages include juniper brandy (*borovicka*) and *slivovica*, a plum brandy.

THE PROPERTY MARKET

Ever since EU accession, Slovakia's property market has been developing at a staggering rate, yet still playing catch-up with markets such as Hungary and the Czech Republic. Unlike countries such as Bulgaria, Slovakia has been steadily attaining moderate levels of capital growth over the past few years without constantly being in the headlines, and has managed to develop without importing the burger bar aspect of Westernism into this staggeringly beautiful country. Between 2003 and 2004, prices were reported to have increased by 50% in some areas and thanks to political and economic stability, coupled with EU memberships and planned euro adoption, the market is tipped to go from strength to strength, making it an ideal investment climate. *A Place in the Sun* magazine ranked Slovakia as seventh in the world for potential market growth, estimating a 307% return on investments in the next 10 years.

With demand from the local population growing and a maturing of the mortgage market, Slovakia is not totally reliant on foreign investment to sustain its immature property market. With more and more Slovaks joining the burgeoning middle class ranks, and as mortgages get cheaper, the Slovakian tendency to buy rather than rent is predicted to put a squeeze on a market which is already short of properties. Slovakia currently has the lowest construction rate in Europe, with a 50,000 house deficit per annum, which is good news for those thinking of buying into an appreciating market.

The market is predominantly focused on Bratislava, something that is set to change as the country is opened up to increasing tourist numbers and as Bratislava prices begin to reach a level with other European capitals. At present there is a shortage of good-quality property in Bratislava, which is helping to sustain the price hikes and as with many emerging markets, prices are much higher in the capital – £200,000 for an apartment – than elsewhere in the country, where you can purchase a villa for £30,000.

Where to buy

Bratislava

When looking at where to buy, Bratislava is still the magnet for overseas buyers. Set to undergo a face lift, the Slovakian government are ensuring that Bratislava is going to be the place to be over the next few years. Regarded as a massively undervalued market, prices in the capital have increased rapidly over the last few years, with 2005 experiencing inflation of 10–15% and 2004 witnessing growth of 25%. These rises seem set to continue for the foreseeable future. While price hikes tapered off after initial rises, they have begun to rocket again as there continues to be a shortage of high-quality homes, and demand from the local market rises.

Bratislava's proximity to Vienna, Prague and Budapest is a major selling point for investors, as is the proximity of two airports within 45 minutes of the capital. Given that Vienna is double the price of Bratislava and a new motorway due to be completed in 2007 will connect the two, demand from Austrian citizens is again set to push prices higher. A good jet-to-let prospect, yields currently sit at around 8–10%.

With 17 residential districts, there is plenty of choice – perhaps too much. Foreigners aspire to purchase in the old town, but if you are looking to buy to let, the downtown area is the prime location for expat workers.

Tatras Mountains

Popular for many years with foreign and local tourists, the country's ski resorts enjoy excellent snow conditions, modern runs and facilities and natural attractions, such as caves, waterfalls, castles and thermal springs. Consequently, they are increasingly acquiring the status of property hotspots, attracting investors as well as second-home buyers. Agents believe that Slovakian ski resorts – and other major tourist centres – will see an increase in interest during 2007 and 2008. Though little is known about them by investors, in some instances they can often offer higher returns than Bratislava. Prices are being fuelled by the interest from wealthy Slovaks, who are willing to pay high prices for a weekend retreat in resorts of the High and Low Tatras, Velka and Mala Fatra. Nevertheless, you can still pick up a three-bedroomed house for £80,000.

Many new developments are planned for the Slovakian ski resorts, fuelled by the millions of euros that have been invested on new ski gondolas, slopes and lifts. If you are thinking of buying to rent here then ensure you buy close to an established resort such as Štrbské Pleso and Smokovce. Liptov and Poprad are also good bets, especially as Poprad has an international airport which is served by Sky Europe from London Stansted, with rumours that Ryanair may soon be flying there too.

Žilina and Trnava

Newly established in terms of interest from foreign investors, the cities of Žilina and Trnava have made it on to the investment radar in 2005–6 due to their recently-built manufacturing plants.

Žilina is Slovakia's third largest city, located in north-western Slovakia, 200km from the capital, Bratislava. An important industrial centre, Žilina is on the confluence of the Váh, Kysuca and Rajčanka rivers and it's surrounded by mountains. Trnava is a much smaller university town, located close to the capital, being only 45km to the northeast of Bratislava. A medieval town surrounded by ancient city walls, Trnava has a rich ecclesiastical heritage and because of the high number of churches within the town walls, it has often been referred to as 'Little Rome', or 'Slovak Rome'.

Both of these markets are very small, with property prices dependant on the location, style, age and type of property. Prices are an average of 30–50% cheaper than Bratislava, with communist built flats in Žilina and Trnava priced for as little as £15,000, with studio or one-bedroomed apartments selling for £30,000. The average price for a newly-built one- to two-bedroomed apartment sits at between £35,000–£70,000, with luxury flats in the centre going for £150,000 – however, these are hard to find. You can find houses for as little as £40,000 in the suburbs, but these are generally in very poor condition. Larger, newer houses can cost more than £400,000.

What to buy

Similar to Prague, Bratislava's market is dominated by newly-built properties and developments, although older properties are selling at a premium – just be sure that if you do look to buy a historic property that you check the title thoroughly. As a popular tourist and second-home location, there are a number of cottages or rural villas which can attract rental income and good rates of appreciation, especially in the Tatras Mountains. Generally speaking, you should steer clear of old communist-style housing, unless you are happy to live or stay there yourself. Giving the growing wealth of the locals, there are stronger resale and rental markets for newly-built modern apartments.

THE BUYING PROCESS

Despite being regarded as a safe place to invest, it is nevertheless essential that you get a reliable estate agent and legal team on board before you even contemplate looking for a property, especially as this is still a relatively unexplored country for foreign buyers.

Stage 1: Restrictions on foreign buyers

There are virtually no limits to foreigners buying a home in Slovakia, with the country lifting restrictions when it joined the EU in May 2004. The only exception is the purchase of forest and agricultural land. This means there's no need for foreigners to set up a company or seek the permission of local officials.

Stage 2: Financing your purchase

Since EU accession, foreigners have been free to apply for mortgages from local Slovakian banks, although the minimum equity required is generally 30% of the purchase price. You will also have to pay an arrangement fee of between 0.5% and 1%, with mortgage rates available at 6–7%.

Other options include using the equity from your UK home to pay for the property or arranging a loan through a specialist UK mortgage company.

Stage 3: Background checks and surveys

It's advisable to let your estate agent or lawyer carry out checks to ensure that the seller of the property you are thinking of buying is actually the registered owner. Some Slovakian properties – particularly the older ones – can have defective titles, so it's imperative that the deeds are checked with the land registry to ensure there are no outstanding debts or disputes over ownership.

Always get a surveyor's report carried out before signing the final contract to make sure there is no structural damage – this is especially important if you are purchasing an older property.

Stage 4: The contract

Once you have found the property you want to buy, you will be required to sign a preliminary contract and pay a deposit of between 10% and 30% in order to take it off the market. From then on, the conveyancing system varies depending on the type of property you are buying.

Buying a resale home

If you are purchasing an old or resale property typically you'll be looking at paying a smaller deposit of between 5% to 10%, with the remainder paid on completion during the signing of the final contract. This final signing requires both the buyer and seller to be present, and the process is witnessed by a notary. The contract will then be sent to the land registry office to allow the property to be transferred into your name, making you the official owner. The registration process takes about 30 days but you can pay to get it fast tracked in 15 days.

Buying off plan

The purchase of a newly-built property differs from that of a resale in terms of the stage payments. Firstly a larger deposit of 30% is paid on the signing of the preliminary contract, with the outstanding balance paid in instalments, the dates of which are written into the contract. Typically, these are broken down into two 30% payments, with the remaining 20% paid on the signing of the final contract. However, developers are increasingly offering a two-stage payment, with a 30% deposit paid initially, followed by the final 70% on completion.

Stage 5: Additional costs

There are few extra fees to be paid, given that the Slovakian government has abolished the payment of stamp duty and transfer tax. Estate agents' fees are generally charged at 3–6% and are normally split between both the buyer and seller – sometimes they are paid just by the seller. Legal costs vary, but are normally around £900, or more for a UK lawyer. Property registration costs £35 and notary fees a total of £100. Generally, the total payable extras come in at around 3–5% of the property's value.

THE LETTINGS MARKET

There isn't a strong culture among Slovakians for renting property, with only 3% of homes in the country let out. This trend has become increasingly apparent as mortgages have become more readily available and affordable to the local market. On average, buy-to-let investors can expect to generate yields of between 8–10% per annum with rental values in the town of Trnava increasing by 15% in the last 12 months.

The first thing to be aware of is that rental income is taxed as ordinary income at a flat rate of 19%, with loans and costs related to the property you are purchasing deductible from the taxable amount. You should also ensure you know which tenant group you intend to target before you start looking for a property. Think about what those tenants are looking for in terms of location and the rent they can afford. If you don't do your research then you may find it hard to make your property appealing to prospective tenants.

Bratislava offers the largest and most diverse rental market, with large demand from students who will pay €300 a month for a shared flat and low-income workers or younger couples who will pay €350. Don't expect to be able to tap into the middle-class market as they generally own their own homes.

In Bratislava, as well as Žilina and Trnava, there is a market to rent to foreign workers and in general these are the tenants you are likely to generate the best income from. However, be aware that they are only interested in high-class accommodation situated in the town centres, and there is a shortage of this in Žilina and Trnava. In Žilina, such rentals can generate €600–€1,200 a month and sometimes more.

RENOVATING A PROPERTY

As with any renovation project, be aware of the potential costs and difficulties you may encounter, made increasingly difficult due to language barriers and finding skilled workers, especially if you are going to be out of the country.

If you are looking to modernise a property, upgrading the bathroom or kitchen, then you will not need to seek planning permission. However, for work that affects the structure or appearance of a property then you will need to secure permission from your Local Buildings Office and this will incur a small fee.

You will be required to submit an application form, proof of ownership – this is obtained from the land registry – and detailed architectural plans of the work you intend to carry out. The application is usually approved or rejected within one month, although given the current levels of development within the country, there may be something of a backlog.

LIVING IN SLOVAKIA

People and daily life

Keen to shed the pall of communism that had previously hung over the country, the Slovaks are embracing their new-found prosperity with open arms. A peaceful people – highlighted by the lack of bloodshed that accompanied the Velvet Revolution of 1989 – the Slovaks are proud of their culture and traditions, which are kept alive today through food, music, poems, dance and song, in memory of the struggle they underwent to maintain their individuality during years of oppression. Friendly, polite and courteous, they are keen to make you feel welcome in their beautiful country.

Visas, permits and residency

EU citizens are entitled to stay in Slovakia for 90 days without applying for a visa and can work without securing a work permit. Any non-EU citizen should consult with their local Slovakian Embassy for visa details. All EU citizens have the right to work in any EU country without restriction and without the need of a work permit. However, for a longer stay, you'll need to apply for a residency permit in order to study or work in the country and this can be obtained from the Slovakian embassy in your country of residence. Applications may take up to 90 days and once you have been granted the permit, you will be required to register with the local police within three days of your arrival in Slovakia.

Utilities

As all utilities in Slovakia are state controlled, you can't choose your supplier, and instead need to go with the local operator. When you purchase your home, you will need to arrange for utilities to be connected and the account put in your name.

Electricity costs may be slightly higher than UK prices, but you do still pay for consumption. To avoid paying a reconnection fee, ensure you let the electricity company know you have occupied the house to avoid the meter being removed – they remove the electric meters within 10 days of the previous owner leaving and there's a £200 reconnection fee. The larger energy companies include Východoslovenská Energetika, a.s. (www.vse.sk), Slovenské Elektrárne, a. s. (www.seas.sk) and CEZ Group (www.cez.sk). Gas is generally only mains supplied in the large cities, with prices based on consumption, while water rates vary dramatically across the country.

Telephone services are generally provided by Slovak Telekom (www.slovaktelekom.sk), who also offer mobile phone coverage with T-Mobile (www.t-mobile.sk) and Orange (www.orange.sk). Broadband and internet services are still not widely available in Slovakia, but you can usually find somewhere in most towns to check your email.

As all utilities are state regulated, you can find out more at www.government.gov.sk, www.teleoff.gov.sk and www.telecom.gov.sk.

Banking and currency

The local currency is the Slovakian crown. One crown consists of 100 haliers and the currency comes in denominations of 5,000, 1,000, 500, 200, 100, 50 and 20 crown banknotes. Coins are circulated in the value of 10, 5, 2 and 1 crowns and 10, 20 and 50 haliers.

Generally open from 9am to 5pm, the Slovakian banking system is very similar to that found throughout Western Europe, with credit cards widely accepted – although there may be a limit on the amount – and ATMs found throughout the country. In order to open a bank account, you will need to produce your passport and possibly proof of residence in the country. Internet banking, loans, savings accounts and mortgages are all available to foreigners from Slovakian banks. The following are some of the larger banks in Slovakia:

- Citibank, www.citibank.com/slovakia
- Ľudová Banka, www.luba.sk
- ISTROBANKA, www.istrobanka.sk
- Tatra Bank, www.tatrabanka.sk
- VUB Banka, www.vub.sk
- Slovenská sporiteľňa, www.slsp.sk
- National Bank of Slovakia, www.nbs.sk.

Taxes

Back in 2004, Slovakia overhauled its tax system, introducing a flat rate of income tax, with inheritance, gift and dividend taxes abolished. Slovakia also has a double taxation treaty with most European countries (including the UK) and America to avoid foreigners paying tax twice.

Foreigners and businesses are only taxed on the income they generate in Slovakia unless they are classed as tax residents in the country. An individual is recognised as a tax resident if they reside in the country for 183 days during a 12-month period and in this class you are liable to be taxed on income earned both in Slovakia and overseas.

Income tax is levied at a flat rate of 19%, as is tax on rental income, corporation tax and capital gains. Although there is no specific capital gains tax, you are liable to pay tax on the profits of a real estate sale. Real estate tax is charged per year and depends on the property type and location. However, it rarely comes to more than £50 a year.

Insurance

You should seek private insurance if you are looking to relocate to Slovakia, largely because state benefits are lower than those in the UK.

In many instances it's better to secure insurance through larger international companies than through smaller Slovakian firms.

- Allianz – Slovenska Poistovna, a. s.,
  www.allianzsp.sk/www.allianz.com

- AIG Insurance, www.amslico.sk

Healthcare

While the government is currently overhauling the healthcare system, they still spend less than half the sum per person of their western counterparts on healthcare and standards fall below EU expectations. With an EHIC card you will be entitled to reduced cost or free treatment in hospitals. If you do have to pay, you will have to do so by cash. If you are working in Slovakia and paying Social Security contributions then you will be entitled to subsidised healthcare. However, it is still recommended that you take out private medical insurance. While doctors are well educated, few speak English. UK prescriptions will not be valid in Slovakia so if you require regular medication you will need to arrange to see a GP as soon as you reach the country.

Dial 155 or 112 for an ambulance.

Retirement

Slovakia is a stunningly beautiful country to retire to, especially around the Tatras Mountain areas – the capital and major towns and cities are more for investors. You will still be able to receive your UK state pension if you relocate to Slovakia. If you retire to Slovakia and secure residency, you may be entitled to a Slovakian pension and if you work in Slovakia you will then be entitled to the same benefits as you would in the UK. Visit the government website (www.government.gov.sk) or Department of Labour, Social Affairs and Family (www.employment.gov.sk) for more details. To be entitled to benefits you need to register at the local Social Security office.

Education

Education in Slovakia is compulsory for ten years and is free. There are also 18 universities in the country, which offer a free education to Slovaks who attended secondary school. Private schooling is reasonably priced but lessons are taught in Slovakian. For English-language teaching, you will need to apply to an international school.

* British International School Bratislava, www.bis.sk

* Forel International School, Bratislava, www.forel.sk

* QSI International School of Bratislava, www.qsi.org

* OSI International School of Kosice, www.qsi.org/ksc_home

Driving

The Slovak Republic is a country going through a great deal of development in its infrastructure and it's easy to get around by car. A driving licence issued by any EU state is valid in Slovakia, as is an International Driving Permit, but if you are going to be staying for longer than one year, you will need to apply for a Slovakian driving licence. This doesn't require you to retake your driving test – you simply fill in the relevant application form and pay £2.

Unleaded petrol, diesel and LPG fuel are all widely available, seatbelts must be worn at all times, it is illegal to talk on your mobile phone while driving and there is zero tolerance to drink driving. Drivers drive on the right-hand side of the road and between the 15th October and 15th March, all vehicles must drive with dipped headlights. If you plan to drive on a toll road, you will need to purchase a toll pass.

Speed limits:

* motorways 130km/h (80mph);

* open roads 90km/h (55mph);

* towns 60km/h (37mph).

Getting around

There are no domestic flights in operation throughout Slovakia, and generally the best way to get around is by car rather than public transport, which is cheap but can be time consuming.

Buses serve most destinations, but may involve a lot of changes. There are regional buses in operation and you can see details of their services at www.slovaklines.sk; they also offer international services.

Slow but scenic, travelling by train in Slovakia can be enjoyable, and prices are low. The railways are state operated by ŽSR (www.zsr.sk) and all details of timetables and prices can be found on their website. Be aware that there are two different types of train: *rýchlik*, which serve the larger towns, and *osobný vlak*, which are local services that are generally slower.

All major cities and towns offer an excellent public transport network, with a choice of buses and trolleybuses – as well as trams in Bratislava and Kosice –to choose from. The website http://cp.atlas.sk offers details on all public transport timetables and fares.

Learning the language

A Slavic language, Slovakian is difficult for English speakers to learn. Pronunciation is sensitive and any mispronunciation can lead to a change of meaning. Outside of Slovakian, Hungarian and German are widely spoken, with a few English speakers. If you can, you should try to learn some basic phrases, but don't try to carry out any transactions without the help of a Slovakian speaker. The Slovaks will appreciate any attempts you make to speak the language and are used to mistakes – this is one of the hardest Slavic tongues to learn.

Post

Post offices – *pošta* – are open between 8am and 5pm, Monday to Friday. Expect your letter to take five days to reach the UK and ten days to reach the USA. The post office provides mail, public telephone and money transfer services and you can find out more at www.slposta.sk.

Crime, corruption and the police

Foreign buyers will not come across corruption when it comes to buying property in Slovakia, especially since the land registration process now offers accelerated registration. In real estate terms, corruption is primarily found in the planning process, and this is a result of the incredibly bureaucratic nature of the system. It's only likely to be eradicated when the legislation gets reformed.

Serious crime is rare in Slovakia, although petty crime does occur in the larger towns and cities. You may be stopped and asked for photographic ID at any time, so ensure you carry your passport with you. The Slovakian police force can be contacted on 158 or 112.

15
Slovenia

COUNTRY PROFILE

Centrally located and breathtakingly beautiful, Slovenia has made itself a haven for foreign investors following the country's accession to the EU, which resulted in an overhaul of the property legislation, making it easier for foreigners to buy here. Giving investors the luxury of choosing from purchasing a vineyard, ski chalet or chic city centre apartment, Slovenia has experienced some of the highest appreciation rates in Eastern Europe, making it an appealing option for those looking to invest their cash wisely.

> **Did you know?**
> A 12-mile stretch of the Ljubljanica River in Slovenia is one of the richest archaeological sites in Europe. Artefacts retrieved date from early Stone Age times, through the medieval period, right up to the Renaissance and 17th century. Archaeologists suspect that the ancients believed the river possessed divine or magical properties and offered material sacrifices to it.

Why buy in Slovenia?

Small but perfectly formed – that's what most people buying in Slovenia think of this beautiful country. It's one of Europe's smallest countries, barely the size of Wales, and it has been much overlooked. Back in the 90s it was relatively unknown, with George W. Bush even famously confusing it with nearby Slovakia. Slovenia has benefited from its central position in Europe as this has helped to develop its blossoming tourist industry – the fastest-growing industry in the country for the last five years – which in turn has encouraged massive levels of foreign investment. Economically, Slovenia is a major success story, with GDP 95% that of Western Europe, while politically the country is stable and well developed, despite being caught up in the collapse of the former Yugoslavia.

Offering outstanding levels of natural beauty and described as 'Europe in miniature', Slovenia offers everything from a sweeping Adriatic coastline, vineyards, towering mountain peaks and lush, green grasslands. It's paradise for lovers of the outdoors, who can choose from hiking, skiing, riding, cycling, climbing, water sports and golfing activities.

Since EU accession, previously antiquated and complex purchasing processes have been replaced by new legislation, making it easier for overseas buyers to invest here. Slovenia is within a short distance of Venice, Vienna, Budapest and Zagreb, and with budget flights offered by both Ryanair (they fly to Maribor airport) and easyJet (they fly to Ljubljana), the country is easy to get to. Given its size, Slovenia is easy to get around, too.

Prices may be more comparable to its European neighbours, but when compared with the UK, you certainly get more for your money. With low crime rates, friendly and welcoming Slovenes, a higher standard of living than Croatia and a lack of congestion – imagine no rush-hour gridlock! – Slovenia is hugely appealing.

Politics and economy

One of Europe's leading economies and the first former Yugoslav country to join the EU and adopt the euro, Slovenia enjoys a firm economic footing. A high-income economy and a prosperous country, Slovenia has a GDP per capita of $23,250, the highest of the newly joined EU countries. Inflation fell in 2006, and Slovenia's economy has started to develop more strongly in the last few years – 5.2% in 2006, with a forecast growth of 4.8% for 2007.

Privatisation has taken place in the banking, telecommunications, and public utility sectors and foreign direct investment is expected to increase over the next few years.

A parliamentary democracy was introduced in Slovenia in 1991, following the declaration of independence in the country, splitting it from Yugoslavia in a thankfully short-lived skirmish – interestingly, Slovenia was remarkably untouched by the Yugoslav conflict and remained a safe country to visit. The current President is Janez Drnovšek and the Prime Minister Janez Janša.

Geography and climate

The third most forested country in Europe and with one of the shortest coastlines – only 46.6km – Slovenia is bordered by Italy, Austria, Croatia and Hungary. It's the meeting point for four geographic regions – the Alps, the Mediterranean, the Pannonian plains and the Dinaric Alps. Fewer than two million people live in Slovenia, with 270,000 of them in the capital, Ljubljana. The country boasts 5,593 square kilometres of grasslands, 363 square kilometres of orchards and 216 square kilometres of vineyards.

The diversity of the landscape is reflected in the climate, with the coast enjoying sub-mediterranean weather, the lowlands a warm continental climate, while the mountainous Alpine areas are characterised by snowfall. Finally, inland areas suffer from heavy rainfall, so don't forget your umbrella!

History and culture

First inhabited in 4,000BC, Slovenia's central location has made it a target for invaders and occupiers for many centuries. Absorbed by the Franks in 745, in later years Slovenia was ruled by the Hapsburgs, and then the Austro-Hungarian Empire.

At the end of WWI, and with the collapse of the Austro-Hungarian Empire, Slovenia formed a united kingdom with the Croats and Serbs, renamed the Kingdom of Yugoslavia in 1929. Declared the Socialist Federal Republic of Yugoslavia at the end of WWII, it wasn't until 1991 that modern-day Slovenia was formed with a declaration of independence from the crumbling Yugoslavian state.

Overflowing with culture, there are more than 200 museums in Slovenia and a number of sacred sites and points of architectural interest. As many as one third of Slovenia's cultural sites are of sacred interest, with antique early Christian basilicas, pre-Romanesque chapels and gothic, renaissance, baroque and neo-Romanesque churches.

Slovenia boasts one of the highest levels of biodiversity in the EU, with 11% of its territory protected land, and it has no fewer than 44 protected areas or parks, including one national park, three regional parks and 40 landscape parks. Slovenia is also home to a number of thermal springs and spas, with many visitors attracted to the country for activity or well-being holidays. There's also plenty for lovers of ancient architecture as there are hundreds of examples in Slovenia, the best being Bled, Podsreda, Brezice, Ljublijana and Velenije.

Religion

The majority of Slovenes declare themselves to be Roman Catholic – 68% – although many do not faithfully practise it. There are also a number of Serbian Orthodox followers (2.3%), Islamic (1.2%) and Christians (0.9%). In total, there are roughly 30 different denominations practised in Slovenia.

Tourism and getting there

The Yugoslav conflict greatly damaged the Slovenian tourist industry, even though the country was free from conflict. Post independence, the most successful year for tourism was 2004 when 2,341,281 tourists visited the country; this was 4.2% more than in 2003 but still 17% less than in 1986.

Given that the country has a year-round tourist industry, with everything from skiing in the winter to hiking in the summer, not only does this mean there's the potential for healthy rental yields, but it also guarantees sustainability in the property market. Tourism is also evenly spread throughout the country, not just focused on the capital, and importantly, Slovakia only receives 3.5% of its GDP from tourism, avoiding reliance on the industry. This is a good sign when it comes to preserving the country's natural environment.

Adria Airways (www.adria.si), Ryanair (www.ryanair.com) and easyJet (www.easyjet.co.uk) fly directly into Slovenia from the UK, and you can also fly directly into nearby Zagreb in Croatia or Graz in Austria.

The cost of living

While you can expect the cost of living to be lower than that of the UK, Slovenia is not as cheap as some of its Eastern European counterparts. However, a UK pensioner would live comfortably here, even though there are fears that the euro adoption will bring prices level with those of neighbouring Italy. A three-course meal for one costs as little as £6.50, while a bottle of beer costs just 96p.

Food and drink

Slovenian culinary fare draws heavily on influences from neighbouring Hungarian, Austrian, Croatian and Italian cooking. Traditional meals vary depending on your location. In the mountainous areas, dishes are meat based and hearty, while along the coast, fish dominates the menu. Goulash is ubiquitous, while two traditional dishes are *zlikrofi* (ravioli filled with potato, onion and bacon) and *zganci*, a porridge often served with sauerkraut. Sour soups are readily found in the Gorenjska, Pohorje and Primorska regions.

As with many post-communist countries, you will find a mix of international cuisine available. Pizzerias are found in most high streets, while pasta dishes are on most restaurant menus.

Slovenia produces some fabulous wines. With 216 square kilometres of vineyards, Slovenes have been making wine for 2,500 years, with 80 million litres produced annually. Slovene wines are generally not as well known as wines from other parts of the world, but there are some very fine examples, especially from some of the larger vineyards. Slovenian wine is mostly red and particularly well known is the Teran variety, which goes well with smoked ham (*prstut*), smoked sausages and local cheeses. Another good tipple is the Dolina wine from Vipava.

PROPERTY MARKET

Sustained by both local and foreign demand – 29% of which are British jet-to-let investors – the Slovenian property market has been performing well over the last two years. This is mainly thanks to the country's economic and political stability, as well as the fact that since EU accession, purchasing property has been made easy. Prior to the entry of Slovenia into the EU, from 2001 to 2004, property prices rose between 35% and 60%, and over the past two years, prices have doubled in some places, such as the province of Gorenska, where it's now hard to find a property for under € 140,000. Figures state that the average price of a property in Slovenia is now € 100,000, with real estate prices predicted to grow by 250% by 2015.

Demand is high, particularly around the picturesque Bohinj valley, while prices in the Kranjska Gora area have rocketed since Slovenia joined the EU in May 2004. Knight Frank have reported that Slovenia offers the best potential for further growth in its property market, and given that Slovenians are getting wealthier and there are increasing numbers of foreign executives relocating here for business purposes, the market is set to continue to experience demand and further growth. This is helped by the fact that Slovenia is a small country and there's a lack of available property, making this a sustainable market.

Where to buy

Vineyard areas

There are three main wine-growing regions in Slovenia: the first is the area which extends northeast from Stajerska and Celje to Ljutomer and Prekmurje; secondly, there's the area extending from Celje into Doljenska and Bela Krajina across to the Croatian border; and finally, there's the area in Primorska around Goriska Brda, Nova Gorica and on to Karst. These regions offer many small vineyards which often come with management facilities, and many British investors are now purchasing as it's only two hours' flight from London. There are also tax breaks for agricultural tax and inheritance tax. Land in this area is highly affordable, with prices starting from as little as £4,064, rising to £10,000 for an up-and-coming vineyard.

Ljubljana

The beating commercial heart of Slovenia, property prices here have risen by 32% in recent years, with prices doubling between 2004 and 2006. There has been increasingly strong demand for city centre property, which offers the best potential for jet-to-let investors, and this has recently spread out into the suburbs as property comes increasingly hard to find. Much sought after are apartments in the historic city centre.

This is not a cheap place to buy, with property costing between €2,000 and €3,500 per square metre. Prices in neighbouring Hungary, as well as in Poland, offer more for your money, but given that Ljubljana is attracting increasing numbers of executives, businesses and tourists, thanks to budget flights, prices are likely to continue rising now that Slovenia is part of the eurozone.

Coastal area

Jet-to-let investors tend to be focusing their attention on the more established and popular tourist resorts of the Primorska region, such as Koper, Izola and Piran. Prices on the Adriatic coast are similar to those of Ljubljana, with a two-bedroomed apartment in Koper costing €174,000, while a three-bedroomed house will cost around €280,000, and a four-bedroomed house €650,000. Prices here are currently 20% higher than those of Turkish coastal regions, but when you consider the stability of the Slovenian market, with the country already being an EU and eurozone member, and a regular destination for budget flights, as supply continues to dwindle and demand to rise, you are pretty much assured appreciation in the market.

Ski resorts

The ski resorts in Slovenia are affordable, accessible and adaptable. Kranjska Gora, Bohinjska Bistrica, Bohinj and Bovec are hugely popular, all sitting within one hour of Ljubljana International airport, which receives numerous budget flights.

New apartments in Bohinjska Bistrica and Maribor are currently attracting many foreign families, and in the Maribor area there is a positive feeling of new growth, especially in the tourist industry. Ryanair have begun flights directly into Maribor airport from the UK, meaning the region is likely to see massive expansion. There are also a number of thermal spas around the Maribor region, which attract many visitors.

Since 2004, property prices have jumped from €1,500 a square metre to €3,350, with the average cost of a home €145,000. Away from Kranjska Gora, where prices have doubled and property costs €5,000 per square metre, ski property is still very affordable, priced at €70,000 for a one-bedroomed apartment of 60 square metres. For the best value, you should look at larger properties that command a lower price per square metre – for example, in Bohinjska Bistrica, a property comprising of four apartments is available for € 395,000.

Ski property in Slovenia can be used during both the winter and summer seasons, and as the Slovenes are outdoor enthusiasts, a home here has the potential for year-round rentals.

What to buy

Those seeking to buy holiday homes are increasingly looking to stable EU countries such as Slovenia, especially as the markets of France and Spain get more saturated. The most popular with foreign buyers are the coastal resorts around Koplar and Piran, where you can find a bargain if you look inland at some of the older properties requiring renovation. However, investors should look to the newly-built developments.

It's a similar story in the capital, where developers have already made inroads into the city centre. Historic properties that have been transformed into apartments are also popular. In the mountains, characterful ski lodges are in high demand for rentals, while there are also a number of small apartments on the slopes, as well as renovation projects.

THE BUYING PROCESS

Anyone living within the EU can buy property in Slovenia, although currently you can't get a mortgage in the country. The process is safe and secure, with an organised land registry system making ownership rights clear. As always, though, professional, independent legal advice should be sought.

Stage 1: Restrictions on foreign buyers

Before Slovenia joined the EU, foreigners trying to buy a property had to go through a long and complicated process, requiring them to obtain permission from the Ministry of Justice prior to purchase – this could take as long as five months.

Thanks to EU membership, this arduous process has been eradicated, meaning the real estate market is free of legal restrictions for EU citizens. However, one caveat remains; for up to seven years after accession, should they choose to, Slovenia may enforce Article 37 of the Accession Treaty, allowing them to reapply restrictions on purchases by non-nationals.

You will be required to get an EMSO (identity) and tax number in order to purchase a Slovenian property. This can be organised by your estate agent and should cost no more than £10.

Stage 2: Financing your purchase

Slovenia is really only for those who are able to finance their own purchase. At present there are no UK firms offering mortgages in the country, and so you're probably looking at re-mortgaging your UK home in order to raise the necessary finances.

Stage 3: The survey

Unlike many Eastern European agents, estate agents in Slovenia do carry out a basic survey on all properties except newly-built ones that come with guarantees. However, if you are looking to buy an older property, it is probably best to have an additional, more detailed survey conducted. The Royal Institute of Chartered Surveyors (RICS – www.rics.org) can recommend a surveyor, or you can ask for a recommendation from a professional you trust.

Stage 4: The contract

Once you've found a property that suits your requirements, your lawyer needs to make an offer in euros and get confirmation as to how much the initial deposit will be and when this should be paid – it's normally 10%

of the valuation price and is paid two weeks after the initial request for the property to be removed from the market. Be aware that in Slovenia, the lawyer normally represents both the buyer and seller. Of course, you can chose to get an independent lawyer to represent you.

If the offer is accepted then your lawyer needs to perform background checks at the land registry office land searches, which can generally be provided within two days. Once this and the survey have taken place, your lawyer will then draw up the initial contract, outlining all conditions of sale – payment schedules, repairs and so on – and once signed, the deposit will need to be paid. The sale is then binding.

Now you can talk to your bank in the UK about a money transfer, which has become increasingly simple since Slovenia adopted the euro. You should also ensure that you get all the documents connected with the sale – including details from the land registry, any management contracts and all insurance policies – translated into English, as it is mandatory in Slovenian law for an official translation of the documents to be present when the contract is signed.

Finally, once you and your lawyer are satisfied with all the details, you can begin completion of the sale by signing the contract in both languages in the presence of a notary, and making arrangements for the deeds to be updated at the land registry, naming you as the legal owner.

Generally, the whole buying transaction usually takes between eight and ten weeks, although in the case of agricultural property, it can take longer.

Stage 4: Additional costs

Before you make an offer to the seller, you need to take into account the extra costs you will be faced with at the end of the purchasing process, such as estate agents' fees, furnishings and equipment.

Estate agents' fees are paid by both the buyer and the seller and are generally 2% of the valuation each, making it a total of 4%. VAT is payable on the sale, but this is a fixed percentage of the agent's fee. For older properties it works out as 2.4% (agents' fee at 2% plus 0.4% VAT).

Legal fees vary. If the agent did most of the legal work in conjunction with the notary then the fees will be around € 250. If the lawyer did the majority of the work then this will rise to around € 600. Translation fees will be around € 100, while to enter the property in the land register, you will be faced with a fee to the government of € 8, with the agent charging about € 83 for carrying out the paperwork on your behalf.

THE LETTINGS MARKET

Rental yields in Slovenia average 6.81% per annum, with rental yields for properties in central Ljubljana ranging from 4.8% to 7%, with income of around € 600 per month. In Ljubljana's suburbs, rental yields are a bit higher at 5.85% to 7.5%, while property prices are much lower at € 1,500 to € 1,650 per square metre. Currently, few people invest in holiday properties in Ljubljana, but there is good long-term rental potential among workers, especially foreign executives, who represent the bulk of the market.

Average rents have been put at € 1,400 in built-up areas, dropping to € 1,000 elsewhere. Given that this is still a relatively immature, undiscovered and under-supplied country, and with tourism set to increase, you can expect to see an upturn in the number of rentals and income generated over the next decade.

RENOVATING A PROPERTY

If you decide you are going to renovate a property in Slovenia, you won't be short of options. While historic city centre apartments may well be worth the renovation costs and all the effort, in rural areas you will find little demand for such homes; these would be more a labour of love.

Generally speaking, fittings in Slovenia are of a comparable cost to the UK, but labour – such as carpenters and electricians – is relatively cheap. As with any renovation project, it won't be easy and it is worth doing significant amounts of research into the average costs and timing prior to taking one on.

LIVING IN SLOVENIA

Daily life and people

It is difficult to be specific about the Slovene people's characteristics. Only independent since 1991, many have Italian, Hungarian, Austrian or Croatian ancestors and very rarely will you come across a 'pure' Slovene. Slovenes themselves are very conscious of this, but happily live with the multi-ethnic make up of their people and their country, with little if any conflict between races. Lovers of the outdoors, the Slovenes have a great rapport with nature and are also calmer than many of their Balkan brethren – although if you do cross a Slovenian, beware – they can be a stubborn bunch!

Visas, permits and residency

Since Slovenia joined the EU in 2004, if you are a EU citizen you do not need a visa to enter the country. However, you may only stay for three months without a visa, and if you intend to stay longer, you must apply for a residency permit. This is usually issued for one year and then needs to be renewed. For more information, visit the Ministry for Foreign Affairs website at www.mzz.gov.si.

Utilities

Transferring utilities can be a tricky process and so it is advisable to ask your estate agent to help you, as you will undoubtedly need someone who speaks the language.

Electricity can be purchased from one of the following companies depending on the region you live in:

* Elektro Celje, www.elektro-celje.si
* Elektro Gorenjska, www.elektro-gorenjska.si
* Elektro Maribor, www.elektro-maribor.si
* Elektro Ljubljana, www.elektro-ljubljana.si

- Elektro Primorska, www.elektro-primorska.si.

While gas is available in the country (Geoplin, www.geoplin.si), most people have oil-fired central heating. Water is charged depending on your rate of consumption, which is monitored by a meter.

Telecommunications are provided by Telecom Slovenije (www.telekom.si/en) who also provide broadband; this is mostly restricted to the larger towns and cities at present. Mobile phones do work in Slovenia as the country has a GSM network which is compatible with the rest of Europe – check on www.gsmworld.com or with your service provider before travelling out there. Mobile phone companies include Mobitel (www.mobitel.si/eng) and Vodafone (www.simobil.si).

Currency and banking

Previously employing the tolar, since 1st January 2007, Slovenia has been using the euro. Notes come in standard euro denominations of €5, €10, €20, €50, and coins of 1, 2, 5, 10, 20, 50 cents, and €1 and €2.

You will need to open a bank account in Slovenia in order to set up standing orders for the payment of utility bills, cable television and any property management charges.

Residents and non-residents are treated differently when it comes to opening a bank account. Those expatriates who are classed as residents – i.e. who have been working in the country for at least six months or have been granted a residential visa – are entitled to all of the banking services offered to Slovenians. Non residents – i.e. those who have visas which are valid for less than six months or who cannot prove they have a temporary residence in Slovenia – may only open personal non-resident accounts. These restrict you to depositing and withdrawing cash and/or carrying out local and international payments and conversion into other currencies. As with most other Eastern European countries, you will generally just need photographic ID in order to open an account.

SKB Banka (www.skb.si) offer a good package of services for internationals living in Slovenia, whether residents or non-residents.

Other useful contacts include:

- Bank of Slovenia, www.bsi.si

- Abanka Vipa d.d., www.abanka.si

- Bank Austria, www.ba-ca.si

- Banka, www.banka-celje.si

- Banka Koper, www.banka-koper.si

- Nova Ljubljanska banka, www.nlb.si.

Taxes

Tax residents in Slovenia are classed as people who hold permanent residency in the country; they will be taxed on both their income secured in Slovenia and that outside of the country. However, there is a double taxation treaty in place with all EU countries, as well as with Croatia, Montenegro, Canada, Turkey, the USA and others.

Income tax rates in Slovenia are high, charged at a progressive rate from 16–50%, while corporate tax is charged at a flat rate of 23% (in 2007, to be reduced to 22% in 2008, 21% in 2009 and 20% for subsequent years). Capital gains tax is not payable if you have owned a property for three years. If the property is not for residential usage, then capital gains is paid at a rate of 25% if it has been in possession of the owner for less than 10 years. VAT is charged at a standard rate of 20%.

For more information, visit The Tax Administration of the Republic of Slovenia website at www.durs.gov.si or the Ministry of Finance at www.gov.si/mf/angl/index.html.

Insurance

As in the UK, you will need to take out house, contents, car and health insurance in Slovenia. There are a number of firms that offer English-language services:

- Adriatic Slovenica, www.adriatic-slovenica.si/

- Zavarovalnica Tilia, www.zav-tilia.si

- Triglav Insurance Company, www.zav-triglav.si.

Healthcare

As Slovenia is part of the EU, all EU citizens are entitled to free medical treatment from government-run hospitals. You just need to ensure that you get an EHIC card (www.ehic.org.uk) to prove your entitlement. Be aware that some Slovenian hospitals may still require payment upfront, but you can claim this back at a later date.

By Western standards, Slovenian healthcare is good, although resources are stretched. It is still advisable to secure private medical treatment and the British Embassy in Ljubljana (www.british-embassy.si) should be able to provide you with a list of private facilities as well as a list of English-speaking doctors and dentists.

Dial 112 for emergency services.

Retirement and benefits

Slovenia is an attractive country for retirees due to the healthy natural surroundings, although it is not as cheap as some might like. Your pension will be payable in Slovenia and if you have worked in Slovenia prior to retirement you may well be entitled to a Slovenian pension.

Your social security rights are the same as those that apply elsewhere within the EEA and if you choose to work in Slovenia, you will contribute to the Slovenian social security system and, consequently, gain the right to benefits.

Education

Schooling is compulsory between the ages of 6 and 15 and education is free to Slovenian nationals. Further and higher education is provided in the form of secondary schools and two universities. In recent years, approximately 6% of GDP has been spent on education and in 2002, 67% of population had at least upper secondary education.

There are several international schools in the country, including:

- QSI International School of Ljubljana, www.qsi.org

- International education in Ljubljana, Gimnazija Bezigrad, www.gimb.org/gimb
- The Second Gymnasium, Maribor, www.druga.org.

Driving

Slovenia has a well-developed road network, with motorways connecting all major towns and cities, as well as neighbouring countries. Signposting is clear, with road signs and traffic rules similar to those used throughout Europe. Vehicles drive on the right-hand side of the road and by law, you need to drive with dimmed lights 24 hours a day. It's illegal to drive while on your mobile phone and you are only permitted to drive with 50mg of alcohol in your bloodstream. You can drive in Slovenia using your UK driving licence – which must include a photo – or an International Driving Permit.

Speed limits are as follows:

- motorways: 130km/h (80mph);
- open roads: 100km/h (62mph);
- towns: 50km/h (31mph).

Getting around

While driving is the best way to see this beautiful country, buses are the fastest method of getting around. The national operator is Avtobusna Postaja Ljubljana d.d. (www.ap-ljubljana.si) which serves destinations throughout the country and internationally. As well as being fast, efficient and comfortable, fares are also cheap.

Trains are reliable, too, with Slovenske Zeleznice (www.slo-zeleznice.si) operating both national and international services which are fast and cheap. It is possible to travel extensively throughout the country by train.

There are no internal flights in Slovenia – the country is simply too small to warrant them.

Meanwhile, getting around the capital is easy. Buses operate throughout Ljubljana all day and in the evenings, and this is also a great city to explore on foot.

Learning the language

The official language of Slovenia is Slovene, with Hungarian, Italian, German and English also widely spoken. Part of the Slavic family of languages, more than two million people worldwide speak Slovene; unsurprisingly, most of them live in Slovenia. Language has always been a politically-charged topic in and around the old Yugoslavia. Slovene was a language that was suppressed for years and consequently Slovenians are extremely proud of their vernacular.

This is a difficult language for English speakers to learn, but it's worth trying to pick up a few words. However, Western Europeans do tend to find the pronunciation very difficult, so don't be surprised if your efforts draw some bemused or blank looks from the locals.

Shopping

In the capital you can expect to encounter a number of modern shops and department stores, including many western labels and fashion boutiques. BTC City (www.btc-city.com) is Ljubljana's largest shopping centre and has 420 shops, which include names such as Mango, Benetton, Top Shop, Miss Selfridge, Cacharel, Evans, Lacoste, Levi's, Hugo Boss and O'Neill.

In the smaller towns, while you can find virtually anything and everything, don't expect to find a huge number of imported products.

The Slovenians pride themselves on their organic produce and some of the local markets offer some delicious fresh foods and are well worth a look.

Post

Post offices in Slovenia are known as *Posta Slovenije*, with bright yellow signs bearing a bugle marking their presence in the high street. You can send letters and faxes, as well as exchanging money. Visit www.posta.si to find your nearest post office.

Crime, corruption and the police

Crime is practically non-existent in Slovenia, with corruption labelled as 'significantly improving' by the Transparency International Coalition Against Corruption (www.transparency.org). The country has been ranked as 28th in the world for perceived corruption, which indicates a low level – Slovenia has a rating of 6.4, with the best rating (no corruption) being 10.

Note that members of the police force in Slovenia are unlikely to speak English, but in the case of an emergency, dial 113.

Case study

Joanna Vaughan is a Lincolnshire-based freelance journalist whose long-term aim is to move to France, either running a campsite or a gîte business.

However, Joanna and her husband realised they were never going to achieve this on their salaries. 'We decided something had to be done,' recalls Jo, 'and the obvious solution seemed to be to invest in a property abroad.'

With their work, Jo and her husband regularly travelled around Europe.

'I knew roughly what the areas we could afford to buy in were like. In the past, Slovenia had charmed me with its scenery, old-fashioned feel and cheap prices. Other places I considered were Italy, East Germany and Croatia. We chose Slovenia as there seemed to be numerous agents dealing specifically with the country, and they could take on the workload for us. Also, Slovenia seemed to be a lower risk option. As house prices were rising rapidly, it was a bit of a no brainer!

'I found a British agent who arranged for a five-day viewing in Slovenia. To be honest, the agent turned out to be a bit of a nightmare – I wish I'd gone through SlovenianProperties.com, who have since helped me out of a couple of holes. During my first trip, the agents didn't turn up when they said they would and I was left sitting at the hotel, but eventually I got to see all the properties and there were two that seemed full of potential. The idea was that I would let it out for as much of the year as possible, although I would occasionally use it myself.

'I eventually brought an apartment in the village of Mojstrana, in the heart of the country's Julien Alps. The initial cost of the apartment was ⇔113,000 for around 50 square metres. To give myself a bit more space I asked if I could also purchase the loft space above the apartment as this would double the size of the property. Amazingly, the owner offered it to me for just ⇔14,000, not realising, I don't think, how useable the space was, as I have since turned it into two bedrooms!

'The main problem I encountered was with the builders. At one stage, my agents told me that their priority was to keep the builders happy, rather than me, as their loyalties lay with the people they'd have to deal with in the future. Consequently, they pushed me to pay the full amount in June when the property was promised to be finished and ready. When I arrived, there were still no staircases or floors, but I still handed over the money – what a mistake! Eventually the apartment was finished in December.

'I also left my agents to sort out my furniture for me, and while it was superb stuff, I paid way more than I should have done. I would advise anyone to speak to a local and spend a week or so looking round the different furniture stores as it will save them a fortune in the long run. I've ended up with what is possibly the most expensively-furnished rental apartment in Slovenia – although from my feedback, my guests are appreciating it!'

Joanna's tips

'Be careful who you buy from, and make sure you get all the facts straight before you enter into any agreement. Don't skip on the extra legwork – it's better to spend a few extra days in Slovenia looking at the smaller details than get caught for some large bills later. Also, get a survey done, secure the services of an independent solicitor, and arrange insurance as soon as possible. Financially , get a bank account from which you can pay all your bills – it's easy to do. I would recommend talking to SlovenianProperties.com as their contacts and service were invaluable to me.'

For more details on renting Jo's apartment, visit www.apartmentmurena.com.

16
Turkey

Factfile

Population: 72 million

Population growth rate: 1.06%

Area: 783,562 sq km

Capital city: Istanbul (population: 1,932,500)

Inflation: 8.16%

GDP growth rate: 7.4%

Unemployment rate: 14.9%

Net migration: 0 migrants per 1,000 people

Currency: New Turkish Lira

Exchange rate: £1 = 2.34TRY

EU status: Working towards membership

Time zone: CET (GMT +2 hours)

COUNTRY PROFILE

An EU hopeful with an already-established property market stretching along the country's southwestern coast, there have been some question marks over the country's economic and political stability, especially due to the country's proximity to the Middle East. Nevertheless, Turkey has a massive economy and hefty tourist market, both of which are positive signs for future growth in the property market.

Did you know?

- Istanbul is the only city in the world built on two continents, Europe and Asia.
- Turkey is the native home of the tulip, which was exported to Holland in the 16th century.
- Noah's Ark is said to have landed on Mount Ararat (Agri Dagi) in Eastern Turkey.
- Turkey is the only secular Muslim country in the world.
- The original Father Christmas was St Nicholas, Bishop of Myra, who lived in Turkey in the third century AD.

Why buy in Turkey?

One of the best-known investment markets in Eastern Europe, Turkey is an incredibly welcoming country, with good food, a wonderful climate, relaxed lifestyle, fabulous surroundings and bags of culture and history. With a low cost of living, 8,333 kilometres of coastline and a staggering 300-plus days of sunshine every year, there are plenty of reasons to buy here, and that's before you look at the good economic health of the country.

Hugely varied, both culturally and historically, Turkey sits at a crossroads, bridging the gap between east and west, and with a bright future ahead of her. Economically, Turkey is a dynamic and vibrant place, although not without challenges. Boasting one of the highest levels of UK buyers outside of Spain and France, with roughly 1.2 million UK and Irish tourists visiting annually, this is a secure destination for those seeking an expat enclave – there are 3,000 Brits living in Bodrum alone.

Property legislation has also been overhauled in recent years and since January 2006, foreigners have been allowed to purchase land under 2.5 hectares in size for personal use. A new mortgage bill was also given the green light at the end of February 2007, meaning foreign buyers can now secure a mortgage and typical rates are 1.5–3% over 15 years.

With prices still incredibly low – as affordable as those of Spain 20 years ago – but with appreciation rates rising as high as 30% in some areas, you can expect good returns. This trend is likely to continue, thanks to the growing affluence of the country and the ability now to secure a mortgage, something that prevented the market from expanding to its potential in previous years.

The infrastructure is good, the country easy and cheap to get to and facilities are excellent, with plenty to do. What's more, the Turks are friendly and welcoming and the country offers a more exotic feel than many in Eastern Europe.

Politics and economy

Short term, the prospects for the Turkish economy are looking positive, thanks to the government's determination to retain tight control of the country's finances while instigating economic reforms and accelerating privatisation of commercial sectors. Turkey's recent economic past has been dominated by a series of crises, particularly that of 1991, which plunged the country into a deep recession. Since then a programme of stringent fiscal reforms has been implemented as Turkey strives to secure EU accession, which is estimated for 2015. Despite the strong economic gains in 2002–2006, due largely to renewed investor interest in emerging markets, IMF backing and tighter fiscal policy, the economy is still burdened by high levels of debt and budget deficits. Inflation has also been a major problem for Turkey. Back in 1997 inflation rates stood at a staggering 85.7%, and while today they have been reduced to a more manageable 8.16%, they are still high when compared with 3.7% in Slovakia and 3.4% in Montenegro.

The public sector still dominates the economy, although the private sector is growing strongly, while the inflow of foreign direct investments reached $12.8 billion dollars in the first nine months of 2006, an increase of over 50% compared to 2005. GDP has grown strongly over the last few years, reaching 9% in 2004, dropping to 5% in 2005, and then settling at an average annual rate of 6.8% over the last two years. The unemployment rate remains worryingly high at 10%, yet this is still below the EU average.

Turkey's improving economic situation, along with efforts to improve human rights, has persuaded the EU to open negotiations for full Turkish membership. A major stumbling block remains Turkey's reluctance to allow free traffic with Cyprus, although talks have already had a positive effect on the economy, increasing the confidence of investors and encouraging foreign interest in the property market.

A parliamentary representative democracy, Turkey's Prime Minister is Recep Tayyip Erdoğan. While being a stable and secure democracy, Turkey has always taken a fairly isolationist line, especially towards the west, although Erdoğan is keen to change this policy, introducing some brave and much-needed social and economic reforms. Disappointed over what he describes as the EU's 'foot-dragging' over Turkey's membership, he is urging them to make a decision one way or the other.

Geography and climate

Surrounded by the Black Sea, the Sea of Marmara, the Mediterranean and the Aegean, Turkey's coastline stretches for 8,333 kilometres. Bordering Bulgaria and Greece to the northwest, Georgia, Armenia and Iran to the east, and Syria and Iraq to the south, the huge number of cultural influences on the country is clear. This is a vast land – it's the 37th largest country in the world, covering 779,452 square kilometres and straddling the continents of Europe and Asia. The landscape is hugely varied, with the vast coastal plains and plateau of Asia Minor, the 3,000-metre-plus peaks of eastern Turkey – home to Mount Arafat – plus the Mediterranean and pine-clad shoreline of the western coast.

The climate is equally varied, with Istanbul experiencing a more Balkan climate and the western coast being more balmy and Mediterranean. The interior can endure harsh climatic conditions, with the Anatolian plateau seeing temperatures drop as low as –30°C, with 120 days of lying snow a year.

History and culture

Home to everyone from the Romans, Greeks and Byzantines the first major empire in Asia Minor was that of the Hittites, who occupied the land from the 18th to 13th century BC. Turkey has seen a fair share of invaders over the years. The Ottoman Empire survived there for 623 years, and it wasn't until it collapsed at the end of WWI that modern day Turkey was born. Occupied by the allies following that war, the Turkish War of Independence raged under the leadership of Mustafa Kemal Pasha, and in September 1922 he succeeded in founding the first Republic of Turkey. Introducing many radical reforms in an effort to eradicate the legacy of Ottoman rule, Mustafa Kemal was given the honorific name of 'Atatürk' (Father of the Turks) in 1934. On the side of the allies in WWII, Turkey joined the UN in 1945. The years that followed saw intervention in Cyprus and the recognition of the Northern Cypriot Republic in 1974. The 1960s to 1980s were periods marked by political instability and coups, and it wasn't until the beginning of economic reform in the 80s that the country began to settle down.

Rich in culture and historical sites, Turkey is home to two of the world's seven ancient wonders: the Temple of Artemis and the Mausoleum of Halicarnassus. While museums are thin on the ground, breathtaking monuments are not and some of the finest include the Blue Mosque, Tokapi Palace, the Grand Bazaar and the various Hittite sites. Numerous amphitheatres and shrines can be found across the country, along with remnants of the Roman age, such as the shrine at Ephesus. Meanwhile, the bustling bazaars are truly exhilarating and a great place to find a bargain.

The country is a blend of Islamic, Ottoman, Western and Oğuz Turkic cultural traditions, and nowhere is this more evident than in Turkish music and literature. Architecturally Byzantine and Ottoman elements feature strongly, as do Islamic. This is particularly evident in the Blue Mosque and Dolmabahçe Palace in Istanbul.

Religion

The only secular Muslim country in the world, 99% of Turks are Muslim. The remainder of the population belong to Christian denominations, Judaism, Yezidism and atheism.

Tourism and getting there

A hugely popular tourist destination, the World Tourism Organisation (UNWTO) have labelled Turkey as the 'star performer in this sub-region', with an increase of 20% for 2005, adding 3.4 million arrivals to the annual numbers visiting the country and passing the 20 million mark. Foreign tourist arrivals increased substantially in Turkey between 2002 and 2005, from 12.8 million to 21.2 million, making the country a top-10 destination in the world for foreign visitors. It generated US$17.5 billion in revenues in 2005 and US$ 15.3 billion between January and October 2006. Consequently, tourism is important to the Turkish government and central to their quest to secure economic prosperity and security. The largest number of visitors are Germans (32% in 2005), followed by Russians (16%) and British (12.5%).

According to figures released by UNWTO, the number of foreign tourists visiting Turkey has increased 15-fold in the last 25 years, with the 1.2 million foreign arrivals in 1980 now dwarfed by 2005's figures. Turkey is currently looking to expand upon its traditional resort-based tourism, with the development of new out-of-season incentives to visitors, including thermal tourism – Turkey has 1,300 thermal sites, more than any other European country – and archaeological tourism. With a detailed tourist plan in place for each Turkish region, the government are working hard to build a healthy industry.

There has been a huge rise in the number of budget flights into Turkey. Turkish Airlines carried the second largest number of passengers in 2005, an increase of 20.4% on 2004, with only Spanish airline Spanair carrying more. There are numerous airlines operating from airports throughout the UK to Bodrum and British Airways, easyJet and Turkish Air all fly into Istanbul. Currently, the budget carriers don't serve the more popular western coast.

Cost of living

Inexpensive to live in, Turkey has become popular with retirees whose pension goes further than it would in the UK, with prices between

30–50% cheaper than in Great Britain. The cost of living is way below European levels, even in the more popular tourist resorts. The cost of a bottle of mineral water is around 40p, while a beer costs around £1. Dinner with local wine in a restaurant typically costs £12 per head although you can eat for a fraction of that outside of the tourist resorts. It is anticipated that EU entry will change this, though.

Food and drink

Turkish cuisine is rated as highly as French and Chinese in many gourmet circles, with traditional recipes dating back to Byzantine and Ottoman times. There is an abundance of fresh fruit and vegetables available in Turkey, depending on the season, while yogurt and local cheeses are a delicacy. Meat is central to the Turkish diet, with a large number of kebab and grilled dishes to sample. Turkish *Meze* is famous worldwide and very tasty, and if you're a vegetarian, you're best off sticking to these dishes – most other recipes include meat stock in some form or another. Sardines, tuna and mullet dishes are also good, while the staple fare tends to be soups, many of which feature beans.

Despite the country's religious status, alcohol is readily available, and Turkey produces some very drinkable wines, particularly from the Thrace and Cappadocia vineyards. There are a number of domestic beers available, although bottled and draught are cheaper than canned beer. Efes Pilsner is the most popular brew, with imported brands available in most supermarkets.

THE PROPERTY MARKET

While many people may look at Turkey as a new and emerging market, in truth it isn't. Boasting Europe's largest population and with a heritage stretching back for 2,000 years, economically Turkey has a strong and proud tradition, with decline only experienced between the 1700s and 1980s. A re-emerging market, the entrepreneurial talents of the educated population, as well as political deregulation, has translated into a strong economy, tourist industry and property market.

Turkey's negotiations with the EU are also helping to prop up the property market. Talks have been going on for decades, and even though it is not guaranteed that EU accession will take place in 2015, the fact that talks are occurring and reforms are moving the country along the path to modernisation means that the tourist industry, economy and property market are benefiting.

Turkey is a secular Muslim state, and while there have been concerns over terrorism and links to Islamic extremism, especially in an age when, sadly, extremism and terrorist threats are all around us, many people have discounted such worries. What's more, it has been proven that recovery rates between incidents of terrorism and economic recovery are getting shorter.

Investment potential is excellent in Turkey. Obviously it depends on where you buy but in general, across the country, capital growth has been averaging 21% per annum for the last couple of years. Thanks to economic and population growth, demand has been sustained from the local market, especially in areas such as Istanbul. Similarly, there have been reports that 95% of housing in Turkey needs to be renovated or is situated in run down areas, meaning there is massive demand from the increasingly affluent population for better quality housing.

While the market has been hampered by a lack of low cost flights to the southwest, there are some cheap flights, although the lack of frequency can damage the rental yields you can expect in Turkey. However, as with Croatia this has resulted in a more discerning and higher-spending tourist, which in turn can help to stimulate capital growth. The market is further set to grow as there are all kinds of properties for all kinds of buyers, meaning there is no sign of a wane in demand.

Where to buy

Prices are far lower than in Western Europe's more established markets, and in some areas you can buy a three-bedroomed villa for less than £125,000. However, in other regions, prices are much higher due to greater demand from foreign buyers. If you are able or willing to look within half an hour of the major resort hotspots, you are more than likely to find a bargain that you can buy for below the average market price.

Bodrum and Fethiye

The major tourist areas, these two towns are experiencing the highest levels of growth, and as Turkey's most exclusive resorts, property is generally low density, low rise and newly-built. Prices vary from between €2,500 to €4,000 per square metre, with appreciation rates averaging 20–30% over the last two years, and the average predicted capital growth per annum predicted to be 10% over the next ten years. Newly-built apartments in a Bodrum development costing £50,000–£60,000 two years ago are now worth £79,000, showing growth of 20–25%. Thanks to Bodrum's international airport it is now easier to get to the Aegean coast and this has helped to develop demand. For a basic, three-bedroomed apartment in a modern development in nearby Altinkum or Alanya prices are lower, starting from as little as £35,000. Of course, for a property with sea views or facilities such as a swimming pool, you should expect to pay more.

Istanbul

Istanbul is seen as one of Turkey's most thriving destinations, and thanks to the estimated 700,000 people who are believed to be emigrating there each year, demand for property is high. With the population booming and urbanisation well under way, property supply is low, helping to push prices up. With lifestyle changes also established, resulting in a decrease in the number of inhabitants per household, the limited amount of quality housing is leading to price hikes and buy-to-let opportunities are huge.

Numerous budget flights arrive in the capital and so accessibility isn't a problem, and this is having a positive knock-on effect on the surrounding area. Couple this with the cultural and historic attractions of the city, and the fact that Istanbul is the economic heartland of Turkey, and you are looking at a stable and appealing investment.

Mediterranean coastline

Areas such as Antalaya, Belek and Side offer better value for money than areas further north around the Bodrum Peninsula, and are more frequented by German and Scandinavian buyers. The population in this area has reportedly risen by 400% in the last 20 years, with prices rising by 25% in recent years. With 11 golf courses in the area, buy-to-let investors can seek to secure year-round interest from the golf market.

Areas such as Kalkan and Kaş are small, but have seen rapid development in recent times. Prices have risen by roughly 12–15% in the last year. With a lack of space for development due to strict zoning regulations, there is a shortage of homes here, despite continued interest.

What to buy

Newly-built property is the most popular choice in Turkey, especially since so much of Turkish resale property is in need of massive renovation – and this can be a minefield of red tape. Most demand tends to be for off-plan property, and this is likely to rent better and appreciate at a greater rate. Apartments and villas are the favoured property type, and along the southern coast – the most popular area with foreign buyers – older properties are fairly non-existent. Buying an older property is always more complicated and takes longer as it's usually owned by several family members and you're required to secure permission from all of them before you can purchase.

THE BUYING PROCESS

With recent years seeing a relaxation of property legislation, it has become easier for foreigners to purchase a home in Turkey. However, this is still not an easy country to buy in, so don't enter into the conveyancing system unprepared – always carry out the correct background checks on the property and vet the estate agents and lawyers before you put your trust – and money – in their hands.

Stage 1: Restrictions on foreign buyers

A foreigner can buy with no legal restrictions in Turkey, although you are not allowed to buy property in areas which are deemed to be important to the military. Foreigners also need to get military permission to buy in the country and by applying for this, it allows the government to ensure you won't be in a militarily sensitive zone, and to carry out a check on your character with the UK government, should they choose to do so. As long as the property is correctly zoned and you are granted permission then you are free to buy it.

Generally, this process only takes two to three months, although there has been a backlog recently, following a government review of property legislation, which put a freeze on sales to foreigners. It is believed that one of the requirements for EU entry will be the removal of military permission, although this has yet to be confirmed.

Stage 2: Financing your purchase

Financing has become easier in the last few months as the government has overhauled the mortgage system. Traditionally, foreign buyers would have to secure a loan or release equity from their property in their home country. However, you can now get a mortgage at a rate of 1.5% to 3% over a 15-year period. It's still early days, though, and these terms are likely to improve.

Stage 3: Land registry, background checks and surveys

One of the most essential things to be aware of when looking to purchase a Turkish property is the *Tapu*, or title deed. The *Tapu* office is the land registry, where details of the property deed will be kept and where your lawyer will need to carry out all the necessary background checks on your property. These checks include making sure that the property is not located within a Military Security Zone, checking that there are no outstanding charges (such as mortgage payments) on the property, and finding out about the ownership situation – you need to make sure that the seller is the registered owner.

When it comes to purchasing, you should also do your research on the developer you are purchasing from, as there is no system in place to protect the buyer should the developer go bust before completion. Therefore, it is imperative that you invest in a trustworthy developer.

Surveys are not normally part of the purchasing process, but if you are buying an old property, you should always get a structural survey carried out; new properties generally tend to come with a guarantee.

Stage 4: The contract

Once you have carried out all of the necessary background checks and are confident you are dealing with trustworthy developers and agents, it is time to take the first step in the conveyancing process. The necessary stages to follow for completion vary, depending on whether you are buying a new-build or old property.

Buying off plan

If you are buying a newly-built property, you will need to pay a reservation fee of 1–2% which is non-refundable and will take the property off the market for 20 days. A contract will then be drawn up between the buyer and the developer, which will contain the payment schedules and terms and conditions for the sale. Once the preliminary contract is agreed, you will then need to sign and pay a deposit of between 10% and 30%. In order for the sale to be finalised, a final contract needs to be signed by both the buyer and seller, and then military clearance needs to be applied for. Once this is received, the *Tapu* can then be transferred to the buyer's name. During construction, you will continue to pay the outstanding balance in instalments, as agreed in the contract. The first payment is usually paid on the signing of the final contract.

Purchasing a resale property

If you are buying an old property you will sign a preliminary contract, with the deposit paid on signing. Once the deposit is paid, you need to ensure the title is clean with the *Tapu*. If it is, the final contract can be signed and your lawyer can apply for military clearance. Once this is received, the title will be transferred into your name, making you the legal owner.

Stage 5: Registering the property

Once all the paperwork and necessary payments have been carried out, you will be able to apply to have the property registered in your name. In order to do this, you'll be required to secure a Turkish tax number and be registered with the tax office. The title deeds can then be sent to the *Tapu* office and you will be registered as the new owner. Be aware that your title deeds will also carry a photo of you.

Stage 6: Additional costs

Earthquake insurance is compulsory in Turkey, although the fee is generally around £50 for the year. With new builds, you should also be prepared to pay management charges, which generally sit at around €5–€10 per square metre per year, depending on the facilities on site.

Generally speaking, additional costs don't normally come to more than 10% of the purchase price and this includes 1.5% stamp duty, 3% for estate agents' fees – payable by both the buyer and seller – legal fees of 5% and transfer tax of 1.5%. You will also be liable to pay an annual property tax based on the declared value of the property, which currently stands at 0.3%.

THE LETTINGS MARKET

Thanks to the low property prices and rapidly expanding tourist industry, buyers can expect to generate rental yields of around 7% per annum. The market is still in its infancy, but it's a good one for jet-to-let investors. The concept of buying to let in Turkey is still a relatively new concept, but there are some fabulous entry points for the canny investor. The best opportunities are in southern Turkey, although things are picking up in

Istanbul too. A three-bedroomed detached villa on the Bodrum Peninsula with sea views can generate around £650 a week in peak season. If the property has its own pool then you would expect to receive an extra £100 to £150 a week.

You will be liable to pay tax in Turkey on any rental income generated in the country. There is a double taxation treaty in place between Turkey and the UK so you won't be paying tax twice. Rental income is taxed as income tax, but Turkish income tax law exempts a certain amount of rental income from residential buildings per annum. For 2007, residential rental income up to YTL2,300 (approximately £800) is exempt from income tax.

RENOVATING A PROPERTY

While inland there is no shortage of renovation properties, on the coast, older homes are scarce and titles can be difficult to check. You will also find that while there are plenty of construction companies and building work is cheap, with workers paid a mere £10 a day, it can be difficult to find a builder who will modernise a property to Western standards. Recommendations are the best way to find reliable workers and architects, but even then, building permission can be hard to secure, with a huge amount of red tape surrounding permits.

LIVING IN TURKEY

People and daily life

The Turkish people are friendly and will always make visitors to their country feel welcome. With a strong entrepreneurial spirit since the economic collapse of the 60s to early 90s, the Turks have helped to rebuild their country's economy and tourist industry. While family has always been central to Turkish life, there has been a lifestyle change as the younger generation seek more independence and an increasing interest in Western values. However, to the east, values remain more traditional. This is a poor, and predominantly agricultural, region and the people in this area tend to be more conservative in their attitudes and beliefs.

Visas, permits and residency

In order to enter Turkey you will need to secure a tourist visa which is valid for three months. This can be arranged prior to leaving the UK through the Turkish Embassy, or on arrival in the airport. Your passport will need to be valid for six months prior to entry and you must have the exact amount in cash to pay for the visa – it costs £10 – as cards and travellers cheques will not be accepted. Tourist visas can be renewed on leaving Turkey, which needs only be a short hop by ferry to one of the Greek islands.

Foreign property owners can apply for residency permits, although be aware that this can involve a considerable amount of paperwork and red tape. Generally you will need to apply for a residency visa eight weeks before departure to Turkey and the cost is £85. You can apply for a three-month visa or a residency permit lasting up to five years. Depending on your circumstances, EU nationals can generally secure a visa within a week, if necessary.

Not only will you need to prove you have enough income to support yourself, but in order to work you will also be required to secure a work permit. Foreigners with a visa who have been in Turkey for longer than five years don't need to apply for residency visas after this period. See http://turkey.embassyhomepage.com for all details and online application forms.

Utilities

Once you get your property registered at the *Tapu* office, you will need to transfer utilities into your name. Many utility companies remain state run in Turkey, such as electricity, which is provided by Türk Elektrik Koruma. Bills can be paid by direct debit or via your bank. Electricity and natural gas are provided by the local distributing and retailing companies, with natural gas only supplied to a limited number of cities: mains gas is only available in Istanbul, Ankara and Izmir. In most parts of Turkey, your gas will be provided in a canister. Water is generally mains-supplied, although some areas will need to have water delivered by tanker. Utility costs generally vary from an average of £50 to £200 per month.

Telecommunications are provided Türk Telekom, previously state owned, but recently privatised to Oger Telecom (www.turktelekom. com.tr). The telephone network is good and wireless internet is now available in most cities and coastal regions.

There is a well-developed mobile phone network and the largest and most reliable operator is Turkcell (www.turkcell.com.tr). If you are living in a rural area you may struggle to get decent reception, though.

Cable television is widely available and a number of English-speaking channels can be received, including Eurosport and BBC World.

Currency and banking

In 2005 the new Turkish lira (YTL) replaced the old Turkish lira, whose value had suffered following years of high inflation. New lira coins are available in denominations of 1, 5, 10, 25, 50 kurus and 1 new lira, while banknotes are available in 1, 5, 10, 20, 50, 100 new lira. One lira is worth 100 kurus.

It is recommended that you open a bank account in Turkey, but to do this you will need to take your Turkish tax number and some ID with you. Foreigners can open a standard bank account, and you can withdraw cash from ATMs with most credit or debit cards. Be aware that bank transfers to and from your Turkish bank account will take at least 10 days.

There is a large choice of high street banks in Turkey:

- Central Bank of the Republic of Turkey, www.tcmb.gov.tr
- Citibank, www.citibank.com.tr
- BankEkspres

327

- Garanti Bank, www.garantibank.com
- Yapi Kredi Bank, www.ykb.com
- Demir Bank, www.hsbc.com.tr.

Taxes

In order for you to be classed as a Turkish tax resident you need to live as a permanent resident in Turkey for six months of the year. You will then be liable to pay tax on Turkish and worldwide income. If you are not classed as a tax resident then you are only taxed on your income earned within Turkey.

The income tax system in Turkey is progressive, with rates varying from 15% to 35%.

Tax %	The tax base (YTL)
15	0 – 7,000 (£0 – £2,594)
20	7,001 – 18,000 (£2,595 – £6,671)
27	18,001 – 40,000 (£6,672 – £14,826)
35	40,001 and over (£14,827+)

Corporate tax is levied at a flat rate of 20%, while capital gains tax for an individual is taxed at the same rate of income tax. You are exempt from paying capital gains if the property has been owned for five years prior to sale. There is a double taxation treaty in place with all EU countries and many others, including America, ensuring that you won't be taxed twice on your income.

Insurance

There are a number of insurance companies in Turkey who can offer all the necessary cover you may need.

- AIG Sigorta A.S., www.aig.com
- Commercial Union Sigorta A.S., www.cusigorta.com.tr

- EGE Sigorta A.S., www.egssigorta.com.tr

- Ak Sigorta, www.aksigorta.com

- Demir Hayat, www.demirhayat.com.tr

Healthcare

Currently there is no reciprocal agreement in place between Turkey and the EU, so you will be required to pay for any treatment you may require. Consequently, it is essential that you take out private health insurance. If you are working in Turkey, then you will be paying the equivalent of national insurance payments and will be entitled to state health care. Private health care in Turkey is of a very high standard and you will find many English speakers, but outside of the private sector you will struggle to find staff who speak English.

Retirement

Turkey is a popular destination for retirees and as you can secure residency, it is possible to retire to the country, especially as you can receive your pension in Turkey. If your pension is not a UK state pension then it depends on the rules governing a private pension as to whether or not you can receive it in Turkey. Contact The Department of Work and Pensions (www.dwp.gov.uk) for more details.

Education

The education system in Turkey is run on the French model, and offers both a state and private school education – the best state schools, known as the *Anadolu Lisesi*, can offer higher standards of education than some private schools.

Foreign children are entitled to state education, but facilities can be stretched. The best option is one of the many private schools which can be found in most towns and cities. See www.english-schools.org/turkey for a comprehensive list.

Driving

Turkey has a good infrastructure which links all major towns and resorts as well as connecting to other European countries. Driving in large cities such as Istanbul can be a hair-raising experience and accident rates are high, so be aware.

In Turkey you drive on the right-hand side of the road, headlights must be switched on at all times and it is illegal to use your car horn, except in emergencies. You can drive with an International Driving Permit but it is illegal to drive while using a mobile phone and you are only allowed 50mg of alcohol in your bloodstream. Seatbelts must be worn at all times.

Speed limits are as follows:

- motorways: 120km/h (74mph);
- open roads: 90km/h (55mph);
- towns: 50km/h (31mph).

Getting around

Given the size of Turkey, there are internal flights between Istanbul, Bodrum, Ankara, Antalya, Izmir and other major cities. Onur Air (www.onurair.com.tr) and Turkish Airlines (www.thy.com) provide a number of services.

The Turkish train network covers 610,200km and overnight services can be a good alternative to flying. State run, the lines are old and buses are often a better alternative unless you are travelling between Turkey's three main centres – Istanbul, Ankara and Izmir. See www.tcdd.gov.tr for details on timetables, services and fares.

Buses are the cheapest and best way to get about, with long-distance buses popular and well used. *Dolmuşes* are one of the easiest ways to get around. This is a minibus service which travels between towns, cities and villages, and the concept is that they don't leave until they are full. Their destination is clearly indicated in the front of the bus.

There are also many other bus companies in operation in Turkey, the following being the main operators:

- Asya Tur
- Hakiki Koç
- Hidayet Turizm
- Istanbul Seyahat
- Kamil Koç
- Metro Turizm
- Pamukkale Seyahat
- Ulusoy
- Varan.

For more information on travelling around Turkey, visit www.turkeytravelplanner.com.

Learning the language

Turkey's official language is Turkish, although Kurdish, Arabic, Greek and Armenian are spoken by many of the population. A member of the Ural-Altaic language family, and closely related to Mongolian and Korean, its grammatical structure makes it very difficult for English and Latin-based language speakers to learn, although you should try to pick up some basic phrases.

Shopping

Modern supermarkets are easily found, especially in the southwestern resort areas of the country. However, there are a number of markets and bazaars where fresh fruit and vegetables can be purchased cheaply. Larger supermarkets do provide some imported products, although locally-produced goods are generally of a high standard. Shops are generally open from 9.30am to 7pm, Monday to Saturday, in the larger resorts and towns. Most close on Sundays.

Post

The postal service in Turkey is state run and services are nearing a par with European levels of service. When sending letters, you will find there is a slot for international and a slot for internal mail, while parcels are best sent by a private courier. Post boxes are rarely found on the street. Details of prices and services are all available at www.ptt.gov.tr.

Crime, corruption and the police

Crime levels in Turkey are low when compared to Western Europe. Violent crime is a rarity, although pickpocketing is an increasing problem. Corruption is a much bigger issue, but has been targeted by the government in their attempt to secure EU membership. Foreign buyers will find that the major problems of corruption they are faced with involve unscrupulous vendors and dodgy title deeds.

The police generally treat tourists with respect and can be contacted on 155. However, they are unlikely to speak English, so try to get a local to ring for you.

Appendix 1 – Country matrix

Country	Ideal for	Why buy there?	Warning!	Average price	Typical properties
The Baltic States	Investors	• High rates of appreciation • Increase in tourism and rental demands • Economic and political stability and rapid economic growth rates • Adoption of the euro looming	• The current rate of economic and property market growth is likely to be unsustainable	• €67,514	• Newly-built, high-quality apartments
Bulgaria	Families, retirees and buy-to-let	• The ski resorts are experiencing massive development for rentals • Just become an EU member (Jan 2007) • Families can enjoy the bucket and spade phenomenon on the coast • Retirees will find large expat community facilities • Experiencing healthy rates of appreciation	• There is a threat of oversupply in the market which will damage appreciation rates • While this is still a young market there is a feeling that you may have missed the boat in investment terms • Don't expect to generate significant rental returns	• €25,000 to €35,000 for a 1-bed apartment in a ski resort. • €73,387 for a 1-bed apartment in a development in Sofia. • €140,000 for a 3-bed villa in a golf/spa development	• Newly-built apartment blocks and ski chalets

Country	Ideal for	Why buy there?	Warning!	Average price	Typical properties
Croatia	Well-heeled second home buyer, families and investors	• 6,000km of beaches, stunning scenery and rich cultural life • Appreciation rates of 20–40% in recent years • Can find a bargain • Low cost of living • Safe and clean country	• This is a very affluent market so be prepared to spend more for better quality • You are unlikely to secure a mortgage to buy in Croatia • Not a member of the EU	• 1-bed apartment: €85,000 • 2-bed apartment: €100,000 • 2-bed houses €145,000 • 4-bed houses €240,000+	• Stone-built rural properties and newly-built apartments
Czech Republic	Buy-to-let investors, weekend breakers and professional couples	• This is a well established market • Healthy economic growth rate and tourist industry • Politically stable • High standard of living, good job opportunities and cheap cost of living • Can secure average price appreciation of 10–20% depending on where you buy, and rental yields of 7%+	• Appreciation rates aren't as high in the capital as in some other Eastern European countries due to the established nature of the market	• Prague: €50,000–€220,000 • Brno: €27,000 for a studio apartment • Ski resorts: €158,501 for a newly-built apartment	• City centre newly-built apartments

334

Country	Ideal for	Why buy there?	Warning!	Average price	Typical properties
Hungary	Buy to let, weekend breakers, young professional and retirees (Lake Balaton)	• Blossoming economy, high FDI and strong tourist industry • Beautiful and cultured country • Established property market • Low cost of living but high living standards • Easy to reach thanks to budget flights • Appreciation rates 10% per annum	• There have been questions raised over the economic and political growth of the country	• Budapest: apartments start at €44,200 • Lake Balaton: €50,000 to €199,000	• Newly-built or historic city centre apartments
Montenegro	Adventurous investors, DIY enthusiasts and second-home buyers	• Significant economic growth and increasing stability • Growing tourist market • Price rises of 20–30% • Low rates of property tax • Stunningly beautiful and extensive coastline	• Still highly undeveloped and not a member of the EU • Has only just become an independent country • Still high levels of corruption • Reliant on the development of tourism and budget flights to sustain economic growth • There are problems with the land registry, with many defective titles	• Prices start at €70,000	• Increasingly newly-built property, but also a large number of traditional stone-built homes to renovate

Country	Ideal for	Why buy there?	Warning!	Average price	Typical properties
Poland	Buy-to-let investors, general investors, young couples	• Boasts the most dynamic economy in Europe • Easy to reach, served by numerous budget airlines • Average price rises of 10% per annum • Local home ownership is rising • Strong demand for property and current supply shortage • High standard of living but low cost of living • Next ten years are predicted to see price growth of almost 400% • Still many undiscovered and growing markets	• Some properties can be of poor quality	• €110,500 to €125,000 for a newly-built 2-bed apartment	• Newly-built or historic city centre apartments
Romania	The adventurous investor	• House prices are cheap, but appreciation rates are high at 30% per annum • There is a lack of property supply • The economy is rapidly growing • Just joined the EU (Jan 2007) • Affluence in the country is rising and the tourist market is expanding	• This is still a very undeveloped market and you need to be careful where you buy • Problems can occur with property titles as the land registry records are very poor	• Some property can be found for €7,500, although the average is €37,000–€66,250	• Dilapidated country houses and newly-built apartments

Country	Ideal for	Why buy there?	Warning!	Average price	Typical properties
Slovakia	Buy-to-let investors	• Regular budget flights • Flat tax rate of 19% • 6% GDP growth per annum • Limited property availability • Growth in construction and mortgage market • Rental yields of 8–10% • Massive price rises of between 25–50%	• It's expensive to live and work here	• Prices are high in Bratislava – €295,000 for an apartment – although outside of the capital you can buy a house for €44,000	• Newly-built apartments and ski chalets in the mountains
Slovenia	Buy-to-let investors and families	• A small country, there is a limited amount of property • Burgeoning tourist industry and economy • EU member and has adopted the euro • Easy to get to thanks to budget flights • Prices predicted to rise by 250% by 2015	• Taxes are high and the cost of living can be very high	• Average property price is €100,000	• Historic city centre apartments and newly-built development property

Country	Ideal for	Why buy there?	Warning!	Average price	Typical properties
Turkey	Families and retirees	• A safe country to live in • Established expat community • Economically vibrant with a strong tourist market • Mortgages have just been introduced • Turkey has been introducing a number of reforms to property legislation, making it easier for foreigners to buy • Appreciation rates are around 30%	• There are few budget flights into Turkey • The country still has a long way to go before securing EU membership • Corruption and bribery can still be problematic • Newly-built developments don't always come with bank guarantees to protect your investment	• €88,000	• Newly-built apartments and villas

Appendix 2 –
Useful information

THE BALTIC STATES

National holidays

Lithuania

January 1 – New Year's Day

February 16 – Independence Day (1918)

March 11 – Restoration of Independence (1990)

March–April – Easter

May 1 – Labour Day

June 24 – Midsummer Festival

July 6 – Coronation of Mindaugas, King of Lithuania (1253)

August 15 – Assumption Day

November 1 – All Saints' Day

December 25-26 – Christmas

Latvia

January 1 – New Year's Day

March–April – Easter

May 1 – Labour Day

May 4 – Declaration of Independence of the Republic of Latvia

The second Sunday in May – Mother's Day

Sunday May/June – Whitsunday

June 23–24 – Ligo Day and Jani

November 18 – Proclamation of the Republic of Latvia

December 25/26 – Christmas

December 31 – New Year's Eve

Estonia

January 1 – New Year's Day

February 24 – Independence Day (1918)

March–April – Good Friday

March–April – Easter Sunday

May 1 – May Day

May 9 – Mother's Day

June 23 – Victory Day

June 24 – St. John's Day (Midsummer)

August 20 – Day of Restoration of Independence

December 25 – Christmas Day

December 26 – Boxing Day

Emergency numbers

Estonia

Ambulance: 112; Fire: 112; Police: 110

Latvia

Ambulance: 03; Fire: 01; Police: 02

Lithuania

Ambulance: 112; Fire: 112; Police: 112

Dialling code

Estonia: +372

Lithuania: +370

Latvia: +371

Climate Charts

Tallinn

	Av high °C	Precip cm
Jan	−2	4.17
Feb	−2	3.24
Mar	2	2.74
Apr	9	2.52
May	15	2.65
Jun	19	4.38
Jul	21	6.08
Aug	20	5.91
Sep	15	4.32
Oct	9	4.94
Nov	3	5.03
Dec	0	4.13

Rīga

	Av high °C	Precip cm
Jan	−1	3.06
Feb	−1	3
Mar	4	2.41
Apr	10	2.42
May	17	4.03
Jun	20	5.33
Jul	22	5.79
Aug	22	5.3
Sep	16	4.88
Oct	10	5.44
Nov	4	4.44
Dec	0	3.45

Vilnius

	Av high °C	Precip cm
Jan	−2	3.28
Feb	−1	2.91
Mar	3	3.05
Apr	11	2.81
May	18	3.63
Jun	20	4.87
Jul	22	5.16
Aug	22	5.3
Sep	16	4.65
Oct	10	4.08
Nov	3	3
Dec	−1	3.7

Glossary of useful terms and phrases

Estonia

Hello – *Tere*

Goodbye – *Nägemiseni*

Hi/Bye – *Tšau* (informal)

Thank you – *Aitäh!/ Tänan*

Please – *Palun*

Yes – *Jah*

No – *Ei*

Id Card – *Id-Kaart*

Personal Identification Document – *Isikut tõendav dokument*

Driving licence – *Juhiluba*

Passport – *Pass*

Post office – *Postkontor*

Envelope – *Ümbrik*

Stamp – *Mark*

Doctor – *Arst*

Dentist – *Hambaarst*

Ambulance – *Kiirabi*

Shop – *Pood*

Restaurant – *Restoran*

Café – *Kohvik*

Bar – *Baar*

Money – *Raha*

Currency exchange – *Valuutavahetus*

Exchange rate – *Vahetuskurss*

Wage/salary – *Palk*

Price – *Hind*

Bill – *Arve*

Free of charge – *Tasuta*

Latvia

Hi – *Sveiki*

Good morning – *Labrīt*

Good day – *Labdien*

Good evening – *Labvakar*

Hello! How are you? – *Labdien! Kājums klājas?*

Glad to see you again – *Priecājos jūs atkal redzēt*

Do you speak English? – *Vai jūs runājat Angliski?*

Excuse me – *Atvainojiet!*

Never mind – *Tas nekas*

I'd like to... – *Es gribeetu ...*

What do you want? – *Ko Jus gribat?*

I like it! – *Man tas patik!*

I don't like it – *Man tas nepatik.*

Do you understand me? – *Vai Jus mani saprotat?*

I don't understand – *Es nesaprotu*

Bank – *Banka*

Private company – *Privāta firma*

Law – *Tieslietas*

Lithuanian

Welcome – *Sveiki atvykę*

Hello – *Labas, Sveikas, Sveiki*

How are you? – *Kaip sekasi? Kaip tau sekasi?*

What's your name? – *Kuo tu vardu?* (informal) *Koks tavo vardas?* (formal)

Mano vardas ... – *My name is ...*

Where are you from? – *Iš kur jūs? Iš kur tu esi?*

Pleased to meet you – *Malonu tave matyti, Malonu susipažinti*

Good morning – *Labas rytas*

Good afternoon – *Laba diena*

Good evening – *Labas vakaras*

Good night – *Labanakt, Labos/Geros nakties*

Goodbye – *Viso gero*

Cheers/Good health! – *Į sveikatą!*

Have a nice day – *Geros dienos!*

I don't understand – *Aš nesuprantu*

Please speak more slowly – *Prašom pakartoti lėtai/Prašom kalbėti lėčiau*

Excuse me – *Atsiprašau!*

How much is this? – *Kiek šitas kainuoja? Kiek tai kainuoja?*

Sorry – *Atsiprašau! Atleiskite!*

Thank you – *Ačiū, De'koju, Labai ačiū*

Yes – *Taip*

No – *Ne*

When? – *Kada?*

Where? – *Kur?*

Who? – *Kas?*

Why? – *Kodel*

BULGARIA

National holidays

In addition to New Year's Day, Easter Monday, Christmas Eve, Christmas Day and Boxing Day, Bulgaria's national holidays are:

March 3 – National Holiday

May 1 – Labour Day

May 6 – St. George's Day and Bulgarian Army Day

May 24 – Cyril and Methodius Day

September 6 – Unification Day

September 22 – Independence Day

November 1 – National Day of the Bulgarian Revival Leaders

Emergency numbers

Fire: 160; Police: 166; Ambulance: 150

Dialling code

+359

Climate chart

Sofia

	Av high °C	Precip cm
Jan	3	2.21
Feb	5	2.37
Mar	10	2.71
Apr	16	4.14
May	21	5.55
Jun	24	5.34
Jul	27	3.62
Aug	27	3.92
Sep	23	3.56
Oct	17	3.31
Nov	9	3.24
Dec	4	3.06

Varna

	Av high °C	Precip cm
Jan	6	2.25
Feb	7	1.99
Mar	10	3.16
Apr	15	3.78
May	20	2.81
Jun	25	3.5
Jul	28	3.24
Aug	28	2.69
Sep	24	4.12
Oct	18	2.94
Nov	12	4.13
Dec	8	2.93

Glossary of useful phrases

Do you speak English? – *Govorite li Angliiski*

I don't understand – *Ne rezbiram*

I don't speak Bulgarian – *Ne govorya Balgarski*

What's your name? – *Kak se kazvash?*

Hello – *Zdravei!*

How are you? – *Kak si?*

What time is it? – *Kolko e chasa?*

Sorry? – *Molya?*

Good/OK/Alright – *Dobre /OK*

Yes/No – Da/Ne

Can I have…/I would like … – *Mozhe li…/Iskam …*

How much? – *Kolko struva?*

I'm sorry – *Izvinete*

Good morning! – *Dobro Ytro!*

Goodbye – *Dovizhdane*

Goodbye – *Chao* (informal)

CROATIA

National holidays

January 1 – New Year's Day

January 6 – Epiphany

March–April – Easter

May 1 – Labour Day

June 7 – Corpus Christi

June 22 – Anti-Fascist Resistance Day

June 25 – Croatian National Day

August 5 – Victory Day and National Thanksgiving Day

October 8 – Independence Day

November 1 – All Saint's Day

December 25–26 – Christmas

Emergency numbers

Ambulance 94; Fire 93; Police 92

Dialling code

+385

Climate chart

Zagreb

	Av high °C	Precip cm
Jan	4	4.33
Feb	7	3.61
Mar	12	3.83
Apr	17	7.53
May	23	6.87
Jun	26	6.79
Jul	27	9.71
Aug	27	7.62
Sep	21	9.91
Oct	16	8.06
Nov	10	7.93
Dec	4	6.25

Dubrovnik

	Av high °C	Precip cm
Jan	12	11.06
Feb	13	8.76
Mar	15	7.84
Apr	17	8.53
May	23	5.31
Jun	27	3.06
Jul	29	2.44
Aug	29	5.76
Sep	25	8.01
Oct	21	12.39
Nov	17	15.27
Dec	13	13.98

Split

	Av high °C	Precip cm
Jan	10	7.52
Feb	11	4.98
Mar	14	4.34
Apr	17	6.65
May	24	5.62
Jun	28	2.7
Jul	30	1.6
Aug	30	4.03
Sep	24	10.13
Oct	20	8.49
Nov	15	12.91
Dec	11	9.41

Glossary of useful terms and phrases

Yes – *Da*

No – *Ne*

Welcome – *Dobrodosil*

Pleased to meet you – *Drago mi je*

Hello – *Dobar dan*

Goodbye – *Dovidenja*

Thank you – *Hvala*

My name is ... – *Zovem se ...*

Do you speak English? – *Govorite li engleski?*

I need help – *Trebam pomoc*

Where is the toilet, please? – *Molim vas, gdje je WC?*

Available – *Dio ponude*

Additional plot – *Dodatna parcela*

Garden/courtyard – *Dvoriste*

Floor – *Kat*

Roof – *Krov*

House – *Kucom*

Family house – *Obiteljska kuca*

Site – *Okucnice*

Gas – *Plin*

Basement – *Podrum*

View – *Pogled*

Business space – *Poslovni prostor*

Access – *Prilaz*

Room/bedroom – *Soba*

Apartment – *Stan, soba*

Old/ to restore – *Stara za adaptacija*

Electricity – *Struja*

Zoned for building – *Urbanizirano*

Planning permission – *Ucrtanom*

Holiday house – *Vikendica*

Water – *Voda*

Land/site – *Zemlista*

CZECH REPUBLIC

Public holidays

January 1 – New Year's Day

April 9 – Easter Monday

May 1 – May Day

May 8 – Liberation Day

July 5 – Day of the Apostles St Cyril and St Methodius

July 6 – Anniversary of the Martyrdom of Jan Hus

September 28 – Czech Statehood Day

October 28 – Independence Day

November 17 – Freedom and Democracy Day

December 24–26 – Christmas

Emergency numbers

Ambulance: 155; Fire: 150; Police: 158;

General emergency: 112

Dialing code

+420

Climate charts
Prague

	Av high °C	Precip cm
Jan	2	1.8
Feb	4	1.78
Mar	8	2.32
Apr	14	1.99
May	20	3.92
Jun	22	5.17
Jul	24	5.61
Aug	24	5.05
Sep	19	3.57
Oct	14	2.14
Nov	6	2.36
Dec	3	2.09

Brno

	Av high °C	Precip cm
Jan	1	1.53
Feb	3	1.56
Mar	8	1.92
Apr	14	2.26
May	20	3.95
Jun	23	5.61
Jul	25	4.88
Aug	25	4.04
Sep	20	3.73
Oct	14	2.56
Nov	6	2.56
Dec	2	2.35

Glossary of useful terms and phrases

Hello (formal) – *Dobrý den*

Hello (informal) – *Ahoj*!

Goodbye – *Na shledanou*

Good evening – *Dobry večer*

Good night – *Dobrou noc*

Yes (formal) – *Ano*

Yes (informal) – *Jo/No*

No – *Ne*

Excuse me – *S dvolením*

Sorry – *Promintě*

Please/You're welcome – *Prosím*

Help – *Pomoc*

I understand – *Rozumím*

I don't understand – *Nerozumím*

Do you speak English? – *Mluvíte anglicky?*

Please speak more slowly – *Mluvte pomalu, prosím*

I don't speak Czech – *Nemluvím Český*

How much is it? – *Kolík to stoji?*

Can you help me? – *Můžete mi pomoci?*

Private Ownership – *OV* (*osobní vlastnictví*)

Cooperative Ownership – *DV* (*družstevní vlastnictví*)

HUNGARY

Public holidays

January 1 – New Year's Day

March 15 – Anniversary of 1848 uprising against Austrian rule

April 9 – Easter Monday

May 1 – Labour Day

May 28 – Whit Monday

August 20 – National Day (Feast of St Stephen)

October 23 – Republic Day (Anniversary of 1956)

November 1 – All Saints' Day

December 25 – Christmas Day

December 26 – Boxing Day

Emergency numbers

Ambulance: 104; Fire: 105; Police: 107;

General emergency: 112

Dialling code

+36

Climate chart

Budapest   **Lake Balaton**

	Av high °C	Precip cm
Jan	2	2.12
Feb	5	1.63
Mar	10	2.15
Apr	16	3.64
May	22	4.3
Jun	25	3.94
Jul	27	5.08
Aug	27	3.76
Sep	22	3.4
Oct	16	2.77
Nov	8	3.71
Dec	3	2.49

	Av high °C	Precip cm
Jan	1	3.26
Feb	5	1.56
Mar	9	2.71
Apr	15	5.38
May	21	4.67
Jun	24	5.82
Jul	26	5.95
Aug	26	7.28
Sep	20	6.09
Oct	15	3.02
Nov	8	4.54
Dec	2	4.23

Glossary of useful terms and phrases

Yes – *Igen*

No/Not – *Nem*

Good morning – *Jó reggelt*

Good day – *Jó napot*

Good evening – *Jó estét*

Good night – *Jó éjszakát*

Good bye – *Viszlát!/Viszontlátásra*

Hi – *Szia (s)*

Hi – *Sziasztok* (pl)

I understand – *Értem*

I don't understand – *Nem értem*

Please – *Kérek/kérem*

Thanks – *Kösz/köszi* (informal)

Thank you – *Köszönöm* (formal)

Thank you very much – *Köszönöm szépen*

Excuse me – *Elnézést*

I'm sorry/I beg your pardon– *Bocsánat/Bocsánatot kérek*

Could you help me, please? – *Tudna segíteni?*

How much is it? – *Mennyibe kerül?*

Help – *Segítség*

Where? – *Hol?*

Which way/in which direction – *Merre?*

When? – *Mikor?*

How? – Hogyan?

Doctor – *Orvos*

Pharmacy – *Gyógyszertár*

Hospital – *Kórház*

Ambulance – *Mentõ*

Fire service – *Tûzoltóság*

Police – *Rendõrség*

MONTENEGRO

Public holidays

January 1 – New Year's Day

January 7 – Orthodox Christmas Day

March–April – Orthodox Good Friday

March– May – Orthodox Easter Monday

April 27 – Statehood Day

May 1–2 – Labour Days

July 13 – Montenegro National Day

Emergency numbers

Ambulance: 94; Fire: 93; Police: 92

Dialling code

+381

Climate charts

Podgorica

	Av high °C	Precip cm
Jan	10	8.32
Feb	11	8.28
Mar	15	8.22
Apr	19	9.85
May	24	5.12
Jun	29	3.21
Jul	32	1.82
Aug	32	3.43
Sep	27	10.82
Oct	22	11.19
Nov	15	14.68
Dec	11	11.89

Tivat

	Av high °C	Precip cm
Jan	12	9.29
Feb	13	10.1
Mar	15	8.67
Apr	18	10.59
May	24	6.7
Jun	27	3.73
Jul	30	2.33
Aug	30	4.15
Sep	26	7.28
Oct	22	8.85
Nov	17	14.52
Dec	13	12.25

Glossary of useful terms and phrases

Hello (informal) – *Zdravo*

Good morning – *Dobro jutro*

Good day (hello) – *Dobar dan*

Yes – *Da*

No – *Ne*

Please – *Molim*

Thank you – *Hvala*

No thank you – *Ne hvala*

Do you speak English? – *Govorite li engleski?*

I don't understand – *Ja ne razumem*

POLAND

Public Holidays

January 1 New Year's Day

April 9 – Easter Monday

May 1 – Labour Day

May 3 – National Day

June 7 – Corpus Christi

August 15 – Assumption

November 1 – All Saints' Day

November 11 – Independence Day

December 25–26 – Christmas

Emergency numbers

Ambulance: 999; Fire: 998; Police: 997

Dialling code

+48

Climate chart

Warsaw

	Av high °C	Precip cm
Jan	0	1.66
Feb	2	2.02
Mar	6	2.2
Apr	13	2.92
May	19	3.43
Jun	22	4.87
Jul	24	5.76
Aug	24	3.83
Sep	18	3.52
Oct	12	2.51
Nov	5	2.8
Dec	1	2.39

Gdańsk

	Av high °C	Precip cm
Jan	2	2.39
Feb	3	1.99
Mar	5	2.43
Apr	10	2.49
May	16	4.72
Jun	19	4.87
Jul	21	10.17
Aug	22	5.8
Sep	18	4.03
Oct	13	4.38
Nov	7	3.43
Dec	3	3.11

Kraków

	Av high °C	Precip cm
Jan	0	2.8
Feb	1	2.8
Mar	7	3.5
Apr	13	4.6
May	20	4.6
Jun	22	9.4
Jul	24	11.1
Aug	23	9.1
Sep	19	6.2
Oct	14	4.9
Nov	6	3.7
Dec	3	3.6

Glossary of useful terms and phrases

Yes – *Tak*

No – *Nie*

OK – *Dobrze*

Excuse me – *Przepraszam*

What? – *Co?*

Where? – *Gdzie?*

When? – *Kiedy?*

Who? – *Kto?*

Why? – *Dlaczego?*

How? – *Jak?*

Good day – *Dzien dobry*

Hi/Bye – *Cześć*

Goodbye – *Do widzenia*

I don't speak Polish – *Nie mowie po polsku*

I speak English – *Mowie po angielsku*

I don't understand – *Nie rozumiem*

Help me please – *Prosze mi pomoc*

ROMANIA

Public holidays

January 1–2 – New Year

January 6 – Epiphany

March–April – Easter Monday (Orthodox)

May 1 – Labour Day

December 1 – National Day

December 25–26 – Christmas

Emergency numbers

Ambulance: 961; Fire: 981; Police: 955;

General emergency: 112

Dialling code

+40

Climate charts

Bucharest

	Av high °C	Precip cm
Jan	2	2.13
Feb	5	1.92
Mar	11	2.62
Apr	18	3.75
May	24	4.21
Jun	27	5.94
Jul	29	5.19
Aug	29	3.51
Sep	24	4.68
Oct	18	4.33
Nov	9	3.18
Dec	3	2.96

Timişoara

	Av high °C	Precip cm
Jan	3	2.09
Feb	6	1.59
Mar	12	1.93
Apr	17	2.83
May	23	3.29
Jun	26	4.4
Jul	28	3.5
Aug	28	3.39
Sep	24	3.12
Oct	18	2.82
Nov	9	2.66
Dec	4	2.69

Glossary of useful terms and phrases

Hello – *Salut*

Yes – *Da*

No – *Nu*

Please – *Va rog*

Please – *Te rog* (informal)

Thank you – *Multumesc*

You're welcome – *Cu placere*

I am sorry – *Imi pare rau*

Help! – *Ajutor!*

Where is the toilet? – *Unde este toaleta?*

Taken! – *Ocupat!*

Goodbye – *La reverede*

Kitchen – *Bucătărie*

Shower – *Duş*

Room – *Cameră*

Bedroom – *Cameră*

Window – *Fereastră*

Apartment – *Apartament*

House – *Casă*

Land – *Teren*

For sale – *De vanzare*

Floor – *Etaj*

Surface – *Suprafata*

Balcony – *Balcoane*

Garage – *Garaj*

Cable TV – *Cablu TV*

Double glazing – *Termopan*

Swimming pool – *Piscină*

SLOVAKIA

Public holidays

January 1 – Slovak Independence Day

January 6 – Feast of the Three Kings

March–April – Good Friday

March–April – Easter

May 1 – May Day

July 5 – Feast of St Cyril and St Methodius

August 29 – Slovak National Uprising (SNP)

September 1 – Constitution of the Slovak Republic

September 15 – Our Lady of Sorrows

November 1– All Saints' Day

December 24– Christmas Eve

December 25– Christmas Day

December 26 – Boxing Day

Emergency numbers

Ambulance: 155; Fire: 150; Police: 158;

General emergency: 112

Dialling code

+421

Climate chart

Bratislava

	Av high °C	Precip cm
Jan	2	2.44
Feb	5	2.61
Mar	10	2.68
Apr	16	2.75
May	22	3.61
Jun	25	4.5
Jul	27	3.97
Aug	27	4.19
Sep	22	4.12
Oct	15	2.95
Nov	8	3.43
Dec	3	3.24

Kosice

	Av high °C	Precip cm
Jan	0	1.59
Feb	3	1.89
Mar	9	1.9
Apr	15	3.85
May	21	4.48
Jun	24	5.99
Jul	25	6.76
Aug	25	5.09
Sep	20	3.57
Oct	14	3.3
Nov	6	2.91
Dec	1	1.97

Glossary of useful terms and phrases

Good morning – *Dobre rano*

Good day – *Dobry den*

Good afternoon – *Dobre popoludnie*

Good evening – *Dobry vecer*

Good night – *Dobru noc*

Goodbye – *Dovidenia*

Hello – *Ahoj*

Welcome – *Vitaj/Vitajte*

How are you? – *Ako sa mas? Ako sa mate?*

This is our house – *Toto je nas dom*

It has two floors – *Ma dve poschodia*

Is your house old or new? – *Je vas dom stary alebo novy?*

Is your house big or small? – *Je vas dom velky alebo maly?*

Do you have a garden? – *Mate zahradu?*

Where is your house? – *Kde je vas dom?*

I'm sorry, I don't understand – *Prepacte, nerozumiem*

Please – *Prosím*

Thank you – *Ďakujem*

Cheers – *Na zdravie*

Excuse me (formal) – *Prepáčte*

I don't understand – *Nerozumiem*

Please repeat – *Opakujte, prosím*

Bank – *Banka*

Post office – *Pošta*

Who? – *Kto?*

What? – *Čo?*

Who is it? – *Kto je to?*

What is it? – *Čo je to?*

SLOVENIA

Public holidays

January 1–2 – New Year

February 8 – Preseren Day (Slovenian Cultural Holiday)

March–April – Easter Monday

April 27 – Resistance Day

May 1–2 – Labour Day Holiday

May 27 – Pentecost

June 25 – National Day

August 15 – Assumption

October 31 – Reformation Day

November 1 – All Saints' Day

December 25 – Christmas Day

December 26 – Independence Day

Emergency numbers

General emergency: 112; Police: 113; Fire and medical: 112

Dialling code

+386

Climate chart

Llubljana

	Av high °C	Precip cm
Jan	4	5.73
Feb	7	5.93
Mar	12	7.05
Apr	16	11.93
May	22	10.28
Jun	26	12.14
Jul	27	13.76
Aug	27	13.6
Sep	21	14.8
Oct	16	14.64
Nov	9	15.39
Dec	4	10.83

Maribor

	Av high °C	Precip cm
Jan	4	2.87
Feb	7	3.02
Mar	12	4.44
Apr	16	7.09
May	22	8.07
Jun	25	10.65
Jul	26	11.96
Aug	26	9.87
Sep	21	10.85
Oct	16	8.14
Nov	9	8.22
Dec	3	6.89

Glossary of useful terms and phrases

Please – *Prosim*

Thank you (very much) – *Hvala (lepa)*

Yes – *Da*

No – *Ne*

Sorry – *Oprostite*

Hello – *Dober Dan*

Hello – *Živijo* (informal)

Goodbye – *Nasvidenje*

Goodbye – *Adijo* (informal)

Pharmacy – *Lekarna*

Hospital – *Bolnica*

Police – *Policija*

Bus Station – *Avtobusna Postaja*

Road – *Cesta*

Street – *Ulica*

Good morning – *Dobro jutro*

Good day/afternoon – *Dober dan*

Good evening – *Dober večer*

How are you? – *Kako ste?*

Do you speak English? – *Ali govorite anglesko?*

I don't understand – *Ne razumem*

How do you say ..? – *Kako se reče ...?*

What does that mean? – *Kaj to pomeni?*

What time is it? – *Koliko je ura?*

How much does it cost? – *Koliko stane?*

TURKEY

Public holidays

January 1 – New Year's Day

January 2 – Bank Holiday

April 23 – National Holiday of the Sovereign and his Children

May 19 – Atatürk Commemoration and Youth & Sports Day

August 30 – Victory Day

September–November – End of Ramadan, (moveable; 3 days plus ½ day preceding)

October 28 (½ day)–Aug 29 – Republic Day

November–January – Eid-ul-Adha, Feast of the Sacrifice (moveable: 70 days after month of Ramadan; 4 days plus ½ day preceding.)

Emergency numbers

Ambulance: 112; Fire: 110; Police: 155

Dialling code

+420

Climate chart

Istanbul

	Av high °C	Precip cm
Jan	8	4.63
Feb	8	4.81
Mar	11	4.151
Apr	16	3.43
May	21	2.21
Jun	26	2.1
Jul	29	1.7
Aug	29	1.8
Sep	25	2.85
Oct	20	4.94
Nov	14	5.93
Dec	10	7.21

Bodrum

	Av high °C	Precip cm
Jan	15	7.26
Feb	15	6.98
Mar	17	8.02
Apr	21	3.29
May	26	1.19
Jun	31	0.14
Jul	34	0.01
Aug	34	0.07
Sep	30	0.72
Oct	26	2.61
Nov	20	7.93
Dec	16	10.82

Ankara

	Av high °C	Precip cm
Jan	4	2.05
Feb	6	1.54
Mar	11	2.3
Apr	17	2.79
May	22	0
Jun	26	2.46
Jul	30	1.15
Aug	30	0
Sep	26	0.81
Oct	20	2.28
Nov	11	2.1
Dec	6	2.78

Glossary of useful terms and phrases

Hello – *Merhaba*

Good morning – *Günaydin*

Good evening – *Iyi aksamlar*

How are you? – *Nasilsiniz?*

Yes – *Evet*

No – *Hayir*

Please – *Lütfen*

Thank you – *Tesekkür ederim*

Excuse me – *Pardon*

What? – *Ne?*

How? – *Nasil?*

How much? – *Ne kadar?*

Who? – *Kim?*

When? – *Ne zaman?*

What time is it? – *Saat kaç?*

Big/small – *Büyük/Küçük*

Hot/cold – *Sicak/Soguk*

Left/right – *Sol/Sag*

Near/far – *Yakin/Uzak*

Early/late – *Erken/Geç*

Good/bad – *Iyi/Kötü*

Street – *Sokak/Cadde*

I don't understand – *Anlamiyorum*

I don't know – *Bilmiyorum*

Water – *Su*

Cheap – *Ucuz*

Expensive – *Pahali*

I don't understand – *Anlamiyorum*

Where is …? – *Nerede …?*

Appendix 3 –
Useful contacts

GENERAL

Air Travel

BA, www.ba.com

EasyJet, www.easyjet.com

Ryanair, www.ryanair.com

Balkan Bulgarian Airlines, www.balkanair.com

Wizz Air, www.wizzair.com

Germanwings, www.germanwings.com

Myair, www.myair.com

Croatian Airlines, www.croatiaairlines.hr

Czech Airlines, www.czechairlines.com

Air Lingus, www.aerlingus.com

SkyEurope, www1.skyeurope.com

Air Berlin, www.airberlin.com

Jet2, www.jet2.com

Montenegro Airlines, www.montenegro-airlines.cg.yu

Yugoslav Airways, www.jatlondon.com

Turkish Airlines, www.thy.com

Adria Airways, www.adria.si

LOT Polish Airlines, www.lot.com

Tarom, www.tarom.ro

Currency exchange

Caxton FX
0845 658 2223,
www.caxtonfx.com

Conti Financial Services
01273 772811
www.mortgagesoverseas.com

Baydon Hill
0871 0705555
www.baydonhill.com

Currencies Direct
0845 3893000
www.currenciesdirect.com

Escape Currency
08000 321 109
www.escapecurrency.com

Globex
020 7253 7183
www.globexfx.com

HIFX PLC
01753 859159
www.hifx.co.uk

Moneycorp
020 7589 3000
www.moneycorp.com

SGM FX
020 7220 1740
www.sgm-fx.com

Expat Advice

www.expatfocus.com

www.expat-blog.com

www.expatnetwork.co.uk

www.internationalliving.com

www.shelteroffshore.com

Government Offices

Department of Health
020 7210 4850
www.dh.gov.uk

Department of Work and Pensions
www.dwp.gov.uk

Foreign and Commonwealth Office
Main switchboard: 020 7008 1500
Services for Britons Overseas: 020 7008 0210
Travel advice: 0845 850 2829
Visa enquiries: 0845 010 5555
www.fco.gov.uk

Jobcentre Plus
www.jobcentreplus.gov.uk

Website of UK Government
www.direct.gov.uk

Legal and Financial

Baydon Hill
0871 070 5555
www.baydonhill.com

Bennetts & Co International Lawyers
0870 428 6177
www.bennett-and-co.com

Blevins Franks Financial Management
020 7336 114/ 020 7015 2158

www.blevinsfranks.com

International Mortgage Plans
01932 830660
www.international-mortgage-plans.com

JD Mortgages
01443 203111
www.jdmortgages.co.uk

The International Law Partnership
020 7061 6700/020 7061 6748
www.lawoverseas.com

The International Property Law Centre
0870 800 4565
www.internationalpropertylaw.com

Insurance

AIG
020 7954 7000
www.aigeurope.co.uk

Allianz
01483 568161
www.allianz.com

Generali Worldwide Insurance Company Limited
01481 715400
www.generali-gw.com

John Wason
0118 956 8800
www.johnwason.co.uk

Motoring

Drive Safe
www.nationaldrivesafe.co.uk

AA Route Planner
http://www.theaa.com/travelwatch/planner_main.jsp

Removals

1st Move International Removals
0117 982 8123
www.shipit.co.uk

Allied Pickfords
0800 289 229
http://gb.allied.com

Anglo Pacific
0800 783 4418
www.anglopacific.co.uk

Britannia
0800 622 535
www.britannia-movers.co.uk

European Removals
www.europeanremovals.com

F+N International Removals
0800 583 4844/01476 579210
www.fnworldwide.com

International Removals
0800 783 1085/020 8324 2066
www.international-removals.com

Relocation Enterprises
+39 06 82 40 60
www.relocationenterprises.com

Robinsons
01235 552266
www.robinsons-intl.com

Telephone and Internet

www.kropla.com, listings of worldwide electrical and
    telephone information

Tax

Worldwide Tax
www.worldwide-tax.com

THE BALTIC STATES

Embassies

Estonian Embassy in London
16 Hyde Park Gate,
London SW7 5DG
020 7589 3428,
Embassy.London@estonia.gov.uk
www.estonia.gov.uk

British Embassy in Tallinn
Wismari 6
10136 Tallinn
Estonia
+372 667 4700
information@britishembassy.ee
www.britishembassy.ee

Embassy of Latvia
45 Nottingham Place,
London W1M 3FE
020 7312 0040
http://latvia.embassy.uk.com or www.am.gov.lv

British Embassy Latvia
5 J Alunana Street
Rīga LV-1010
Latvia
+371 777 4700
www.britishembassy.gov.uk/latvia

Lithuanian Embassy
84 Gloucester Place
London W1U 6AU
020 7486 6401
http://uk.mfa.lt

British Embassy Lithuania
Antakalnio 2
Vilnius LT-10308
Lithuania
+370 5 246 2900
www.britishembassy.gov.uk/lithuania

Tourist Boards

Latvian Tourist Board; www.latviatourism.lv

Lithuanian Tourist Board, www.tourism.lt

Estonian Tourist Board, www.visitestonia.com / www.tourism.ee

Banks

Latvia; www.bank.lv

Lithuania; www.lb.lt

Estonia; www.eestipank.info

Department of Statistics

Latvia; www.csb.lv

Lithuania; www.stat.gov.lt

Estonia; www.stat.ee

Government

Latvia: Parliament, www.saeima.lv; Ministry of Foreign Affairs,
www.mfa.gov.lv

Lithuania: Ministry of Foreign Affairs, www.urm.lt

Estonia Government: www.riik.ee/en; Estonian Institute, www.einst.ee

Invest in the Baltic States

Latvia; www.liaa.gov.lv

Lithuania; www.businesslithuania.com

Estonia; www.investinestonia.com

English Media

The Baltic Times, www.baltictimes.com

Estate Agents

Someplace Else, www.someplaceelse.co.uk, 020 7731 2200

BULGARIA

Embassies

Embassy of the Republic of Bulgaria
186-188 Queen's Gate
London SW7 5HL
020 7584 9400/020 7584 9433
www.bulgarianembassy-london.org

British Embassy Sofia
9 Moskovska Str.
Sofia 1000
+ 359 2 933 9222
www.britishembassy.gov.uk/bulgaria

Bulgarian National Bank

www.bnb.bg

Bulgarian Statistical Office

www.nsi.bg

Invest in Bulgaria

www.investbg.government.bg

Tourism in Bulgaria

www.bulgariatravel.org

www.discover-bulgaria.com

Bulgarian Government

www.government.bg

English Media

Sofia Echo, www.sofiaecho.com

Estate Agents

Bulgarian Gateway; www.bulgariangateway.com, 0845 8381438

CROATIA

Embassies

Embassy of Croatia
21 Conway Street
London W1P 5HL
020 7387 2022
http://croatia.embassyhomepage.com

British Embassy Zagreb
Ivana Lucica 4
10000 Zagreb
+385 (0)1 600 9100
www.britishembassy.gov.uk/croatia

Croatian National Bank

www.hnb.hr

Croatian Statistical Office

www.dzs.hr

Invest in Croatia

www.investments.hr

Tourism in Croatia

www.croatia.hr

www.visit-croatia.co.uk

Croatian Government

www.vlada.hr

Croatian Foreign Office

http://uk.mfa.hr

Estate Agents

Croatian Property Services, www.croatiapropertyservices.com, 00385 98 182 6240

Selection Property, www.selectionproperty.com, 020 8533 9988

CZECH REPUBLIC

Embassies

British Embassy in the Czech Republic
Thunovska 14
118 00 Prague 1
Czech Republic
Tel: +420 257 402 111
Fax: +402 257 402 296
www.britain.cz

Embassy of the Czech Republic in the UK
26–30 Kensington Palace Gardens
London W8 4QY
Tel: 020 7243 1115
Fax: 020 7727 9654
www.mzv.cz/wwwo/?zu=london

Czech National Bank

www.cnb.cz

Czech Statistical Office

www.czso.cz

Invest in Czech Republic

www.czechinvest.org

Tourism in Czech Republic

www.czechtourism.com

Czech Government

www.czech.cz

English Newspapers

www.praguepost.com

www.praguemonitor.com

Estate Agents

CzechPoint101, www.czechpoint101.com, 020 7019 6326

HUNGARY

Embassies

Hungarian Embassy London
35 Eaton Place
London SW1X 8BY
020 7235 8767
www.mfa.gov.hu

British Embassy Budapest
051 Budapest
Harmincad utca 6
+36 1 266 2888
www.britishembassy.hu

Hungarian National Bank

www.mnb.hu

Hungarian Statistical Office

http://portal.ksh.hu

Invest in Hungary

www.itdh.hu

Tourism Office Hungary

www.hungarytourism.hu

www.gotohungary.co.uk

Hungarian Government

www.meh.hu/english

English Newspapers

The Budapest Sun, www.budapestsun.com

Estate Agents

A1 Real Estate, www.a1realestate.hu, +36 1 219 5505

MONTENEGRO

Embassies

At the time of going to print there was no Montenegrin diplomatic representation in the UK. For further information see www.fco.gov.uk.

British Embassy, Podgorica
Bulevar Svetog Petra Cetinjskog 149,
First Floor, No.3
81000 Podgorica
Montenegro
+381 (81) 205 460

Central Bank of Montenegro

www.cb-mn.org

Tourism Office Montenegro

www.visit-montenegro.com

Montenegro Government

www.montenet.org

Estate Agents

Montenegro Living, www.montenegro-living.com,
    +381 (0)88 350 485/+381 (0)82 322 294

POLAND

Embassies

Polish Embassy London
47 Portland Place
London W1B 1JH
0870 774 2700
http://london.polemb.net

British Embassy Warsaw
Al. Róż 1
00-556 Warszawa
+48 22 311 00 00
www.britishembassy.pl

Polish National Bank

www.nbp.pl

Polish Statistical Office

www.stat.gov.pl

Invest in Poland

www.paiz.gov.pl

Tourism Office Poland

www.polandtour.org
www.visitpoland.org

Polish Government

http://poland.pl

English Newspapers

The Warsaw Voice, www.warsawvoice.pl

Estate Agents

Property Krakow, www.property-krakow.com, office@property-krakow.com

Poland Venture, www.polandventure.co.uk

ROMANIA .

Embassies

Embassy of Romania
Arundel House, 4 Palace Green
London, W8 4QD
020 7937 9666
http://londra.mae.ro

British Embassy Romania
24 Jules Michelet, Sector 1
010463 Bucharest
+40 (21) 2017200
www.britishembassy.gov.uk/romania

Romanian National Bank

www.bnro.ro

Romanian Statistical Office

www.insse.ro

Invest in Romania

http://factbook.net

www.aneir-cpce.ro

Tourism Office Romania

www.romaniatourism.com

Romanian Government

www.gov.ro

English Newspapers

Bucharest Daily News

Bucharest Business Week, www.bbw.ro

The Diplomat, www.thediplomat.ro

Estate Agents

Romanian Properties Ltd, www.romanianpropertiesltd.co.uk,
   0870 224 2942

SLOVAKIA

Embassies

Embassy of Slovakia
25 Kensington Palace Gardens
London W8 4QY
020 7313 6470
www.slovakembassy.co.uk

British Embassy Slovakia
Panská 16
811 01 Bratislava
Slovak Republic
+421 2 5998 2000
www.britemb.sk

Slovakia National Bank

www.nbs.sk

Slovakia Statistical Office

www.statistics.sk

Invest in Slovakia

www.sario.sk

Tourism Office Slovakia

www.slovakia.org

www.sacr.sk

www.slovakia.com

Slovakian Government

www.government.gov.sk

English Newspapers

The Slovak Spectator, www.slovakspectator.sk

Estate Agents

Slovakia Investment Properties, www.slovakiainvestmentproperty.com,
020 7152 4014

SLOVENIA

Embassies

Embassy of Slovenia
10 Little College Street
London SW1P 3SJ
020 7222 5700
www.gov.si/mzz-dkp/veleposlanistva/eng/london/index.shtml

British Embassy Ljubljana
Trg republike 3
1000 Ljubljana
Slovenia
+386 1 200 3919
www.british-embassy.si

Slovenian National Bank

www.bsi.si

Slovenian Statistical Office

www.stat.si

Invest in Slovenia

www.investslovenia.org

Tourism Office Slovenia

www.slovenia.info

www.ljubljana-tourism.si

Slovenian Government

www.sigov.si

English Newspapers

Ljubljana Life, www.ljubljanalife.com

Estate Agents

Slovenian Properties, www.slovenianproperties.com

TURKEY

Embassies

Turkish Embassy,
43 Belgrave Square,
London, SW1X 8PA
020 7393 0202
http://turkishembassylondon.org

British Embassy Ankara
Şehit Ersan Caddesi 46/A
Cankaya 06680
Ankara
+90 312 455 3344
www.britishembassy.org.tr

Turkish National Bank

www.tcmb.gov.tr

Turkish Statistical Office

www.die.gov.tr

Tourism Office Turkey

www.turkeytourism.org

www.gototurkey.co.uk

Turkish Government

www.tbmm.gov.tr

Turkish Economy

www.turkisheconomy.org.uk

English Newspapers

Today's Zaman, www.todayszaman.com

Turkish Daily News, www.turkishdailynews.com.tr

Turkish Press, www.turkishpress.com

Estate Agents

Cumberland Properties, www.cumberland-properties.com,
    020 7435 8113

Appendix 4 – Relocation checklist

5–6 weeks before moving

Ensure all family passports and visas are valid and up-to-date and check whether you will need to apply for work permits, residency permits or a driving licence. ❏

Collate all necessary travel documentation and tickets for the journey abroad, as well as personal documents such as birth certificates, medical records (you need to obtain these from your GP) and marriage certificates. ❏

Set up a mail redirect service with the post office (www.postoffice.co.uk). ❏

Notify your children's schools and advise your solicitor, bank, doctor, dentist, insurance company and building society of your move, along with any creditors. ❏

Secure quotes for the removal of your items abroad. ❏

Ensure you have found suitable rental information in the country you are relocating to (if necessary) and find a school for your child/children. ❏

Hand in your notice at work and arrange for any references you may need. ❏

3–4 weeks to go

Cancel all subscriptions to newspapers, clubs and magazines and any club cards you may have. ❏

You will need to keep hold of all invoices for new purchases in order to import them through customs. ❑

Get copies of repeat prescriptions. ❑

Have a clear out and get rid of any unecessary items, either by taking them to charity shops, having a car boot sale or on ebay (www.ebay.co.uk). ❑

Compile an inventory of all items that you will be transporting to your new home. ❑

Arrange with your utility providers to have all services disconnected on the day of your departure and try to ensure that all utilities are connected in your new home. ❑

Arrange for someone in the UK to be used as a contact point for any outstanding queries/bills and supply your new contact details to the relevant people/companies. ❑

Pay any debitors and cancel any rental agreements. ❑

Begin to run down all stocks of food and drink. ❑

Confirm your removal date and decide which items you will pack, and begin to collect packing materials. ❑

Make a list of names, addresses and numbers you will need or want to remember, including any local businesses. ❑

Make arrangements to move your pets and secure a Pet Passport (see www.defra.gov.uk). ❑

1–2 weeks to go

Clean and empty garden sheds and clean garden tools and bicycles that you want to take with you – they must be clean for importing. ❑

Arrange for mains services to be disconnected. ❑

Let newsagents and milkmen know your day of departure and pay their final accounts. ❑

Clear out school lockers and desks at work. ❑

Return any items you have loaned out or retrieve any
you have lent to friends and family. ❏

Dispose of plants and perishable food. ❏

Finalise travel arrangements and get your car MOT'd
and serviced if you are driving abroad. ❏

Correctly dispose of any flammables and white goods. ❏

If moving your TV antenna or satellite dish, make
arrangements to have it taken down. ❏

Transfer bank and savings accounts and ensure you have
access to funds abroad. ❏

Begin packing! ❏

Have the house throughly cleaned, including carpets. If you
are taking any rugs or curtains with you, have these cleaned
and packaged in protective bags. ❏

Cancel any unnecessary direct debits. ❏

1–2 days to go

Pack all items you will need during your journey and when
you get to your destination separately to those that are going
to be shipped, e.g. keys, passports, tickets, clothes, money. ❏

Disconnect and clean any electrical appliances that you are
taking with you. ❏

Pack a box of things you'll need as soon as you arrive and
ensure it is packed at the entrance of the removal van so it
will be the first thing off. ❏

Say your goodbyes and have a leaving party! ❏

On moving day

Leave enough food available for breakfast/packed lunches.
Invest in some plastic cutlery and paper plates. ❏

Make a list of things to check before you leave, such as
cupboards, garage, loft and so on. Check the house to see
if there is any damage – for example, floors or walls. ❑

Never leave before the removals company as they may
have questions. ❑

Triple check that you have passports and travel documents. ❑

Ticklist of people to notify

Family and friends ❑

Work colleagues ❑

GP and dentist ❑

Gym and fitness club ❑

Insurance companies ❑

DVLA

Banks and building societies ❑

Utiltity companies (gas, electric, water, oil, telephone, internet) ❑

Inland Revenue ❑

School/college/nightclass ❑

Council ❑

Newspaper/magazine subscription department ❑

Clubs and organisations ❑

Vet ❑

Milkman ❑

Cable provider ❑

Church/place of worship ❑

Credit card and loan company ❑

Landlord (if renting) ❑

Tenants (if renting property anywhere). ❑

Index